Gil Stieglitz

Breaking Satanic Bondage

Intensive Training In Spiritual Warfare

Breaking Satanic Bondage

© Gil Stieglitz 2013

Published by Principles to Live By, Roseville CA 95661
www.ptlb.com

Cover by John Chase

All Rights reserved. No part of this publication may be reproduced, stored in a retrieval system, or transmitted in any way by an means-electronic, mechanical, photocopy, recording, or otherwise-without the prior permission of the copyright holder, except as provided by USA copyright law.

All Scripture verses are from the New American Standard Bible unless otherwise indicated.
New American Standard Bible: 1995 update.
1995 La Habra, CA: The Lockman Foundation.

ISBN 978-0-9838602-4-2
Christian Living

Printed in the United States of America

Dedication

This book is dedicated to

Jenny Williamson and

the Courage Worldwide Team

for the incredible work they do in rescuing

young ladies from the horrors of sex trafficking

Table of Contents

Forward	7
Introduction to Spiritual Warfare	9
Chapter 1: Seeing the Whole Picture	25
Chapter 2: SPECIALISTS: Ghostbusters to the Rescue	39
Chapter 3: EXORCISM: Making the Demons Tremble	77
Chapter 4: POWER: Flexing Your Spiritual Muscles	99
Chapter 5: RESISTANCE: Building the Impenetrable Fort	135
Chapter 6: COUNSELING: Focusing on the Battle for the Mind	191
Chapter 7: TRUTH: Exposing the Truth and the Lies	239
Chapter 8: Putting All the Tools in the Bag	311
Notes	341
Bibliography	347
About the Author	351

FOREWORD

Demons were thought to be a dead issue, but they have risen from a psychological graveyard with new vigor and vengeance in our present day. William James said, more than a century ago, when demonic bondage was being buried as the antiquated myth of a superstitious people:

> The refusal of the modem 'enlightenment' to treat 'Possession' as a hypothesis to be spoken of as even possible in spite of the massive human tradition based on concrete experience in its favor has always seemed to me a curious example of the power of fashion in things scientific. That the demon theory will have its innings again is to my mind absolutely certain.[1]

The Christian, at the beginning of the third millennium since Christ, is faced with a resurgent spiritual world. Draped in the garb of the New Age, animism and even open Satanism is making a strong comeback. Christians no longer live in a world filled with only philosophic alternatives of which they have the best and most consistent option. We are being thrust back into a world resembling the first century. At that time Christianity won the day because Christians had an answer for the spiritual affliction and oppression which plagued all mankind because of its involvement in false religion and worship.

INTRODUCTION TO SPIRITUAL WARFARE

Spiritual Warfare is the process of claiming the abundant life that God has planned for us (John 10:10). Spiritual Warfare means fighting to fulfill all the good works God has planned for us (Ephesians 2:10). Spiritual Warfare means realizing there are numerous enemies that are trying to keep us from enjoying all that God wants our life to be about.

The book of Joshua is a metaphor for the spiritual warfare that all of us are engaged in. God told Joshua and the people of Israel that He gave them the land of Israel. They were given the right to occupy the whole of the land flowing with milk and honey. Some of the parts of the land have cities they didn't build. Some of the land are fields they didn't plant. Some of the places are untamed areas waiting for their development. It is all theirs to occupy and develop.

The Promised Land is a metaphor for the abundant life God has planned for us. All we have to do is claim it. God told Joshua to be strong and courageous and claim the land God had provided. God told Joshua that every place the sole of their feet tread was given to them. God told Joshua they would be invincible, but they would actually have to go to all the parts of the land and fight to claim what had already been given to them. This is the perfect picture of our lives and spiritual warfare. God has promised us an abundant life filled with good works (John 10:10; Ephesians 2:10), but we have to actually claim it. If we don't fight for it and claim, it we won't see it and we won't have it.

The Israelites, under Moses, shrank away from winning their promised land because of rebellion, unbelief, fear, pride, and false worship. They left their promised land in the hand of squatters. For forty years they wandered in the wilderness with little resources while the full potential of their lives waited just over the Jordan River. They refused to fight to claim what was rightfully theirs. They didn't want to trust God that He could give them the power and means to take control of their promised land. They wanted it to be easy. They wanted God to throw out the people of the land without any effort on their part. But God said He would not do that because He wanted the nation to be involved in the claiming of their prize.

In order to claim the life God had promised to them, Joshua starts in the center of the country with the city of Jericho and the powerful kings in the central part of the country. Joshua then moves south, gaining control over the powerful cities and kings in the southern region of Palestine. Then Joshua moves north to capture those powerful cities and kings in the north. Remember, if Joshua does not lead the people into that region, then they do not get to have, use, or have benefit from this part of their destiny. At each section of his campaign he lists the kings he has defeated by God's power. Each one is a separate battle, a separate strategy, and a separate display of God's power. Each stronghold must be attacked and fought or there will be no one living in that part of the promised land. Look at this list of kings Joshua conquered in Joshua 12:7-24:

> *Now these are the kings of the land whom Joshua and the sons of Israel defeated beyond the Jordan toward the west, from Baal-gad in the valley of Lebanon even as far as Mount Halak, which rises toward Seir; and Joshua gave it to the tribes of Israel as a possession according to their divisions, in the hill country, in the lowland, in the Arabah, on the slopes, and in the wilderness, and in the Negev; the Hittite, the Amorite and the Canaanite, the*

Perizzite, the Hivite and the Jebusite: the king of Jericho, one; the king of Ai, which is beside Bethel, one; the king of Jerusalem, one; the king of Hebron, one; the king of Jarmuth, one; the king of Lachish, one; the king of Eglon, one; the king of Gezer, one; the king of Debir, one; the king of Geder, one; the king of Hormah, one; the king of Arad, one; the king of Libnah, one; the king of Adullam, one; the king of Makkedah, one; the king of Bethel, one; the king of Tappuah, one; the king of Hepher, one; the king of Aphek, one; the king of Lasharon, one; the king of Madon, one; the king of Hazor, one; the king of Shimron-meron, one; the king of Achshaph, one; the king of Taanach, one; the king of Megiddo, one; the king of Kedesh, one; the king of Jokneam in Carmel, one; the king of Dor in the heights of Dor, one; the king of Goiim in Gilgal, one; the king of Tirzah, one: in all, thirty-one kings.

In the same way our lives are waiting to be claimed. God has planned out a wonderful life for us. He knows all that could be accomplished by us during our lives. He has the needed help, blessing, knowledge, training, and resources waiting at those locations and at those times if we will just trust Him to fight for the abundant lives He has promised. Yes, there are kings of fear, anger, addiction, and temptation, to conquer and subdue. Some have power because of mistakes of our past; some are there because of family patterns; some exist in everyone's life; but all of these obstacles and enemies must be grappled with in order to live the abundant life God has planned for us. Each of the people I have worked with and the few that are mentioned in this book had to cooperate with God and through faith claim what He had already given them. Most people are not as bound and enslaved as the people mentioned in the chapters of this book, but they still need to claim their lives.

God wants you and me to claim the life He has planned for us. He is not going to hand us the fully-realized abundant life already planned for us. He wants you to be a part of winning it. He wants you to trust Him in the process of building it. He wants you to learn skills and knowledge in the process of claiming the abundant life He built you for. If you shrink away from the battles, the learning, and the hard times, then you will never know the full potential of your life.

Realize that the Almighty God could have adopted a lottery mentality and dropped huge piles of money, blessings, and relationships on us and then told us to enjoy; but He knew that this kind of blessing would destroy us. He knows that what we are involved in claiming and what we are motivated to maintain and appreciate. What we have planned for and fought for is what we can rejoice in having. He has specifically designed this life to be a process of claiming all He will allow. He has a wonderful plan for all of us. Some don't try and claim it at all. Some try and cheat their way to the prize of an abundant life. Some give up half way there. Few continue to trust or to press on until they reach the fullness of God's calling for them. God loves us and He does have a wonderful plan for our lives. We must be ready to trust Him and fight for the life He destined us for, that fight is spiritual warfare.

Usually when someone talks about spiritual warfare they are talking about liberating those who are held as prisoners of war in this conflict. Those who have become so oppressed and afflicted need serious and significant help to realize the life they were destined to have. This book is an exposition of techniques the Christian church has used to set people free since the power of Jesus Christ's life, death, and resurrection have been available to His followers. There are other aspects of spiritual warfare that every Christian faces each day. We face temptations, attacks, and schemes that will not immediately lead to enslavement by the Devil but will diminish our ability to enjoy the abundant life of Christ. Enjoy the book, but realize that even though your own experience of spiritual warfare may not be as intense as mentioned in this book, you are at war to claim the life God has planned for you to have.

BREAKING SATANIC BONDAGE

With the interest in all things spiritual and especially the dark side of spirituality (vampires, witches, spells, curses) in Western culture, the Christian church must come to a unified and biblically-supported position on healing the demonized. The modern church is becoming inundated with fragmented techniques on how to cast our demons or heal the demonized. The different techniques have hardened into methodologies that war with each other. The early church did not battle over how to heal the demonized but used each deliverance as an apologetic for the faith. Justin Marty wrote:

> For numberless demoniacs throughout the whole world and in your city, many of our Christian men exorcising them in the name of Jesus Christ, who was crucified under Pontus Pilate, have healed and do heal, rendering helpless and driving the possessing demons out of the men though they could not be cured by all

other exorcists and those who use incantations and drugs. [1]

One historian's summation of the church during this period is accurate: "Every exorcism was a triumph by Him who was crucified on Calvary over the pagan divinities, a new proof of the divinity of Christianity."[2] The early church worked in unison toward the goal of applying the wonder of Christ to every area of life. At present it is common to hear the following sentiment as expressed by the writer John White: "I grow concerned about what seems an overzealous use of the techniques of deliverance. I wonder whether some advocates of spiritual warfare do more harm than good."[3]

Demonic oppression takes many forms -- from mild to severe. There is no form of demonic oppression that Christ cannot heal, if we will trust him. Jesus' victory on the cross was the complete and final payment for the sins of the world. It is the application of that payment that is being done in Christian deliverance.

There are a number of questions that arise in this area of Spiritual Warfare and Christian Deliverance. Are demons behind every sin? No, the Scriptures tell us that we make choices to sin and we are responsible for our choices. (Galatians 6:7; James 1:14,15) Are there demons everywhere? No, but the spirit world is all around us and is occupied by God, angels, and demons of various ranks and types. (Ephesians 6:10-18). Is it possible for a true Christian to be possessed by wicked spirits? The answer is, No. The Scripture is clear that those who are owned by God through salvation cannot be owned or completely controlled by the Devil. The Apostle John states clearly that the one who is born of God is protected by Christ and the Devil does not touch (own) him. (1 John 5:18) Is it possible for a Christian to be oppressed by demonic spirits? It seems clear from Scripture that the Christian can be attacked, tempted, and even oppressed. Scripture confirms this as Paul states in 1 Corinthians 5:5 that he was handing over to Satan, the man who was involved in heinous unrepentant immorality. The apostle also states we should not give in to anger for long periods lest we give the Devil a place in our life. (Ephesians 4:26,27) Is it possible for a Christian to be plagued, tormented, and redirected from God's best for them by giving into sin? The answer to this is, yes. This is why Peter warns Christians to be alert, for the Devil prowls around like a roaring lion seeking someone to devour. (1 Peter 5:8) A godly path must be followed through the grace of Christ. The question of whether a demonic spirit can be inside or outside of the body of a Christian is not an appropriate question as the issue is one of influence, not location. The skin of a believer or unbeliever does not form an impenetrable barrier to the spirit world; it is the choices that the soul makes that are crucial. Spiritual oppression is the result of giving over control of some portion or aspect of your life to the Devil and his minions through one's choices. The demonic realm cannot control the essence of the Christian, but they can lay claim to large amounts of the soul and body through sinful choices. (1 John 5:18) This is why the battle is often called a battle for the mind (soul). Just as Satan could speak through Peter when he told Jesus He did not need to die, so we too could be the spokesperson for the enemy in various ways.

There are some aspects of Christian deliverance that are controversial. I submit this overview of Christian Deliverance through history and across denominational boundaries is empowering. I fully realize that some Christians will never use or feel comfortable with some forms of deliverance mentioned here. My main goal has been to put an accurate overview into the hands of the Christian church so that as our modernistic period is ending and a new post-modern world is beginning, Christians will be able to help the demonically-afflicted wherever they are found. There is radical power in Christ to see people set free from the slave labor camps of the Devil.

THE FOUNDATION OF CHRISTIAN DELIVERANCE

Christian deliverance from spiritual bondage has existed for two millennia. When taken as a whole, Christian deliverance is a cohesive, permanently liberating application of the life and work of Jesus Christ, the Son of God. Throughout church history, wherever or whenever Jesus Christ and His finished work was truly applied (either in person or through His ambassadors) men and women were liberated from the power of the Devil. Jesus Himself said, "You shall know the truth and the truth shall make you free." (John 8:32) Jesus Christ is the whole truth and the whole of deliverance. Every aspect and successful work in deliverance is bedrocked in Jesus Christ and what He has done for the believer. There are numerous techniques and practices within deliverance, but all find their strength and authority in Christ. Applying who He is and what He did is the whole of Christian deliverance. Unfortunately, over the last sixteen-hundred years of church history (largely since the fourth century), different aspects of Christ's person and work within the Christian deliverance process have been promoted as the whole of deliverance and have been placed at odds with the other aspects of deliverance. This unfortunate development has limited the effectiveness of the Christian church in fighting its true enemy — Satan. Christians must understand and utilize all the weapons which the Lord has given to the believer — those for the right hand and the left. (2 Corinthians 6:7; Ephesians 6:10)

Introduction

It is absolutely crucial for one to embrace with clarity what spiritual warfare is about. It is about choice. It is about the control of one's choices. Spiritual warfare is a battle for the soul but more specifically the island of our choices. We can choose what we think about, what we do, what we emote, what we say, etc. It is these choices that are the focus of all spiritual war. God tells us we are responsible for our choices. (Galatians 6:7) We have in some measure the ability to choose. The Bible makes it clear that we are all bent towards selfishness and evil and will choose those choices if left to ourselves. (Romans 3:10-15) This is why it is important to lead a person toward Christ who is the source of grace, energy, and power to choose righteously. There is much debate about the extent of our choices, the process of our choices, and the influences impacting our choices. God puts all around us righteous opportunities, and we can choose them through His grace. It may be small righteousnesses like being nice instead of nasty, helpful instead of selfish, quiet instead of angry, friends instead of a bottle. There are always righteous choices for us rather than the sinful and selfish choices of our past. We cannot, with one choice, overcome all the bad choices of the past; but God does give us grace and a path of choices out of the hole we have dug for ourselves. There is always a righteous choice. Spiritual warfare is always about those choices. The blessed, free, powerful life we ideally want may be fifty to one-hundred choices away but it is available. The three enemies of the Christian (the world, the flesh, and the Devil) all want to hide, distract, and turn us away from the righteous choices God is offering. These enemies win when we follow their influences and their choices rather than God's. When spiritual warfare is stripped down to its bare essentials, it is about choices. If the world system can get you to chase money, fame, power, or pleasure, then you are not choosing the righteous things that your life could be about. If your flesh can get you to follow its desires into sensuality, strife, bitterness, carousing, and the like, then you have not made the righteous choices God wanted you to make. (Galatians 5:19-21) If the Devil can lure you into following his decision tree then he has devoured you and kept you from making your life count for righteous things. (1 Peter 5:8)

Remember Galatians 6:7 is the core spiritual warfare verse. *Do not be deceived God is not mocked, whatsoever a man sows that shall he also reap.* What does this verse tell us? We can choose what happens to us. Yes, we may have had awful things happen to us. We may have been severely influenced by something, but we ultimately choose a certain path or not choose a certain path. It is those choices in your past that determine what is happening right now in your life. Even the most extreme forms of demonic control are over one's choices. People must choose to invite demons to control them. People must give over control to spiritual powers by choices, requests, spells, oaths, to have high levels of demonic powers plaguing their life. They must choose Jesus Christ and the application of His grace into the areas of their life that they gave to the enemy. God tells us in the Word that our lives are about our choices. Yes, others can mess with us. Yes, people can do evil things to us. Yes, we can be lied to but ultimately we are still responsible for our choices. Start making righteous choices now. Embrace the grace of God and start making righteous choices.

Remember when the two men who were infested with the legions of demons met Jesus on the sea shore? What were they doing? They were walking toward Jesus. Where was the last place that those thousands of demons wanted to be? They did not want to be in the presence of Jesus. Even though those men could not speak or make some choices, they had the ability to walk toward Jesus and Jesus seemed to take their movement toward him as evidence they wanted to be free, so He set them free.

When the Apostle Paul was being hounded by the demonized slave girl, he seemed to finally realize that her shouting out that he was a servant of the true God was her only way of saying please set me free. It was her choice to want to be free. So he did in the power of Christ. If a person wants to be free from the control of demonic powers, then they can be set free in Christ. If they don't really want to be set free in Christ and learn Christ's way of life, then the demonic powers will not let it happen. It is a battle for the island of choice.

The author's own files provide useful examples of the various deliverance processes. A young lady came to see me who was having multiple unusual problems. She would become violently angry for no apparent reason or would fall asleep and/or go into a trance-like state whenever she tried to read the Bible. She was increasingly crippled by these emotional and spiritual reactions. She consulted pastors, counselors, psychologists, and various xperts. She confessed all known sin. She ... in lengthy prayer vigils. She participated in ......ings to throw any spirits out. Yet any release she enjoyed was short-lived until she was handed a copy of the results of Christ's victory on the cross.[4] Armed with this list of the doctrines of salvation and its benefits to her she began to memorize the verses and claim her place in Christ. Only through this detailed application of the person and work of Christ did she know any permanent relief.

THE SIX STREAMS OF CHRISTIAN DELIVERANCE

The process of Christian Deliverance may be divided into six streams of which any one or all may be used on a specific case. The six different streams of Christian Deliverance may be roughly stated as: **The Specialist strategy, The Exorcism strategy, The Power strategy, The Resistance strategy, The Counseling strategy, and The Teaching strategy.** Each one is a unique reflector of the glory of Christ. This book will examine each approach and critique each for its strengths and weaknesses, as well as provide a framework for effective ministry to those who are being deceived, oppressed, and abused by the spirit world.

This book will isolate each aspect of Christian deliverance and show its contributions, weaknesses, limitations, and excesses. Each separate methodology within deliverance is like a thread in a larger tapestry of a particular strength, texture, and color. Even though it may borrow techniques from other methods, it basically retains its own identity. No one strategy or technique within a strategy should have to stand alone. Each strategy and technique of applying Christ to a spiritual problem a person encounters has strengths, weaknesses, and areas prone to ineffectiveness and even error.

In recent years there has been much more cooperation and cross-training between the above aspects of Christian deliverance methodologies. However, the overall Christ-desired unity has not yet been achieved. (John 17:21) This book hopes to aid in the church fighting the Devil instead of one another. There are numerous hurdles (emotional, theological, and cultural) to be overcome to see all of these aspects as joining in the fight to defeat a common foe. It is hoped that in detailing the rationale and practices of the different aspects of deliverance and showing how they all can be parts of a greater whole, the gap between deliverance methodologies will be reduced. Each of the separate methodologies will be seen as a single thread in the whole fabric of Christian deliverance. All of the different aspects claim victories in battle with the Devil, and each has been perplexed with inability to solve certain cases. In other words, each aspect has been found incomplete when used exclusively. Under the guidance of the Holy Spirit, the Lord Jesus Christ must be allowed to use all aspects and applications of His person and of His saving work to liberate those afflicted by the Devil.

An example of this inclusive approach can be supplied from a case in which the author was involved. A young woman with a difficult background came to Christ and was working through her troubled past in counseling. She was asked to renounce the sins of her past and openly declare herself free in Christ from any spiritual influences which may have been attached to her life because of the sins she committed. At that point, all types of demonic strongholds were uncovered and intense battles with demons took place over a number of days. She made good progress for a while but then began to regress. The next time, a more exorcistic approach was used in driving the demons from her. This approach worked and freed her to enjoy the wonder of Christ again. During the proceeding calm before the next spiritual storm, she was schooled in righteous living. This resulted in even more freedom. There was, however, another regression or so it seemed at the time. Voices returned, along with a spiritual oppression and an intense depression. Within this part of the battle the greatest freedom was gained by teaching her who she was in Christ and helping her realize her destructive mental thought patterns. She was referred to a Christian counselor who helped her work through various psychological problems. During this time she was going through intense prayer sessions with what can only be described as supernatural inner healing, as the Lord redirected a number of her memories to show His love, providence, and protection. This woman still has her "evil" days as the Devil tries to keep this woman from greater Christlikeness, but there is not the destructive demonic powers driving her into sin and psychological upheaval. The process of freedom for this woman involved numerous aspects and long periods of time in which all the aspects of the truths of Christian deliverance became necessary.

All the methodologies share the desire to free the afflicted from bondage. It is best to see that each methodology has vital truth to impart to the whole of Christian deliverance. Any one of the six methodologies is incomplete by itself and cannot stand alone under the varied and subtle attacks of the Enemy. Limiting the Holy Spirit to only one portion of the weapons He has given will cost the coming generation dearly as it fights an intensifying battle with Satan. Even though each methodology has cultural, personal, and theological reasons for ignoring or disapproving one or all of the other aspects of Christian deliverance, it is time to come together under the common banner of Christ and His revealed Word and move on to victory in the power of the Spirit over the demonic host arrayed against us. It is clear that Christian deliverance can be divided into different aspects, with each aspect fulfilling a potentially vital role in any or all deliverance.

THE INCEPTION OF THIS BOOK

This book is the direct result of many years of hands-on battles with the spiritual forces of wickedness. Each methodology discussed in this book was at one time thought to be the solution to the problem of demonization. Each new method discovered through reading or conversation with others was evaluated against Scripture and then employed.

The final popular form of this book is the result of sifting through numerous documents from church leaders, my own files, various church traditions, and a detailed look at Scripture, weaving their information through modern stories of personal encounters with wicked spirits. This story-telling approach seemed the best to convey the conclusion of the hours of research.

RESEARCH AND DEVELOPMENT

This project was researched in three ways: on my knees in the Word of God, on my feet in the heat of battle, and on my seat in numerous libraries. Many times in counseling and research I had to stop and open my Bible and pray. The one Book I knew would not lead me astray or limit the work of God was the Bible, and it has been the ultimate judge of all methodologies and techniques. God was gracious and prompted me with verses and stories which correct, encourage, or offer insight. I do not pretend to understand all that the Bible says about the subject of spiritual warfare, but I know research begins and ends in that Book.

1
Seeing the Whole Picture

Normally one does not expect a pastoral visit to develop into an open and direct confrontation with the powers of darkness, but that is what happened one night when I was visiting a young couple in their home. Jerry and Tammy knew there was more depth, joy, and freedom in the Christian life than they were experiencing. They wanted to make a break from the sins of their past and move forward in their Christian commitment. They invited me, their pastor, to their home to help them grow deeper. As I learned more about their background and history, it became clear that some of the immorality, drug use, and party orientation of their past were still effecting their lives. I suggested they should spend some time in prayer agreeing with God that what they had done in the past was sin and asking Jesus to apply the blood of Christ to these actions of their past. I thought they would spend some time during the week praying as a couple over these various sinful actions. Instead, they asked me to lead them personally in a time of prayer of confession and cleansing.

I agreed to lead them. I told them I would pray a prayer over them of protection and divining guidance. I would then ask Jerry to pray a prayer of submission to the Lord Jesus Christ and direction for the coming time. If God wanted them to confess a particular sin, then He should bring it to their mind and they would agree with God it was wrong and put it under the blood of Christ. Then I would lead Tammy through a prayer of confession and to a new level of embrace of the truth of Christ. I will never forget what happened next. Three sentences into the prayer, I watched as her fingers bent backward in an impossible way, her eyes opened and then looked up into her head disappearing above her eye brows and a deep guttural voice spoke, "We won't let her do this!!!" I was stunned. Jerry looked over at me as the voice continued to speak out of his wife and her hands continued to contort. He had a look that said, "Thank God the pastor is here." I thought about the course I had taken in seminary about confronting demonic spirits. Someone was supposed to challenge these voices with Scripture in the power of Christ. I was the pastor and so I began quoting Scripture and challenging this voice as to what it was and what right it had to resist this woman's complete surrender to the Lord Jesus Christ.

A snarling hateful wicked spirit manifested spitting insults at Christ, me, and everything that had to do with Christianity. The voice, much different from the woman's, continued bellowing "She's ours!! We won't let her go!!" I had never faced this before, nor had I been trained in depth to deal with these situations if they arose. This forced me to put my theology into practice. All the things I had learned about the power, victory, and freedom of Christ had to be translated into actual steps of action immediately. Much of what I had learned about how to be a pastor did not fit this situation. Most "How to be a Pastor" books didn't have a section on what to do if a demon manifests during a pastoral call. Over the next four days I explored and utilized everything I knew about Christ and Scripture. The Lord, with great power, set this woman free in spite of my lack of knowledge and experience. What I learned in this and many other situations over twenty years is the content of this book.

After this incident I examined almost everything the Christian church used to expel demons over the last two-thousand years. I discovered, at one time, Christ's power over demons was one of the cornerstones of the church's witness.[1] In the early church (the first three-hundred years), thousands of people converted to Christianity because Christ offered the only permanent solution to spiritual oppression. At that time, Christian deliverance was defined as any method led by the Spirit of Christ which removed the demons from the afflicted and allowed them to choose to act, think, speak, or emote righteously. Tragically, as the centuries of Christian experience rolled along, divisions began appearing in regards to the appropriate methods of handling demonic deliverance.[2] When the Christian church became the officially recognized religion of the Roman Empire (after 313AD), some methods were considered inappropriate, other methods were sanctioned, and a few methods the church had used for hundreds of years were outlawed. The methods that were outlawed were not condemned because of a biblical flaw but rather as a way to promote organizational conformity and reflect the church's new-found political favor. This caused Christian deliverance to eventually fracture into six basic approaches to the demonic problem: specialists, exorcism, power, resistance, counseling, and truth. This fracturing of deliverance into isolated methodologies left any one method incomplete. This book examines the various methodologies (techniques, strengths, weaknesses, and limitations) of Christian deliverance and presents an inclusive model for handling demonic cases which provides the greatest opportunity for the full power of Christ to be applied to the afflicted. Any one of these methods, with its preferred practices and perspectives, is insufficient to handle all the spiritual attacks and oppression in our sinful world. Only when we look at all of the various methods in the light of the Scripture will it bring a wholistic approach to the application of the victory that comes through Christ in His life, death, and resurrection.

The Basic Approaches to Deliverance

What are the ways to bring this woman back to normal consciousness and to liberate her from the bondage of the spirits that claimed ownership of her life? What are the different methods that could be used to set her free? How does each method approach the problem?

The Specialist Model

Many churches depend on a recognized specialist in deliverance to use his/her experience and knowledge as he/she chooses. The "specialist" methodology depends on the specialist to solve demonic problems that crop up in churches. Many deliverance methodologies utilize one key person in the deliverance process. The specialist methodology either explicitly or implicitly insists that only certain people (specialists) should be involved in helping or directing the deliverance process. These specialists may be recognized through gifting, calling, authority, personality, or effectiveness. The Roman Catholic Church explicitly states that only the priest can perform deliverance. The Protestant church often falls into a practical specialist model by bringing all demonic cases to the pastor. The Pentecostal/Charismatic church often looks to a traveling healer or exorcist to deal with deliverance problems. Specialists of all types typically use the following techniques: anointing oil, specific prayers, laying on of hands, strong or dominant personalities, shouting and/or yelling, and renunciation statements. This methodology seems to grow out of the clear need for a knowledgeable individual to sort through this complex area of evil supernaturalism. If the deliverance process can be corralled and controlled by recognized and respected specialists, many people believe that most of the excesses and extreme behavior will be eliminated. It is important to note that the whole arena of evil supernaturalism is extreme. Even Jesus had cases that were not tidy and quiet affairs. One father brought his boy to Jesus and the demon slammed the boy to the ground in his presence before the boy could be delivered. (Luke 9:42)

The Exorcism Model

This model focuses all its energy on driving the demons out of the person. It uses techniques which afflict demons and commands the demons to leave. It is believed demons will release their grip on the individual to escape the discomfort and pain. This model does not permanently liberate the person, and it does not deal with the causes of the demonic presence in the life of the afflicted. The goal of this form of deliverance is the immediate removal of the demonic spirits. This type of deliverance is practiced by Catholics, Protestants, and Pentecostals.

Those who use this model exclusively often cannot see their victories are aimed at temporary improvement. The Scriptures declare that if demons are driven from a person but there is no permanent solution then seven demons worse than the first will come back seeking to re-control the individual. (Matthew 12:43-45) Their techniques usually include praise and adoration of the Father, Son, and Holy Spirit in the presence of the demons. Godly music is usually played to the afflicted one. The exorcist will read or recite Scriptures, pray specific prayers, and make those who are afflicted confess their position in Christ, and submit to Him and, in some cases, make the demons admit Christ's superiority.

The Power Model

The "power" model emphasizes using the power of Christ over the power of the demons. The power model advises the deliverer to cloak themselves in the power and name of Christ and battle the demonic forces until they are forced to surrender before the greater might of the Lord Jesus Christ.

Power deliverance focuses on manifesting the demonic, and combating the demonic element with the power and authority of Christ. The manifestation of the demonic often results in pitched battles which can take hours and can occur over several days. Demons are asked questions to reveal their work, whether they receive power from certain objects, and what sins they claim as their reason to be present. Power deliverance relies on the name of the Lord Jesus Christ and His power and authority to set people free. Further techniques used in the power model are binding and loosing, specific spiritual gifts, renunciation of past sins, and information supplied by the demons. This model differs from the previous type of deliverance in that one attempts to eliminate the sinful source or choice which gives authority for the demonic presence.

Power deliverance often appeals to those performing the deliverance because of their ability to "see and hear" the invisible enemy. At the same time, it is a very distressing methodology to the afflicted because in order to allow the spirits to answer questions, a part of conscious control is surrendered to the demons. Also, there can be a great deal of physical pain associated with answering certain questions. There is controversy over the wisdom and validity of allowing demons to speak through an individual. Some see this as a way to demonstrate Christ's power over demons, to warn and encourage the afflicted person. Some critics suggest that allowing demonic spirits to manifest and give information, even for their own destruction, is not much different from a séance.

The Resistance Model

The resistance model of deliverance is interested in the person taking back volitional control of his/her own life. This model seeks to eliminate any manifestation of the demons. The presence and power of evil spirits is acknowledged but direct interaction is not desired or used. The goal is to teach the individual to confess his/her sins to the Lord and live righteously, especially staying away from certain types of "demonic" sins: pride, rebellion, bitterness, anger, lust, occultic involvement, and transference. Jesus' words to the paralytic in John 5:14 is the idea in this model. *Behold, you have been healed; do not sin anymore, so that nothing worse may befall you.*

This form of deliverance avoids direct contact with the spirit world by focusing on sin and righteous living. Any contact with the spirit world is held to a minimum. This deliverance methodology goes to the root of the afflicted person's problem, and deals with the specific sins (selfish and evil choices) which act like a magnet attracting demons. This inevitably leads to great stress being placed on the seven "demonic" sins: pride, rebellion, bitterness, anger, lust, occultic involvement, and transference.

The resistance model typically narrows the contact with the demonic to renunciation commands, prayers of resistance and expulsion after full confession, and repentance by the victim. Recently those using the resistance model have expanded the emphasis on confession to include confession of ancestor's sins and canceling any curses, hexes, vexes, charms, spells, omens, or any other occultic phenomena.

The Counseling Model

This model focuses on the mental processes and experiences which might cause aberrant demonic and/or occult behavior. This method usually refers the individual to a Christian psychiatrist or Christian psychotherapist. This is called the "counseling" model because of its stress on environmental and mental aspects of the problem. The counseling model recognizes it is the thought process and emotional responses that are the places of demonic attack. If those processes and reactions can be understood, then the evil influence can be exposed and avoided in the power of Christ.

This method has been developed relatively recently in Christian history. The counseling model does not usually acknowledge the demonic element as a cause of aberrant behavior. It chooses not to directly attack the spiritual influences but to overcome the emotional and environmental pressures shaping the afflicted person's life. In other words, if one can understand certain promptings or desires as evil or destructive, then they can be resisted and ignored.

The techniques in this model focus on the logical aspect of the afflicted person. Great emphasis is placed on uncovering and correcting environmental pressures, emotional traumas, and the thinking process. The techniques used to uncover these pressures include intensive listening, detailing family and personal histories, developing new mental perspectives, labeling, and encouraging an emotional attachment between the counselor and counselee. This process depends upon learning, insight, time, family and cultural patterns and relationships to correct the effects of spiritual problems.

The Teaching Model

This model emphasizes the person's understanding and appropriation of scriptural truth as the key to permanent freedom. It seeks to eliminate the manifestation through direct appeal to the person's consciousness while utilizing the teacher or deliverer's authority in Christ to command the demons to release the individual. Then begins the process of teaching one's position in Christ and how to uncover and resist the temptation, deception, and strongholds of Satan. This strand of deliverance is called the "teaching" model because of its emphasis on teaching the truth of Scripture.

This method focuses on the believer's position in Christ and the liberating ability of those truths. The teaching model seeks to direct the afflicted person's attention to the battle for the mind. ==This model believes it is the truths of Christ (His death, resurrection, ascension, and present ministry in heaven), when understood and applied by the afflicted, will liberate the oppress==ed. It also is formed around the idea that the New Testament supports a teaching model for deliverance. (John 8:31, 32; 2 Corinthians 2:11; 2 Timothy 2:24-26) It contends that permanent freedom from demonic bondage is only possible when the individual makes choices to live out the believer's strong and powerful position in Christ.

Summary

All the methodologies share the desire to free the afflicted from bondage. Each methodology exhibits case studies showing its effectiveness. Yet each differs on how to accomplish the permanent freedom of the afflicted. It is best to see that all these methodologies include vital truth for the whole of Christian deliverance. Any one strand is incomplete and cannot stand alone under the varied attack of the Enemy.

A New Mental Construct About Christian Deliverance

How we think about Christian deliverance and the overarching mental pictures we hold about demons and the spiritual world can significantly change our approach. Christian deliverance in the 21st century is in need of a new mental construct. We tend to see demons as invaders or armed robbers who come to pillage the lives of largely innocent people. This seems to come from a misunderstanding of Matthew 12:29. This invader model means that these surprise aggressors need to be found, arrested, removed, and locked away (preferably in the abyss). If this is the way we see demons, then their presence is always a surprise. This seems like an unwarranted tip of the hat to the naturalistic Enlightenment view of the world. But those involved in deliverance know that demons are not rare. They are almost everywhere. As one church leader remarked, "Demons are like pigeons in the park." "They are everywhere." I believe there is a better overarching mental picture for Christian deliverance than the invader imagery.

It is better to understand Christian deliverance as fumigation. Let me suggest we see demons as the maggots and cockroaches of the spiritual and moral world. This is not a perfect analogy, but I believe it is biblical and helpful. Is this not what Jesus suggests about demons, hell, and deliverance in Matthew 9:44-48; 12:44? We know demons are attracted to and seem to feed off of moral decay and wickedness. (Ephesians 6:12) In the natural world soon after there is death or filth, decay sets in and a host of molds, maggots, and insects gather. The same is true in the spiritual and moral world. When, through our choices, we promote or allow immorality and moral decay, the spiritual maggots gather. Not only does sin bring oppression and guilt, it invites demons. All of the strategies and techniques of Christian deliverance fit within this understanding of the demonic world, and it answers many of our questions.

Let me draw out this analogy a little further. In the physical world we are surrounded by bacteria and insects all the time. It is our positive life, our cleanliness, and our vigilance that keeps them at bay. In much the same way our moral actions or inactions give or deny these spiritual cockroaches a place in our lives. (Ephesians 4:26) The demons are always ready to strike, to grow, and to spread. It is our positive purity and love that keep these demonic beings at bay.

Think about the physical world again. Whenever and where ever people allow decay, filth, and unkempt conditions, the bugs will begin to take over. If the owners of a home sweep, clean, spray, and disinfect, then the bugs will be kept at bay by those activities. Isn't this the analogy Jesus uses about demons wanting to return to a house swept and cleaned, but the owner is not vigilant and truly occupying the house? (Matthew 12:44)

Sin is moral filth and if enough sin is piled upon itself, it creates a moral garbage dump crawling with spiritual maggots and cockroaches. This environment becomes spiritually and morally toxic for its perpetrators and those who are forced to relate to and live with them. The moral depravity of some can force others to be victims, living on a moral garbage dump. Eventually those victims become accustomed to living life on a garbage pile as normal even though nothing about it is normal. God calls us to rescue those who want to leave life on the decaying landfills of sin. Christ has said He wants to rescue people through us and He has supplied all the resources that are necessary to do it through His life, death, ascension, and ministry in heaven for us. Whoever will hear His voice and respond will be saved. (John 3:16; 36; 6:40; 47; Hebrews 3:7-11; 4:7)

This fumigation construct allows us to have a better picture of what is really happening when people sin. It allows us to understand what the Apostle Paul meant when he said in Ephesians 4:26 "Do not give the devil a place." Demons of various levels and desires are everywhere waiting for moral decay and moral filth so they can do their soul-killing work.

The fumigation model causes people to realize they must be alive, morally clean, and vigilant or they will be overrun by spiritual maggots. Morals matter. There is a huge difference between being moral and being immoral.

Our lives should be about glorifying Jesus Christ with all we say and do. When we have sinned, we need to confess and clean it up. Demons are present everywhere, but our focus should be on glorifying God through love and not on the demons. (Matthew 22:37-39) We do not need to be fumigation experts or consumed with demons, we just need to keep our lives morally pure so we can love from a pure heart. (1 Timothy 1:5) It is the signs of a loving, moral life that will keep the demonic world at bay.

2

SPECIALISTS:

Ghostbusters to the Rescue

Jenette[1] was a Christian struggling under terrible spiritual oppression. She was unable to read the Bible without falling asleep or going into a trance. Going to church was an awful strain as a multitude of voices demanded her to leave. She often flew into fits of rage and verbally attacked her husband or children for no apparent reason. In spite of this growing agony, she refused to allow anyone except a recognized specialist to pray for her or work on the problem. She insisted only an experienced, knowledgeable person should even know that she struggled. After hearing that I had helped others and was knowledgeable in this area, Jenette came to see me.

Jenette's case is ==an example of an unhealthy dependence on the specialist model of Christian deliverance==. The specialist model is the explicit or implicit belief that one needs a recognized expert to work in the demonic realm. While the specialist may utilize many different techniques in the deliverance process, the emphasis is that he/she is the only one operative in the process. This is the popular concept of how to deal with any bizarre spiritual problem. It was popularized in movies like *Ghostbusters*, where an elite (if not wacky) team of specialists is called in to deal with problems of ghosts, haunting, and demons. The movie, *The*

Exorcist, focused the attention on the problem of the demonic and those who were trained to deal with it. There are three forms the specialist model has taken corresponding with three large divisions of Christianity.

The Roman Catholic Form

The Roman Catholic Church has developed the most explicit version of the specialist model. The Catholic Church refuses to allow deliverance to take place, without the permission of the local bishop, using a qualified priest. The selected priest must have passed the requirements for the order of exorcism and must have been prepared ahead of time to use the sanctioned ceremonies of the Catholic Church.[2]

The Protestant Form

The Protestant church uses a de facto specialist model. In most Protestant churches, the pastor is the specialist on all spiritual matters including deliverance. Some pastors do shun this area altogether and refuse to admit the possibilities of demonic invasion. This means the pastor is operating as a specialist in ruling out the demons as a source of the person's problems. If the pastor does allow deliverance ministries, he usually reinforces a specialist mentality by a refusal to involve others in the deliverance process. It is common for pastors to form a prayer team around themselves and not trust others in deliverance other than to pray.

The Pentecostal/Charismatic form

The Pentecostal/Charismatic churches place special emphasis on the miraculous (healing the sick, casting out demons, etc.). Within Pentecostal/Charismatic theology, this miraculous emphasis is supposed to spread to every Christian so all can perform a deliverance. There has been, however, a specialist model even within this group. A specialist surfaces as a particular healer and gathers a reputation (Wigglesworth, Roberts, etc.) within a local congregation, region, or nationality. This person is then regarded as the expert and is expected to heal all spiritual problems.

History of the Expert Model

The specialist model became the dominant position of the Catholic Church following the fourth century. The fourth century witnessed three critical events which pushed the Christian church to officially sanction the specialist model as the only Christian deliverance procedure. Since the specialist model is only one of the six ways of dealing with the demonic, the effectiveness of the church suffered.

The three events which led to the ascendancy of the specialist model of deliverance were: the conversion of the Emperor Constantine, the official recognition of Christianity as a religion of the Roman Empire, and the Council of Laodicea. The first of these three – the conversion of the Emperor – released the church from persistent persecution. No longer under persecution, the church grew explosively. The church was not prepared for the problems of social acceptance. It had existed as an outcast minority for three centuries. The pressures of social acceptability and material prosperity made controlling apostasy, blasphemy, and licentiousness difficult. Rapid growth and social acceptability made the church soft and unwilling to expose satanic schemes in people who had worldly and fleshly reasons to want to be a part of the church.[3]

The second major event of the fourth century was the recognition of Christianity as the official religion of the Roman Empire. This opened the door for an even greater social acceptance of Christianity. This had two profound effects upon the church in terms of her dealings with the demonic. First, the church had a huge influx of the unconverted who tried to embrace to the empire's new religion. Their lack of conversion meant they operated as change agents within Christianity for their old beliefs systems. Second, because Christianity was the official religion, the Emperor could begin waging a war against the forces of paganism within the empire. He could not battle spiritually, only physically. The effect was that he began persecuting non-Christians in the same way Christians had been persecuted a few years before. This forced those under demonic influence to go underground. These two results of the official sanction of Christianity diminished the number of demonic confrontations and, therefore, reduced the number of deliverance cases. This led to the third of the major developments of the fourth century-- the development of the specialist emphasis.[4]

The third major event of the fourth century which altered the emphasis of deliverance within the church was the Council of Laodicea near the end of the fourth century. This Council outlawed anyone except deliverance specialists from performing exorcisms. This established the specialist model as the only approved method of deliverance. This was a radical departure from the church's early position. In the first and second centuries the Church had numerous individuals involved in deliverance. There was not a formalized way, nor approved individual to deliver the afflicted. Origen, an early church scholar, states: "The ejection of demons was not a specialty among Christians but available to all. In fact it was usually the unlettered, who made manifest the grace of God and despicable weakness of demons."[5]

All Christians in the early church were acknowledged as capable of being involved in the deliverance process. Certain believers, however, because of knowledge, giftedness, or experience were the ones that usually led in these matters. As the church became larger and more organized, those involved in deliverance came under the auspices of the Bishop. This led to the formation of the office of "exorcist." When the Bishop identified someone who could carry on this vital work, he appointed that person to the office of exorcist. Upon being appointed to this office, the person was given a book of prayers and adjurations (a manual on deliverance) to be used against the Devil.[6] These manuals were designed to increase the newly appointed exorcist's knowledge and effectiveness in this area. These local church manuals eventually became elaborate systems written under the pseudonyms of the great saints of the Church (Ambrose, Augustine, etc.). Using the office of exorcist and the manuals, the bishop exercised a growing control over the activity and actions of those involved in deliverance. The need for exorcists and the desire for greater control eventually led to adding "exorcist" to the steps of the priesthood. This was also done to save the church from the extremes and excesses of novices working among the demonized. By the end of the fourth century the popularity of the church and the church-state mix made exorcism an unpleasant and unacceptable activity. Therefore, the church moved to control those involved in deliverance by outlawing "exorcism" except by the ordained clergy.[7]

The Council of Laodicea, which belongs to the end of the fourth century, forbade in its canon twenty-six exorcisms by those who have not received ordination. These exorcisms must be understood literally; they do not mean catechetical instruction. Here the church is reserving to the bishops, priests, and deacons the monopoly of exorcism.[8]

Foundation of the Specialist Model

There are three essential prerequisites for utilizing a specialist approach to demonic deliverance. They are knowledge, experience, and giftedness.

Knowledge

There are four specific kinds of knowledge that are needed to become a specialist in spiritual warfare. First, a deep abiding knowledge of God and a regular practice of the classic spiritual disciplines that will create a deep intimacy with God. If a person enters into intense spiritual warfare and does not truly know God through the Lord Jesus Christ, then they will be attacked severely as the exorcists were attacked in Acts 19:13-16:

> *But also some of the Jewish exorcists, who went from place to place, attempted to name over those who had the evil spirits the name of the Lord Jesus, saying, "I adjure you by Jesus whom Paul preaches." Seven sons of one Sceva, a Jewish chief priest, were doing this. And the evil spirit answered and said to them, "I recognize Jesus, and I know about Paul, but who are you?" And the man, in whom was the evil spirit, leaped on them and subdued all of them and overpowered them, so that they fled out of that house naked and wounded.*

This need for accurate theological information has caused many to seek formal seminary education which can be helpful, but it is also possible to pursue theological education through intense Bible study and reading sound theological books about God, such as, *Knowing God* by JI Packer, *Knowledge of the Holy* by AW Tozer, *Mere Christianity* by CS Lewis and *The Pursuit of God* by AW Tozer. These are just a few of the great books that will build a solid foundation for understanding and relating to the Almighty God.

It is not enough to just have an intellectual knowledge of God; one must have a deep relationship with the Almighty. The Apostle John tells us the goal is to "know Him who was from the beginning." (1 John 2:12-14) The regular practice of the classic spiritual disciplines is what brings a deep, abiding comfortability with the presence and wisdom of God. These practices would include confession, yielding to the Holy Spirit, biblical meditation, biblical memorization, Bible study, various practices and disciplines of prayer, service, worship, fellowship with other believers of differing spiritual levels, practice of communion, believer baptism, witnessing, fasting, solitude, other disciplines of abstinence, and loving by faith, giving, and the development of a generous spirit. There are a number of good books in this area of spiritual formation that can inspire people to begin practicing these disciplines and drawing nearer to the Lord. I wrote a practical book on how to actually practice each of these disciplines called *Spiritual Disciplines of a C.H.R.I.S.T.I.A.N.* In order to effectively war in the spirit realm, one must truly have an active faith and relationship with Jesus Christ.

The second crucial area of knowledge that is needed for effective spiritual warfare is deep understanding of the aspects of salvation and its benefits. The writer to the book of Hebrews reminds us we have "so great a salvation," and we should not neglect to learn about it and take advantage of it in fullest measure. The salvation Jesus won on the cross for those who would believe is amazingly deep and wide. The New Testament takes considerable time to detail the various aspects of our salvation. There are at least twenty-seven different elements of salvation that have practical application for every believer. The following is a listing of these dynamic aspects of salvation. Every person who wants to go into intense spiritual warfare should understand these aspects of salvation:

God's foreknowledge
Election
The Creation of the world

The Restraining ministry of Holy Spirit
The Holy Spirit's ministry of conviction
God's call
Conversion
Justification
Regeneration
Union with Christ
Adoption
Spirit baptism
The Indwelling Holy Spirit
Sealing of Holy Spirit
Sanctification
The Filling ministry of Holy Spirit
Spiritual gifts
Perseverance
Glorification
Redemption of the body
Marriage supper of the lamb
New heavens and new earth

Each theological tradition will see these aspects of salvation slightly differently. Unfortunately, because of these differences between Christian camps, we have not declared the truths of our great salvation enough. Christians need to know what Jesus the Christ bought for them on the cross of Calvary.

The third area of knowledge that is important for the warrior in a spiritual war is the knowledge of the angelic realm and the absolute division between good and evil. We cannot afford to be naïve about the nature of the spirit world, the levels of angelic beings, their powers and limitations. The Scriptures clearly declare there are at least four types of angels: Cherubim, Seraphim, Archangels, and finally angels. There has been Christian theological speculation about ten levels and/or kinds of angels. The Scriptures also declare that one third of the holy angels fell in sin and rebellion with Lucifer. (Revelation 12:4) These evil angels have arrayed themselves in a ranking under Lucifer's headship: "For our struggle is not against flesh and blood, but against the rulers, against the powers, against the world forces of this darkness, against the spiritual forces of wickedness in the heavenly places." (Ephesians 6:12) Again there are several good books that detail the basic Christian theological understanding of angels. *Angels: Elect and Evil* by Fred Dickenson is becoming a classic theological tome. On a more popular level, *Angels* by Billy Graham gives an accurate theological understanding and stories involving angels. There are a number of sensational and speculative books about angels, so it would be best to talk with a trusted pastor or professor about which books would be best to read in this area.

The third area of essential information and understanding for the spiritual warrior is knowledge of the schemes of Satan. In 2 Corinthians 2:11, we hear the Apostle Paul tell us we are not ignorant of the schemes of Satan and yet most Christians are completely naïve when it comes to the strategies and devices Satan uses to destroy our faith and our churches. The Scripture has not been silent about what the Devil and the demons will try and do, but we as Christians have not been paying attention. God has "hidden" the schemes of Satan in the names He has given to this unholy angel throughout the Scriptures. The following is a listing of these names which will give you the schemes that the demons will be using. It is possible you will see what he is trying to do to you right now through looking at this list and defining the names.

> Lucifer: Isaiah 14:12
> Satan: Job 1
> Devil: 1 Peter 5:8
> Deceiver: Revelation 12:9
> Tempter: Matthew 4:3
> Murder: John 8:44
> Sinner: 1 John 3:8
> Beelzebub: Matthew 12:24
> Father of Lies: John 8:44
> Enemy: Matthew 13:39
> Evil One: Matthew 13:39
> Angel of light: 2 Corinthians 11:13
> Roaring Lion: 1 Peter 5:8
> Belial: 2 Corinthians 6:15
> God of this world: 2 Corinthians 4:4
> Dragon: Revelation 13
> Serpent/Snake: Genesis 3
> Prince of the power of the air: Ephesians 2
> Ruler of this world: John 17
> Wicked One: Matthew 13:19, Ephesians 6:16

Satan is alive and well and living on planet earth. He is our enemy and wants to destroy our faith, our reputation, and the churches we so desperately need for support and refuge. The spiritual warrior must not fall victim to a scheme of Satan. Realize that if you go into helping people out of their bondage to the Devil and his demons, you will be attacked. You should know what form those attacks will take. You must stand firm against these schemes.

The above types of knowledge allow an individual to point the way to freedom. (John 8: 31, 32) Some have sought to enter into deliverance ministry based on their spiritual giftedness or experience watching others work among the demonically afflicted. However, without a proper grounding in the doctrines of Scripture, even a conscientious worker can be led astray by the half-truths of Satan. Mark Bubeck details the need for knowledge if one is to sustain a ministry in this area.

> "The counselor must not be presumptuous or trifling in these matters. Such bold warfare should always be accompanied by deep and full commitment to the Lordship of Jesus Christ and requires careful doctrinal study on the ground of our victory. Scripture memorization should be practiced so the sword of the Spirit will be ready for use. The snarling, wicked powers of darkness will do all they can to intimidate and frighten the counselor in such encounters. Their tricks and deceptions are varied and numerous. Complete dependence upon the Holy Spirit and the victory of Christ alone will suffice to see one through to victory."[9]

Experience

One of the key elements in being able to work among the demonized is experience. The Apostle John tells us that one of the crucial growth steps in the Christian life is "overcoming the evil one." (1 John 2:12-14) This means we must begin to recognize our skirmishes with him, and we should be involved in helping set people free as apprentices. There are a number of books, tapes, and even DVD's available where the growing Christian can watch and learn from different "experts" in the field of spiritual warfare. This book is one such resource but there are dozens of others from every type of theological stripe.

==Even the apostles were needing experience== under Jesus' tutelage as they were unable to deliver the demon-possessed boy at the foot of the Mount of Transfiguration. Look at this passage in Matthew 17:14-24 and notice the growing experience of the apostles:

> *When they came to the crowd, a man came up to Jesus, falling on his knees before Him and saying, "Lord, have mercy on my son, for he is a lunatic and is very ill; for he often falls into the fire and often into the water. I brought him to Your disciples, and they could not cure him." And Jesus answered and said, "You unbelieving and perverted generation, how long shall I be with you? How long shall I put up with you? Bring him here to Me." And Jesus rebuked him, and the demon came out of him, and the boy was cured at once. Then the disciples came to Jesus privately and said, "Why could we not drive it out?" And He said to them, "Because of the littleness of your faith; for truly I say to you, if you have faith the size of a mustard seed, you will say to this mountain, 'Move from here to there,' and it will move; and nothing will be impossible to you. ["But this kind does not go out except by*

prayer and fasting."] And while they were gathering together in Galilee, Jesus said to them, "The Son of Man is going to be delivered into the hands of men; and they will kill Him, and He will be raised on the third day." And they were deeply grieved.

The more one works with this area of Christianity, the more competent one becomes. There are some bits of knowledge and understanding that are only gained through practice and pattern recognition. You have seen this before and you remember the last time you made the wrong choice or your mentor did something that was unusual, it worked powerfully. It is almost a surety that a Christian speaker who mentions working in this area will receive a number of phone calls or requests to work with the person. Experience allows a person not to be challenged by some new wrinkle in a particular case. Experience allows the use of a variety of techniques that can be employed. Experience allows a sense of pace and decorum in working with demons and the afflicted. Those who have witnessed deliverance sessions or have been a part of a ministry team will often be thrust into this specialist role.

Overall Giftedness

Throughout the centuries, Christians have recognized there are certain people specially gifted to work in this area of demonic deliverance. It is often thought there is a "gift" of deliverance given to an individual by God. However, there is no gift of deliverance listed in Scripture. Instead of a specific gift, it is best to see giftedness divided into two areas: a specific call to work among the demonic and the possession of a group of gifts (such as knowledge, wisdom, discernment of spirits, etc.) which eases the deliverance process.

In relation to the specific call of God to work among the demonically afflicted, the church has historically recognized a special anointing upon certain individuals to perform this type of ministry. Also the church has often recognized a threefold division in the concept of spiritual giftedness: the gift, the ministry, the effect. This threefold division grows out of I Corinthians 12:4-7. "Now there are varieties of gifts, but the same Spirit. And there are varieties of ministries but the same Lord. And there are varieties of effects, but the same God works all things and all persons."

The early church saw deliverance as a ministry the Lord specifically equipped certain people to accomplish even though anyone could do it. The modern church has not recognized a ministry position involving deliverance. It may be only a few years off as the need continues to rise. At present the church has a growing number of people in this area who feel called of God to continue long-term in this type of ministry. Kurt Koch writes, "In order to counsel such [those oppressed by demons] people, a Christian needs a commission from God in the equipment provided by the Holy Spirit."[11]

Koch adds a word of warning involving volunteering to which God has not called them:

> Without a commission from God, a Christian should not venture too far into the area of the demonic occult. There are certain rules that have to be obeyed. People with a sensitive nervous system

or with past oppression of their own should not attempt to do any work in this field. Recent converts should also refrain from this type of work. A Christian working in this field must also live soberly and have their life clearly founded upon the teachings of the Bible. Fanatics, extremists are unfit for this type of work. There is value in some form of medical training and/or psychological training.[12]

Giftedness

There are specific gifts that are very useful in the fight against Satan. The primary gift is the discernment of spirits, which is the special ability God has given to some believers to know when evil spirits are present. When this gift is a refined and developed, there is the ability to know the name, work, and attachment point of a demonic spirit. No one starts out with the gift operating at this level. One woman I have worked with had the gift of the discernment of spirits. She had developed this gift to a high degree. On one occasion when she did not accompany the deliverance team, I called her on the phone to ask her name of the demon and its work. She prayed and gave me a name and an activity. I went back to the session armed with her information and made substantial progress in the session. The other gifts which are especially helpful for a deliverance ministry are words of knowledge (the special ability to know information not normally available) and words of wisdom (the special ability to know how to apply the truth to a person's life). These gifts greatly reduce the typical struggle involved in deliverance. These gifts (discernment of spirits, word of knowledge, and words of wisdom), however, seem to work best when spread among a few individuals on a deliverance team rather than concentrated in one individual. Too often, if one person has a concentration of these gifts, the temptation to pride and power is overwhelming. These gift clusters are special tools given by the Lord to help in a deliverance type of ministry. These valuable instruments must not be cast aside.

Working with the demonically afflicted is perseverant and at times exhausting work. It is usually individualistic work. People who have been afflicted by the work of the enemy in severe ways need to rebuild the way they think, act, and the way they talk with others. This highly individualized work usually is handled by a person with a shepherding gift and/or a mercy gift. Prayer teams and counselors are usually people gifted by God with shepherding gifts and mercy gifts which allow them to focus on one individual at a time and stay with people over a long period of time. Therefore one usually does not find a person with high leadership gifts involved in long-term work with the demonically afflicted because leadership gifts are used for large groups of people.

Techniques of the Specialist

The specialist utilizes a number of techniques to free people from demonic bondage. Each technique needs to be explored as to its ways of application and reason for inclusion in this type of deliverance.

Anointing Oil

James 5:16 tells the members of the congregation to call for the elders if they are sick. The elders are told to anoint the afflicted person with oil and pray for them. Demonization (mild to severe) has historically come under this type of cure. Although the particulars of the anointing differ, Christian leaders have practiced this biblical mandate and have seen God heal. This way of utilizing God's healing power is a specialist technique, for the Bible restricts it to elders.

My church uses this technique in the following way. A person who is sick asks the elders to come and pray. At least two members of the elder board meet with the individual and go through a set procedure. The elders let the person know there are five potential reasons for an illness (sickness unto death, sickness because of sin, sickness from reproof, sickness for God's glory through healing, sickness for God's glory through remaining sick with greater grace), and we must discern why God has allowed this illness before we can pray properly. The individual must confess any sin in his/her life. After the elders agree as to why this person is sick, then they can pray according to God's will about healing. God has done miraculous things in many churches through this anointing process.

It is appropriate to touch a drop of olive oil to the forehead of the afflicted to be a symbol of dedication to the Lord Jesus and a desire for the presence of the Holy Spirit. The afflicted person needs to be in agreement that they want this done. The anointing oil is a powerful symbol of the Holy Spirit in the spirit world. Use it.

Most spiritual warriors have found the use of anointing oil to dedicate a house to the Lord Jesus and the presence of the Holy Spirit is very powerful. The anointing oil is a symbol of the Holy Spirit and when used with prayer and a sincere faith, it can be a significant block to demonic activity.

It is appropriate to anoint the doorposts of a house with olive oil and thereby declare that the house belongs to the Lord Jesus. I can remember being asked to go to dozens of houses and anoint the doorposts and the doors to bedrooms with anointing oil. I was always pleased when people would report back to me there was a new spirit of calm in the house and the spiritual problems were not present as they had been before.

One family came to me because their son had severe terrors and was highly reactive to the name of Jesus during these periods. I went to the home and dedicated the home to the Lord Jesus, anointed the front door with olive oil, the bedrooms, and then the young boy's bed. At each point we stopped to pray and asked for a strong presence of the Holy Spirit to be there in association with the oil. The whole family was there and in agreement with this dedication process. Later that night when it was time for the young man to be put to bed, during their prayer time he flew into a rage and began screaming, "I want that oil off my bed." After talking and praying in the other room, the young man agreed he wanted the Lord Jesus and the Holy Spirit to protect him during the night. He laid down and slept soundly and the night terrors have not been a problem. This young man needed to give his blessing and permission to this dedication process. When he gave his permission, then there could be no further agitation in the spirit realm.

Particular Prayers

Throughout the centuries Christians have found certain types of prayers have had greater impact in the demonic arena than others. These types of prayers are called warfare prayers. They are full of claims on God's promises and salvation. They take a strong and powerful, if not attacking, tone. In older centuries there was a tendency to directly address the Devil. In recent years, it seems better to use the tactic of Michael the Archangel when he disputed with the Devil over the body of Moses (Jude 1:9) by asking the Lord to rebuke the Devil. The following are two examples of this type of prayer. The first is the older version. The second was written recently.

Prayer one: "I come against you, most unclean damned spirit; you are grown old in evil, the substance of crimes, the origin of sin; you delight in deceits, sacrileges, defilements, slaughters. Invoking the name of our Lord Jesus Christ we rebuke you and adjure you through His majesty and power, passion and resurrection, advent and judgment, that in whatever part of the members you are hiding, you manifest yourself by your own confession, and that, shaken by spiritual flames and invisible torments, you flee from the vessel that you believe yourself in possession of, leaving it purged for the Lord after having been your dwelling place. Let it suffice that in former ages you ruled over almost the whole of the world and in the hearts of men. Now day by day your kingdom will be destroyed and may your weapons daily grow ineffectual until the end. What you suffer now was long ago prefigured. Already you were devastated by the plagues of the Egyptians, you were drowned in Pharoah, destroyed in Jericho, prostrated in the seven Cannaanite nations, defeated by Samson in the Philistines, cut off by David in Goliath, hanged by Mordecai in Haman, cast down by Daniel in Bel, punished in the dragon, pierced through by Judith in Holofernes, subjugated by the Lord to human commands, blinded by Paul in the magician, burned in the serpent, burst open by Peter in Simon; by all the saints you are put to rout, tortured, lacerated, consigned to eternal flames and infernal darkness, from where our Lord Jesus Christ in a second Adam rescues man while He triumphs over you. Depart, depart, from where you are, and seek no more to enter bodies dedicated to God. May they be forbidden to you forever, in the name of the Father and the Son and Holy Spirit, and in the glory of the Lord's passion, by whose blood they are saved, whose advent they await, whose judgment they confess."[13]

Prayer two: "Heavenly Father, I bow in worship and praise before You. I cover myself with the blood of the Lord Jesus Christ as my protection during this time of prayer. I surrender myself completely and unreservedly in every area of my life to Yourself. I do take a stand against all the workings of Satan that would hinder me in this time of prayer, and I address myself only to the true and living God and refuse any involvement of Satan in my prayer.

"Satan, I command you, in the name of the Lord Jesus Christ, to leave my presence with all your demons, and I bring the blood of the Lord Jesus Christ between us. Heavenly Father, I worship You, and I give You praise. I recognize that You are worthy to receive all glory and honor and praise. I renew my allegiance to You and pray that the blessed Holy Spirit would enable me in this time of prayer. I am thankful, Heavenly Father, that You have loved me from ty that You sent the Lord Jesus Christ into the world to die as my substitute that I would be redeemed. I am thankful that the Lord Jesus Christ came as my representative and that through him You have completely forgiven me; You have given me eternal life; You have given me the perfect righteousness of the Lord Jesus Christ, so I am now justified. I am thankful that in Him You have made me complete, and that You have offered Yourself to me to be my daily help and strength.

"Heavenly Father, come and open my eyes that I might see how great You are and how complete Your provision is for this new day. I do in the name of the Lord Jesus Christ, take my place with Christ in the heavenlies with all powers of darkness and wicked spirits under my feet. I am thankful that the victory the Lord Jesus Christ is in the heavenlies; therefore, I declare that all wicked spirits are subject to me in the name of the Lord Jesus Christ.

"I am thankful for the armor You have provided, and I put on the girdle of truth, the breastplate of righteousness, the sandals of peace, and the helmet of salvation. I lift up the shield of faith against all the fiery darts of the Enemy, and take in my hand the sword of the spirit, the Word of God. I use Your Word against all the forces of evil in my life, and I put on this armor and live and pray in complete dependence upon You, blessed Holy Spirit.

"I am grateful, Heavenly Father, that the Lord Jesus Christ spoiled all the demonic powers and made a show of them openly and triumphed over them in Himself. I claim all that victory for my life today. I reject out of my life all the insinuations, the accusations, and the temptations of Satan. I affirm that the Word of God is true, and I choose to live today in the light of God's Word. I choose, Heavenly Father, to live in obedience to You and in fellowship with Yourself. Open my eyes and show me the areas of my life that would not please You. Work in my life that there be no ground to give Satan a foothold against me. Show me any area of weakness. Show me any area of my life that I must deal with so that I would please You. I do in every way today stand for You and the ministry of the Holy Spirit in my life.

"By faith and in dependence upon You, I put off the old man and stand into all the victory of the crucifixion where the Lord Jesus Christ provided cleansing from the old nature. I put on the new man and stand into all the victory of the resurrection and the provision He has made for me there to live above sin. Therefore, in this day, I put off the old nature with its selfishness, and I put on the new nature with its love. I put off the old nature with its fear and I put on the new nature with its strength. I put off today the old nature with all its deceitful lusts and I put on the new nature with all its righteousness and purity.

"I do in every way stand in the victory of the ascension and the glorification of the Son of God where all principalities and powers were made subject to Him I claim my place in Christ victorious with Him over all the enemies of my soul. Blessed Holy Spirit, I pray that You would fill me. Come into my life, break down every idol. And cast out every foe.

"I am thankful, Heavenly Father, for the expression of your will for my daily life as You have shown me in Your Word. I therefore claim all the will of God for today. I am thankful that You have blessed me with all spiritual blessings in heavenly places in Christ Jesus. I am thankful that You have begotten me unto a living hope by the resurrection of Jesus Christ from the dead. I am thankful that You have made a provision so that today I can live filled with the Spirit of God with love and joy and self-control in my life. I recognize that this is Your will for me, and I therefore reject and resist all the endeavors of Satan and of his demons to rob me of the will of God.

"I refuse in this day to believe my feelings, and I hold up the shield of faith against all the accusations and against all the insinuations that Satan would put in my mind. I claim the fullness of the will of God for today.

"I do, in the name of the Lord Jesus Christ, completely surrender myself to You, Heavenly Father, as a living sacrifice. I choose not to be conformed to this world. I choose to be transformed by the renewing of my mind, and I pray that You would show me Your will and enable me to walk in all the fullness of the will of God today.

"I am thankful, Heavenly Father, that the weapons of our warfare are not carnal, but mighty through God to the pulling down of strongholds, to casting down of imaginations and every high thing that exalted itself against the knowledge of God, and to bring every thought into obedience to the Lord Jesus Christ. Therefore in my own life today I tear down the strongholds of Satan, and I smash the plans of Satan that have been formed against me. I tear down the strongholds of Satan against my mind, and I surrender my mind to You, blessed Holy Spirit. I affirm, Heavenly Father, that You have not given us the spirit of fear, but of power and of love and of a sound mind. I break and smash the strongholds of Satan formed against my emotions today, and I give my emotions to You. I smash the strongholds of Satan formed against my will today and I give my will to You and choose to make the right decisions of faith. I smash the strongholds of Satan formed against my body today, and I give my body to You, recognizing that I am Your temple; and I rejoice in Your mercy and Your goodness.

"Heavenly Father, I pray that now through this day You would quicken me; show me the way that Satan is hindering, tempting, lying, counterfeiting, and distorting the truth in my life. Enable me to be the kind of person that would please You. Enable me to be aggressive in prayer. Enable me to be aggressive mentally and to think Your thoughts after You, and to give You Your rightful place in my life.

"Again, I now cover myself with the blood of the Lord Jesus Christ and pray that You, blessed Holy Spirit, would bring all the work of the crucifixion, all the work of the resurrection, all the work of the glorification, and all the work of Pentecost in to my life today. I surrender myself to You. I refuse to be discouraged. You are God of all hope. You have proven Your power by resurrecting Jesus Christ from the dead, and I claim in every way Your victory over all satanic forces active in my life, and I reject these forces; and I pray in the name of the Lord Jesus Christ with thanksgiving. Amen".[14]

The reaction to this type of prayer is varied and at times spectacular. Mark Bubeck, the author, speaks of the reactions in the following:

> The Devil hates this prayer. Usually before working with anyone who has deep demonic affliction, I will request that we read this prayer in

unison. Many times the oppressed one can read only with great difficulty. Sometimes sight problems, voice problems, or mind confusion become so intense that the afflicted person can continue only with great effort. It is the truth of God that Satan cannot resist, and he vigorously fights it being applied against him. Those serious about warfare should daily use a prayer of this type along with other prayer examples shared in this book.[15]

Laying on of Hands

The New Testament records numerous occasions where the apostles or elders laid hands upon people to transfer spiritual authority or power to certain individuals. (Mark 8:23; 10:16; Luke 4:40; Acts 8:17-18; 9:17; 2 Timothy 1:6) This continues in some churches today. One woman who was plagued by demons operating through bizarre eating disorders and a counterfeit gift of tongues did not begin to become free until I laid my hands upon her forehead as the rest of the team prayed. The laying on of hands was a visible way to transfer the faith and spiritual authority of the team to the young woman.

When a spiritual warrior is praying for an afflicted person, it can be very appropriate to place a hand on their head or hover the hand just above the head while one is praying for the person. It must be clear it is not the touch of the specialist's hand that transfers power to the afflicted. It is the faith of the specialist, the faith of the afflicted, and the faith of the prayer team along with the power of prayer that brings relief. The Devil would like to trick people into believing it is the physical act of touching the afflicted that releases the power of God. If he can get a naïve spiritual warrior to believe the power is in them and is released through their specific touch, then he can get people touching in inappropriate ways and places to try and "release" the power of God.

Personality or Emotional Strength

Throughout history those involved in a long-term ministry to the demonically afflicted have been those with a strong or dominant personality or great emotional strength. Joseph Turmeil in his book the, *The Life of the Devil,* suggests the following reasons:

> Theoretically, it (exorcism) was accessible to all Christians. But, to exercise it fruitfully, it was necessary to be capable of intimidating the demons, that is to say, the demoniacs; and this required aplomb, a powerful voice and imperious gestures. Tertullian exaggerates, according to his custom, when he tells us that the first-comer among the Christians casts out the demons. But we can, on the contrary, believe Origen, who tells us that the exorcisms were, above all, performed by uncultured persons. The timid, the refined, failed miserably, and such incapable persons were found, above all, in cultivated circles. In short, the well frequented exorcist, those who had a large clientele and much work, constituted a closed corporation; closed by means of elimination, since all the incapable were excluded from it by the force of circumstances. [16]

It is important to note all Christians can be involved in deliverance, but sustained involvement requires great personality strength.

Shouting or Yelling

One technique often used by those who deal with the demonically afflicted is to shout or yell at the demons when they manifest themselves. Although it is rarely advocated, it is often practiced. It often results from frustration or righteous indignation with a desire to demonstrate the power of Christ over the demonic invader. It results from frustration or righteous indignation. It has the effect of letting the afflicted know who is in control and seeking to intimidate the demons. Calls for the demons to leave or for the person to re-emerge often need to be stated forcefully, but they do not need to be done with loudness or strain. The spirit world obeys authority and Christ is the ultimate authority in the world. Remember when the Centurion came to Jesus and told Him he understood authority and all Jesus had to do to heal his son was to say the word. Remember that Jesus marveled at this man's faith. The spirit world obeys rules. There is cause and effect in the spirit realm. What the Christian authority wants should take place unless there is some technicality or willfulness on the part of the afflicted. There is a need to be clear, forceful in Christ, and powerful in the use of the victory Christ won; but there is not usually a need to yell or shout.

This practice can result in the counselor beginning to rely on the power of his voice or his own anger, frustration, or energy to drive away the demons rather than on Christ's power. A shift to a personal power source in combating wicked spirits leads to destructive results. It can subtly introduce a psychological abuse of the counselee. It can wear out the leader because of the higher level of energy and emotional expenditure. It can suggest to the leader that deliverance is dependent upon their exertions rather than Christ's power.

Renunciation Statements

All branches of Christianity utilize renunciation statements to cancel out the power of Satan's work in the life of a person. Sin (especially occultic sin) is like signing a contract with the enemy and giving him power to influence and control the person. Therefore it is crucial to renounce the sins committed in the past. Renunciation statements include personal confession and renunciation as well as ancestral confession and renunciation. Ancestral confession and renunciation is needed because of contracts and sin which hang like a plague over family lines. This will be dealt with in greater detail in the section on confession in the resistance model. When a person renounces past sins and the sins of their ancestors, contracts the Devil is holding against the person are cancelled. An example of a personal confession and renunciation is:

> On the authority of the Lord Jesus Christ I render inoperative all wicked spirits having to do with (name of counselee). We take for him the full victory the Lord Jesus Christ as won over Satan and all his forces. We cancel all ground and consent he had ever given to the Devil and wicked spirits. (Name of counselee) is bought with the blood of the Lord Jesus Christ and is to be entirely to His glory. On the authority of the Lord Jesus Christ we resist you, Satan. Loose

your hold upon (name of counselee) and be gone from him. On the authority of the Lord Jesus Christ I command all wicked spirits to leave him and go where Christ sends them, never to return.

After making the command, have the counselee pray, "Lord Jesus, deliver me from all the power of Satan." Then lead him in speaking aloud the above declaration himself as you personalize it and give it to him clause by clause. Finally, thank the Lord for what He has done and pray for the counselee to be healed of all the works of the wicked ones. Instruct him to surrender anew to the Lord Jesus Christ and to ask to be filled with the Holy Spirit. [17]

An example of the second type of renunciation prayer is:

In the name of Jesus Christ I renounce all the works of the Devil together with the occult practices of my forefathers, and I subscribe myself to the Lord Jesus Christ, my Lord and Savior, both now and forever. In the name of the Father, and of the Son, and of the Holy Spirit, Amen. [18]

While this process is needed in most cases of demonization, it can often result in an outburst of bizarre activity when used with the severely demonized. Therefore it should be utilized in the presence of a prayer team and after other techniques are used. [19]

CRITIQUE

Since the days of the early church, some have had greater effectiveness than others in working with demons. In most cases, those who did deliverance work were involved in sustained ministries.[20] Therefore, it is naive to suggest there are no specialists or authorities in this field. It is, however, time to examine the relative strengths, weaknesses and limitations of this approach to deliverance.

Strengths

1. There is scriptural support and precedence for the specialist model.

In Matthew 10:1, Jesus pulled His twelve apostles aside from the larger mass of disciples which followed Him and gave those twelve power to cast out demons. He made them specialists by the authority and instruction He gave them. In 1 Corinthians 12:7-11, the Apostle Paul lists the distinguishing of spirits as a spiritual gift. This suggests God specially equips certain believers to work in this area to distinguish between demonic agency and the movement of the Holy Spirit. In II Timothy 2:24-26, the Apostle Paul states that the pastor must be especially kind, gentle, and knowledgeable to lead those caught by the snare of the Devil to do His will into repentance. Even James 5:13-16 suggests the elders are specialists in the area of damage done as a result of sin. They are specialists simply because they are elders. There is, therefore, scriptural precedence for the elevation and promotion of some to the position of expertise in the area of spiritual warfare. This is not to suggest the rest of the body can remain ignorant about spiritual warfare, for clear warnings are given about the degree of readiness which the whole body must display. (2 Corinthians 2:10-11; Ephesians 6:10-18; 1 Peter 5:8,9) It is also clear some rise above the norm in knowledge, giftedness, or experience in spiritual warfare.

2. The specialist model deals with the demonic in the most natural way to the average person. Bring a complex problem to a specialist.

One of the greatest strengths of the specialist model is that it is one of the most natural ways of dealing with a complex or fearful problem. Average Christians naturally go to their pastor when they are overwhelmed by a spiritual problem. The pastor needs an above-average understanding of the spiritual realm and a specialist beyond himself to whom to refer the lay people. It is inconceivable that a pastor would say to a hurting parishioner that he does not have special knowledge about this area. The church will never escape the need for the specialist model as the brokenness of sin continues to bring destruction into people's lives.

3. The specialist model provides and emphasizes that a knowledgeable and experienced person should handle these complex spiritual problems.

A major strength of the specialist methodology is that it provides the afflicted with a recognized, knowledgeable, and experienced (God ordained) person to handle a difficult and delicate problem. In the absence of this type of person, the church has surrendered countless thousands of people over to others who further cloud the problem under false solutions.

4. The specialist methodology brings order and direction to the area of deliverance.

The specialist methodology provides a leader and director to monitor progress and prescribe techniques (e.g., oil. laying on of hands, renunciations statements, etc.) in order to free people. It is usually too confusing for afflicted people to direct their own deliverances (especially in cases of severe demonization). The specialist model can provide an objective process that is not dependent on subjective feelings and volition of the counselee.

This approach to the deliverance process gives hope because it focuses the "road to recovery" upon following the specialist's instructions. In the absence of this type of person, the afflicted will usually "christen" an untrained willing person and follow his/her advice. Having a trained, experienced person is also much better than saying, "Read this book" or "Read your Bible." People with problems or questions need to talk to an expert with answers.

Weaknesses

The weaknesses of this methodology can be broken down into four major categories.

1. Too many volunteer to be involved in this spectacular ministry without the calling of God, the maturity, or the theological background.

    God has set apart some to be specialists in working with the demonically afflicted; this cannot be a hastily started ministry. Those whom God has set apart for this ministry must be given time to mature in wisdom and in biblical truth. It is dangerous to rush into this arena. Many run afoul of Satan's schemes for their hasty entrance into this area. The church must develop procedures and opportunities for those called of God to mature in this type of ministry.

2. Specialists are determined by effectiveness and not ecclesiastical decree.

God does not always set apart for His purposes those who are acceptable to men. To suggest specialists exist is to raise the issue of who appoints the specialists. This appointment process can be the greatest weakness of any specialist methodology. "Specialists" who are acceptable to a church hierarchy, but are not effective, are useless or destructive. The fourth and fifth century church went down this road and eventually lost the use of the specialists because their specialists were acceptable but ineffective.[21]

3. Those who are set apart by God for this ministry can begin to believe they are experts.

Pride will quickly destroy one's ministry. One of the keys to any God-ordained work is continual dependence upon the Lord. When the specialist begins to believe what people are saying about him, Satan is waiting at the door to pounce and destroy his ministry, life, and hope. One must adopt the attitude expressed by Rev. Ernest Rockstad:

> Much is yet to be learned in the realm of spiritual warfare. Every person who is involved in the work of deliverance could probably write a book (or books) and set forth truths not covered by any of the others. No one arrives at the place where he is an "expert" in this field. In the final analysis, we know so little about the spirit realm. New problems and new situations are constantly confronted. One who seeks to help the oppressed will find he must repeatedly seek God for wisdom and grace. Although I have been involved in this work in some degree for over thirty years, and with considerable intensity for sixteen years, I am today less confident of my

knowledge and experience than I was ten years ago.[22]

4. The specialist methodology tends to place too much emphasis on what the specialist is doing instead of what God is doing and what God wants the afflicted to do.

Deliverance is the process of the afflicted moving into the freedom that is offered in Christ. There must be an active choosing on the part of the afflicted. The specialist is only the God-appointed director or prompter for afflicted people to take the right steps themselves. If afflicted people do not enter into the process of embracing Christ, they will slip back into a state of bondage.

Limitations

The limitations of the specialist methodology are in many ways the same as the strengths.

1. The specialist methodology is limited by the person who is labeled as the specialist.

The church has a habit of rallying around certain individuals, and in this area there is no exception. The specialist methodology can become a limitation when a church or denomination limits itself to the techniques and conclusions of one specialist.

2. God is not limited to using a specialist to set someone free in Christ.

The simple prayers of a friend or loved one, applying a new aspect of one's union with Christ can help set a person free. Saying no to a particular sin can result in freedom from spiritual bondage.

One must be careful not to deify those who are specially gifted by God to work in this area.

The essence of the spiritual warfare is to have the individuals take ownership over their own lives and, with the Lord, build the righteous positive life God has planned for them. God sends specialists, but He uses ordinary Christians with faith to do remarkable things in their lives and in the lives of others.

3. The church is slow in recognizing and training the people God sends to it.

This reluctance often results in the few doing too much. The church as a whole is slow to recognize the problem of the demonic and the need for trained people to meet this need. Therefore, it is not developing the needed curriculum and resources to do the training. It is also true most pastors try to do too much of the work themselves instead of recognizing gifts and training others to do the work.

SUMMARY

At the beginning of the third millennium since Christ, the rise of Satanism, Islam, animistic beliefs, and a desire for that which is spiritual will force the church to combat growing occultic bondage. Specifically trained and Holy Spirit-equipped men and women are a significant part of the answer. These men and women can be at the forefront of setting people free in Christ. The local church should have at its disposal a number of Holy Spirit-directed believers who can work with the afflicted. This will increasingly become a vital ministry for the local church and could consume all the pastor's time if he is not careful and diligent.

The local church should form teams to support and assist those God calls into a deliverance ministry. A number of churches already have these type of teams under the name "Prayer Teams." This is better than the more flashy title "Deliverance Teams." These local church teams can be monitored by an elder or pastor and function as one of many ministries the church offers.

If people feel God calling them to this type of ministry, they should not rush into the work. They should learn, watch, pray, and keep in mind what other specialists say about this type of ministry.

This is a ministry in which you must be prepared to be brought repeatedly to the end of yourself. Every case is different and when you think you know something about the subject, you will discover you actually know very little. You will be cast constantly upon the Lord for wisdom and direction. You will need to call upon Him repeatedly for His grace and enabling. He will not fail you. Only your self-sufficiency will fail. Jesus Christ is Lord ! This is the truth which wicked spirits will not confess, but because of it they must yield. "Greater is He that is in you, than he that is in the world." (I John 4:4) "We are more than conquerors through Him that loved us." (Romans 8:37)[23]

I would say humbly no one ever becomes an expert in these times of confronting the enemy head on. The moment he regards himself as such, he will be quickly humbled. Our only ground of victory over these powers is our union with the Lord Jesus Christ and the ministry of the Holy Spirit. Almost every time one faces a confrontation against darkness, he will find himself completely baffled as to what to do next. The powers of darkness are unpredictable and very crafty. Constant dependence upon the Holy Spirit for wisdom is necessary.[24]

While it is critical to acknowledge some are called to sustained ministries of deliverance, there are other methods which have been developed to free the afflicted from bondage to Satan.

3

EXORCISM:

Making the Demons Tremble

I was called to the home of a long-time member of our church, Jane. Jane had come to the church for years but her husband Stan didn't want to have anything to do with church; he was having too much fun living an immoral life. Stan, however was increasingly being plagued by voices and uncontrollable anger. He wanted help. When I arrived and sat across from him in the living room of his home, after some small talk, I asked him about the voices and what they suggested. I asked him about his anger and if he could look inside of himself and find where his anger was. Very quickly he found his anger and it was screaming and shouting at me. It was no longer him but instead a snarling, hateful demon that wanted nothing to do with the preacher or with Jesus Christ. As I was quoting Scripture and calling for Stan to come back, I was praying asking God what I should do. God reminded me of the incident in which Paul just commanded the demons to leave the slave girl in Acts 16:16-18 and prompted me to do the same. I commanded the demons to leave in the name of the Lord Jesus Christ and they did. All of us were somewhat shocked at the sudden turn of events. Stan was back and in his right mind without the voices or the anger. I let him know this "deliverance" was a temporary situation unless he surrendered to Jesus Christ at a new level and removed the gross, sinful choices he was making. I showed him Matthew 12:43-45 and warned him he needed to make some changes. I began meeting with him weekly to help him with the changes.

This type of deliverance has been used for thousands of years. When the Gaderene demoniac approached Jesus in Mark 5:1-17, his actions demonstrated he desired to be free. Jesus granted his unspoken wish and sent the evil spirits into a herd of swine. There was no counseling or confession prior to freedom. This same type of situation is also recorded in Acts 16:16-18 with the Apostle Paul. Paul casts out the demons from the slave girl without seeking her permission or talking to her.

Exorcism is one type of deliverance and it is crucial to understand the difference between exorcism and complete deliverance. Exorcism is the process by which the evil spirits are made uncomfortable, afraid, and/or afflicted. The tormentors are tormented until they want to leave. Wicked spirits are tormented by reading of the Scriptures, by sincere praise of God, by all talk of Christ's atoning sacrifice for sins, and by confession of sins in Christ's name. In an exorcism the spirits are forced to abandon their position in and/or around the individual. Exorcism drives the demons out of the person with little or no regard to how or why they are there or whether they will come back. The personal choices the individual made that gave the spirits power in their life are left untouched. Hopefully they will be dealt with soon after the exorcism. If the reason the spirits are plaguing the individual are not dealt with then what Jesus said in Matthew 12:43-45 will take place. The demons who left will bring seven more demons back, more powerful than themselves and the last condition of the person will be worse than the first. Exorcism is interested in immediate relief. Deliverance, on the other hand, is the desire to permanently liberate the afflicted person from the work of demonic spirits. Deliverance, therefore, is much deeper in its treatment. Deliverance uncovers and eliminates the reasons for the demonic affliction as well as the demons themselves. Deliverance also helps the person begin making righteous choices. It is possible to speak of exorcism as a form of temporary deliverance.

HISTORY OF THE EXORCISM MODEL

Exorcism exists in all religions – Christian and non-Christian. The desire to rid an afflicted person from demonic working is as old as humanity. Other religions use magic (incantations, ceremonies, rituals, etc.), superstitions (cloves of garlic, horseshoes, salt, etc.), and physical torture (flailing the skin, fasting, beatings, etc.) to try and make the demons leave. However after the death and resurrection of Christ, a new form of exorcism entered the field. Secular historians in this area attribute the exorcistic abilities of Christianity to "the greatest name magic the world has ever seen."[1] Eventually this began to codify the power of the death and resurrection of Christ into the following practices in exorcism: the name of Jesus, praise of the Tri-une God, and the truths connected with Jesus Christ's redemptive work. Exorcism developed into a system by collecting the techniques and successful ideas of Christians involved in relieving the affliction of the oppressed and deliverance. If a technique proved successful and transferable, it was recorded in a manual and circulated. Eventually there were enough of these manuals that their contents could be collated and standardized. Starting after the official acceptance of Christianity as the religion of the Roman Empire and increasing during the Middle Ages, Christianity began borrowing many of the pagan practices of other religions to exorcise demonic problems. These practices, however, are not the Christian solution. Unexamined pagan practices crept into the Christian church through this method and stood beside godly applications of Christian truth and diluted the power of Christian exorcism and deliverance.[2]

TECHNIQUES

The following is a listing and explanation of those Christian techniques which are effective in making the demons uncomfortable and/or driving them out of an individual. These techniques can be used in conjunction with other deliverance methods or can form a separate methodology of deliverance, exorcism.

Praise and Adoration

The first technique in the exorcism model is praise and adoration. The demons seem tortured by sincere praise of God. In one episode the author was involved with demonic powers that took hold of a young woman and would not let go. I directed the entire prayer team to begin to praise God, the Father, the Son, and the Holy Spirit. As the different members spoke out the praises, shouts and deep guttural groans rang out from the woman's mouth, "Stop that. I hate that!" Knowing the young woman was a Christian and loved the Lord Jesus, I discerned this strong, guttural voice was a demon. The more we praised the Lord and adored the Tri-une God, the more tormented the demons were, and the more they loosened their grip on the person. Ernest Rockstad in his *Deliverance Papers* says this about praise:

> Praise is an effective weapon, and it should be liberally employed. Praise God for the glory and grace of our Lord Jesus Christ, our redemption in Him, His triumph over the powers of darkness, and our deliverance from them. Every victory is a call to praise. Prayer and praise to the living God are a torment and a

torture to the wicked spirits and often bring about subjugation when they seem to be particularly stubborn.[3]

Godly Music

Another powerful tool in the process of dislodging demonic strongholds is godly music. When King Saul was tormented by demons after his serious sinful choices, (1 Samuel 15-18) David, the sweet singer of Israel, was brought to sing and ease Saul's pain. The incredible effect of music was demonstrated in a counseling session where a demon manifested. I asked if Christian music could be played to encourage the oppressed person and to pressure the demons to leave. One of the prayer team members put on the album of a well-known Christian artist who has sung many beautiful praise songs. What began to play was not praise music, but this artist's experimentation with a new style of music. The atmosphere changed. Rather than being bothered by the music, the demons seemed to be encouraged by this type of music. The music was then changed to other songs played by the artist. The whole atmosphere of the room changed again. The wicked spirits were disturbed by the music. The afflicted person relaxed. The prayer team was strengthened. Music has an impact on the war with supernatural evil. The Catholic Church in most of its ancient exorcistic rituals uses a choir singing praises in the background and at times taking center stage in the exorcism itself.[4]

Reading or Reciting Scripture

One of the most powerful things a Christian can do, when facing wicked spirits, is read or quote Scripture. Demons hate hearing the truth of their defeat and the victory of Jesus Christ over sin. Specifically Scriptures about the death burial, and resurrection of the Lord Jesus Christ are especially powerful. Psalm 22; Isaiah 53;

Isaiah 9; Luke 1:31-34; 46-55; 68-79; 23:33-48; 24:1-12; Acts 1:1-11; Romans 1:1-6; 16,17; 4:7,8; 5:8; 1 Corinthians 15:1-3; Revelation 5:9,10; etc. When reading through the rites of Solemn Exorcism of the Catholic Church, one is struck by how much of the ceremony is based on Scripture. This suggests that the saints of old found spoken Scripture to be invaluable in arresting demonic control. Scripture is a powerful tool in warfare with Satan. The reading and/or reciting of Scripture dealing with redemption, atonement, and the final defeat of Satan are like swords thrusting deep into the wicked spirits. Bubeck in his book *Overcoming the Adversary* says this about the power of the Word of God:

> The sword of the Word has the power to penetrate one's life. It is meant to do corrective surgery within the soul, spirit, thoughts, and attitudes of the believer. That is perhaps the secret of its power against Satan. As the believer uses it, the Word can penetrate, cleanse, and change the believer's life and in so doing, cut away Satan's grip upon that life.
>
> Nothing is quite as important in spiritual warfare as getting the Word of God into the mind and heart of the believer. That one thing will accomplish more in setting a person free from Satan's oppression and affliction than any other method I know.[5]

The Apostle Paul suggests this technique in the famous passage in Ephesians 6:10-18. He calls the Word of God the sword of the Spirit. He uses the word *rhema* rather than *logos* for the

Word of God, suggesting the power of the Scripture comes into play when it is spoken in a battle with wicked spirits.

In the cases of severe or strong oppression it is helpful to have the Scriptures read out loud to the afflicted person. This can be done with an audio book copy of the Scriptures. This practice of having the Scriptures read out loud can so torment the wicked spirits they loosen their grip in the life of the person. The trembling of the spirits at the reading of the Scripture can help the afflicted person "see" the difference between themselves and the demonic agencies.

Doctrinal Praying or Recitation

Another exorcistic technique is to pray or recite the doctrinal truths of the Scripture. An expounding of the doctrine of redemption, atonement, justification by faith, sanctification, union with Christ, glorification, and the return of Christ, etc., encourages the afflicted and torments the demons. In one case, a woman had been in the habit of giving in to spiritistic trances. Any time she was angry or challenged in any way, she would go into a transitive state. She experienced a great deal of freedom by reciting out loud the great doctrines of Scripture with their accompanying Scriptural verses. The more she said them, the more she began to believe them. The more she believed them, the more the vice grip of rage and anger were released.

It must be stated that success in deliverance goes back to the victory Christ won on the Cross. The benefits stream from His person and work are applicable to anyone who embraces Him in faith. This is the basic victory of Christianity. Forgiveness from God and freedom from spiritual oppression is available through Christ to everyone who believes. It is not just for the upright, the generally moral, the upper class, the church goer. No, the benefits of Christ's life, death, and resurrection are for everyone. Every technique of deliverance is an application of the benefits Christ offers. Therefore, the practice of reciting the myriad of blessings which are available to the believer is torture to the demonic realm. Their job is to blind the eyes of the world to the great freedom that is available in Christ.

Commands for the Demons to Leave

At some point in any exorcistic process, someone must command the demons to leave. This command must be in the name of the Lord Jesus Christ. The Apostle Paul commanded the demon in the slave girl in Acts 16, "I charge you in the name of Jesus Christ to come out of her." The one who commands the demon to leave must put his/her complete faith in the Lord Jesus Christ or the wicked spirits will not usually move from their host. At times those working with the afflicted become entrenched in a pattern of deliverance (specialist, power, resistance, teaching, etc) and do not listen to the Spirit's gentle voice prompting the demon should just be ordered out. We must always be ready to stand in the name of the Lord Jesus and demand the demons leave.

Two cases come to mind where people did not need more counseling. They needed relief from the tormenting thoughts and emotions. In one situation, a man was plagued by uncontrolled anger and sexual passion. The demons were so strong it was useless to counsel with him. At a frustrating point, it seemed that the Lord wanted me to order the demons out. Acting by faith, I commanded the demons to leave this man alone in the name of the Lord Jesus. I am somewhat ashamed to say I was shocked when they left. The demons left and allowed the man a clear mind when listening to why the spirits were present in his life. After some counseling, we were able to determine the man was not a Christian. Tragically, after explaining the plan of salvation and this man's need of the Savior, he rejected Christ. He was later visited by more powerful demonic spirits. It is important to remind the reader that the exorcistic model does not aim at permanent freedom, just immediate removal. The second case is of a woman who would go into a trance when our counseling started to work. The prayer team finally knelt in prayer and requested God drive the demons out of the woman in the name of the Lord Jesus. After five to ten minutes of prayer, the woman was free. She then needed to start making new choices that would keep them from coming back. She began spending considerable time reading, studying and reciting Scripture. It was very energizing and ultimately protective as she was not re-attacked or at least was sufficiently bathed in Scripture to repel the attack.

The Righteousness of Those Helping

Those involved in deliverance need to live righteous lives or else their lack of righteousness will be evident in a lack of spiritual power. On numerous occasions when a deliverance session is producing nothing, the Lord may bring an unconfessed sin to someone's mind. It is important for the team member to excuse him/herself, spend some time confessing the sin to the Lord, and then return to the counseling session. The dramatic difference in spiritual power is amazing. God will not use a dirty vessel. The demons do not tremble before a filthy saint. Another incident demonstrates the power of righteousness in deliverance counseling. We had assembled a prayer team to work with a woman. The work was going slowly and there was little progress. I could not understand why Christ did not deliver the woman. After a few hours, one of the members of the prayer team turned to me and said, "I have to get out of here. I don't know why, but the Lord does not want me in here." I resisted and would not let him leave.

A few minutes later he just left the room. When he did, the power of Christ began to work. The woman became free and began to rejoice in the Lord. I then went into the hall and began to talk to the fellow who left. He said there were unconfessed sins in his life that needed to be cleared up. The next day he unburdened his heart before the Lord and was released from his own spiritual oppression.

Church history reveals that when pastors were given the sole responsibility for exorcising demons (following the Council of Laodicea) the number of official exorcism dropped dramatically. However, "illegal" exorcisms increased among the monks.[5] The reason seems to be the righteousness of the monks outshined that of the priests. Even though they were not called to be exorcists, their piety tormented the demons. This torture inflicted on the demons because of the monks' righteous living made them the unofficial exorcists of the day. The annals of history are full of the pious causing demons to flee because of their righteousness and love for Christ.

Exorcistic Spiritual Gifts

There are certain spiritual gifts that make the demons uncomfortable or loosen their grip when used properly. These are somewhat controversial in some theological circles because of misuse or false claims. This is the list of gifts that have an exorcistic element in them when used properly: Tongues; Interpretation of Tongues; Discernment of Spirits, Prophecy. Let me explain why I suggest these are gifts with powerful exorcistic effect, and how I have seen these used with great effect.

The gift of tongues as used in Scripture is a gift of praise to God by the Holy Spirit speaking through a believer. The power, presence, and truth of the Holy Spirit speaking audibly is devastating to the demons. They just let go when confronted with the Holy Spirit in this way. I can remember praying for a man who was under severe attack from demons. Nothing we tried was making any difference in the choking attack. At one point a man who had joined the prayer team began praying in tongues, and it was so powerful that the afflicted man had immediate relief and was able to think clearly and was free.

The gift of interpretation of tongues means that a person is supernaturally gifted to translate the message of the Holy Spirit that was given in a foreign tongue. The message of the Holy Spirit was a message of praise, adoration, and truth to God from God. Therefore this message is powerful whatever language it is in and whether it is in the delivered second-hand through the interpretation or first-hand by the Holy Spirit in the tongue.

The gift of discernment of spirits is a supernatural ability to sense, see, hear, or smell the presence of demons. The person with this gift, when developed, can ask the Lord what is the name, work, and anchor point of a demon and they will be told. This is so powerful when helping a person to be released from the oppression of demons. I have helped raise up a number of people who have been specifically given this gift. When I call on them as a part of the prayer team or on the phone, they always know what we should aim for and vital statistics for winning the battle.

The gift of prophecy means the person has the supernatural ability to discern the thoughts and intents of the heart of people when God activates that gift in a person. One of the things demons do is they hide the sins and secrets of the afflicted so they cannot be exposed and thrown out. The person with the supernatural gift of prophecy can reveal these truths, which usually shocks the person who has had their secrets and sins revealed. It also usually produces a new level of awe and worship for the Lord Jesus Christ which allows the demons to be driven out.

These four gifts are deliverance gifts but can be used in an exorcistic way in that they can bring temporary relief while the afflicted person deals with the issues in their life.

CRITIQUE

A careful analysis of the exorcism methodology shows its positive contributions to deliverance as a whole and its serious weaknesses and limitations. It is important to consider this controversial deliverance methodology to learn from its strengths instead of just discarding it as a relic of the past.

Strengths

1. The exorcism model is scriptural.

On numerous occasions Jesus and the Apostle Paul do not conduct pre-deliverance interviews with those seeking freedom from demonic bondage; they just cast the demons out with a word of command. In Jesus' episode with the Gaderene demonic, the demons ask if He was there to torment them. The Apostle Paul casts the demon out to the slave girl in Acts 16 with the simple word of command. In the Old Testament David soothed the mad ravings of Saul with godly music – perhaps the Psalms.

2. The exorcism methodology recognizes the power of Christ to deliver immediately by word of command.

No one disputes God can free a person instantaneously, but there is often a gap between theory and practice. The exorcism methodology insists this type of deliverance be practiced regularly. We must not abandon the immediate and powerful application of the name of Christ. This is a critical technique in our age. We are so accustomed to tracing the cause and effect sequence that we can eliminate room for the miraculous power of God. God wants, at times, to set the person free and have them grow into their place of freedom and grace from the position of freedom rather than the slow pealing back of demonic powers that can be present in other methods.

3. The exorcism methodology stresses the absolute necessity to treat the wicked spirits as despicable enemies.

Some deliverance models treat demonic thoughts as expressions of the afflicted person's psyche and confuse the person and consoling of the darts of the enemies. There is no room for pity or pandering of demons or their thoughts. Christians should declare their anger, hatred, and displeasure at evil. Christians are trained to love and respect so much they are sometimes timid to hate demons and their work. Angelic beings who have corrupted their natural holy estate should be despised and driven to destruction. There is a place for hatred and wrath. It should be directed at evil. One can be righteously angry at the wicked spirits who seek the destruction of a person.

4. The exorcism methodology exalts the power of godly music to strengthen the believer and drive wickedness away.

There is power in music. David exercised great power in the court of Saul because of his ability with godly music. The Christian world is chasing after secular music and its entertainment value. There is a need again to emphasize that Christian music is different. It is aimed at a different target, hoping for a different effect.

In our day and age, Christians have not been told or taught about the power of saturating their life with Godly music. Christians listen to secular music stations, letting the ideas and perspectives of the world bathe their subconscious mind. It is no wonder the laws and principles of Scripture seem foreign and limiting.

5. The exorcism methodology prioritizes the need to know the great doctrinal truths in order to speak them out.

Christians are largely ignorant of theology. This leads to weakness in belief and life. Christians need to understand who God is and His essence, attributes, nature, names, and great works. Christians need to know much more about Christ and His work on our behalf. Christians need to understand the wonder and depth of our salvation. Christians need to grasp and cooperate with the work of the Holy Spirit in their lives. Christians need to embrace the truth of Christ's return. Christians need to connect with God's organism, the church. All these truths of Christianity help set a person free. When a Christian knows what Christ did for them at the Cross and what He is doing for them in Heaven, they can stand firm against the schemes of the Devil. In order to use these doctrines effectively in deliverance, reading, studying, reciting, and even memorizing of these truths is needed. These doctrines, when memorized and contemplated, powerfully affect the demons and the strengthen the believer.

6. The exorcism methodology uses scripture as an offensive weapon.

When the Apostle Paul was seeing the elders of the Ephesian church for the last time, he commended them to God and His Word. (Acts 20) One of the great gifts of God is the Scriptures and the truths contained in it. The quoting or reciting of Scripture to torment or torture wicked spirits is an offensive thrust with the sword of the Spirit. It strikes a blow against the kingdom of darkness. Most often scripture is outlined as a defensive weapon to protect against temptation (Psalm 119:11) or used to comfort in a time of discouragement. (Philippians 4:7, 8) It is important to retain in actual practice the use of Scripture as a means of fighting the forces of darkness.

7. The exorcism methodology places proper stress on practical daily righteousness.

Righteousness, in many Christian circles, is a negative list of rules and limitations instead of a powerful dynamic obedience to the commands of God. Righteous living is love, joy, peace, patience, kindness, gentleness, faithfulness, and self-control by the Holy Spirit. Righteousness of life is a powerful force in the life of the Christian. Remember, the whole of Spiritual warfare is about the control of your choices. If demons or the world system or your own flesh can keep you from choosing to cooperate with the Holy Spirit in doing righteousness, then they have won. They do not have to get you to sin in great ways. All they want to do is to keep you from doing and saying righteous things. As the world goes further and further from the boundaries of the Ten Commandments, Christians must again emphasize the power of a righteous life focused not on pleasure and self-serving but instead on holy compassion and good works. Unfortunately an emphasis on legalistic adherence to a set of antiquated rules has made righteousness and holiness something negative instead of the positive force that it truly is. A life devoted to love, compassion, joy, peace, and devotion is a powerful life. This method of deliverance highlights the power and need of practical righteousness. The exorcistic techniques put an emphasis on listening to the Holy Spirit and doing and saying righteous things because these torment the demons.

Weaknesses

1. The exorcism methodology can and often does overlook the causes of demonic invasion.

It is not enough to just be free of demonic influence. The person must live in the grace of God and allow the power of God's grace to change the choices they make. In the exorcistic model, a great stress is placed on the departure of the demons which can cause the reason for the demonic presence to be overlooked or dismissed in the euphoria over their leaving. I have seen numerous cases of demonic invasion where people were set free but afterwards did not want to follow up on the process of protecting themselves. The sins in their lives were not confessed, the deception was not countered with truth, and the negative patterns were not substituted with positive actions. They eventually fell into greater demonic bondage.

2. The exorcism methodology can raise unrealistic expectations that God will instantaneously deliver every afflicted person.

All those who come to Christ for relief and comfort need to realize that, at times, God can work in our lives in different ways. He can instantly deliver us from the results of our past. He can ask us to slowly appropriate His grace to overcome the problems of the past. He can quickly help us overcome some problems and slowly have us deal with others. Just as He had the Israelites personally conquer each square foot of the promised land, so He often has a person deal with every aspect of their past, present, and future. Sometimes when the afflicted believe all deliverance is instantaneous, it can damage their faith to be involved in a seven-year battle with the wicked spirits of their past. Even if the Lord did miraculously deliver the person, there is work that must be done to change lifestyle patterns and learn the truths of Scripture. Because the expectations of some people rise by the "advertising" of an exorcist, they can lose faith in God when no instantaneous miracle takes place or when work is required after the deliverance. Some people think deliverance is like a vending machine in which they can choose the kind of healing they want. They can come to believe they are in charge of their deliverance.

3. The exorcism methodology can cripple the spirit and emotions in a person.

One of the truths about demonic influence is that it can truncate normal emotional and mental maturity. A person has been allowing the demon to do a lot of the thinking and feeling for them. If they are set free quickly, they can be lost or emotionally vulnerable. God often allows the process of deliverance to take time: One, so they may grow up emotionally and mentally to handle life without the wicked spirits guidance; Two, so those who are afflicted will not allow this type of sin or deception to re-enter their lives; Three, some that are delivered easily turn the mercy of God into a license by believing that they can be redelivered easily if they are oppressed again. This flippancy about the consequences of sin is a trap.

4. The exorcism methodology leaves the afflicted person passive in the deliverance process.

One definition of demonic influence is any passivity induced by demons. In other words, wicked spirits come to control and take away volitional choice, intellectual analysis, and normal emotional response. The exorcistic methodology can, and often does, reinforce the passive position of the afflicted. The oppressed is not active in the word of command, the reciting of Scripture, or the other techniques involved in this model. This can reinforce the passive tendencies in the person instead of cooperation with the Spirit of God, which is the normal Christian life. A person is only going to win against the schemes of the Devil long term by becoming active in their spiritual life. (Ephesians 6:10-18)

Whatever deliverance methodology is used to help people, eventually the person must become an active part of their continued freedom in Christ from sinful influence and control. God can, at times, not allow the exorcistic techniques to work so the passivity must end. The person must become more engaged in their own deliverance. This is not like the removal of a wart from your toe. True deliverance requires an embrace of Christ and a working out of our salvation in fear and trembling. (Philippians 2:13-15)

5. The exorcism methodology can leave those who have been freed unable to defend the liberated areas of their lives.

It is often true the demonized person allowed the demons to be their emotional support and strength. When the demons leave, a person can be reduced to the emotional age of the beginning of control. For instance, if a twenty-five year old invited the demonic control into his life when he was thirteen, then removing the demon can cause some level of reversion to the emotional maturity of a thirteen-year-old. The strain of facing life with these immature reactions and emotions leads many to give into new vices and demonic control. Like the butterfly needs the struggle to be free from the cocoon in order to prepare its wings for flight, many times the afflicted may need the struggle to become free of the demonic oppression to cope with life.

God could have handed the Promised Land over to the Israelites with no enemy people living there, but He tells them He wanted them to trust Him in the conquering of the land. He also tells them He did not want the land overrun with wild beasts which would have taken place if all the inhabitants had been removed.

6. The exorcism methodology can focus attention on the exit of the demons, rather than the embrace of Christ.

Christ is the author of true freedom. His embrace of the believer and the believer's embrace of Christ results in life. The demonic hosts seek to make themselves the center of attention even in their departure. One of the true weaknesses of this method is it tends to make the departure of the demons the climax of the process. All of one's problems are not solved when the demons leave. Rather, the departure of the demons is an opportunity to fully embrace Christ. Those involved in deliverance are often guilty of focusing attention on the demons and what they are doing, or have done, instead of emphasizing life lived with Christ in control. Therefore if this method is used, it is important to help everyone see what Christ is doing and to focus on Christ rather than the demons.

I have often asked those who are set free from demonic powers to serve the prayer team a snack immediately after the deliverance. I have also asked the person to listen hard for assignments to love, joy, peace, patience, kindness, gentleness, faithfulness, and self-control. If the person is not quickly directed to listening for the promptings of the Spirit of Christ, the deliverance can be seen as freedom to do as I please without the old consequences.

Limitations

1. The exorcism methodology will not work in every case.

God, in His matchless sovereignty, chooses to deliver some in an instant and others by learning obedience through a process of deliverance and discipleship. It must not be believed that more faith will produce instantaneous deliverance. It is my experience that complete, instantaneous deliverance can produce a nonchalance in regard to the Devil and sin, as well as an inability to live in the newly-found freedom.

I was sitting in the living room of one of the couples of our church. They had invited me to come over to help a friend of theirs who was troubled by constant voices in his head. After some preliminary discussions and interactions, I began to pray and speak directly to any spirits that were in the young man. He began screaming, "Make them go away. Make them go away," There was a team of people from the church praying for him in an adjacent room. As we probed, it became clear he was not crazy but was truly afflicted by wicked spirits. He had been tormented for over five years with bizarre voices and insane thoughts. He had done many crazy things in obedience to their suggestions – at one point jumping off a bridge in order to commit suicide. He was now desperate to get rid of them.

He was not, however, interested in doing any of the work himself. He wanted me or someone else to drive them out. His desire for me to force the demons to leave (without dealing with why they might be there) is what exorcism is all about. He did not want counseling. He would not give me any background information into his family or personal actions that might have caused the voices. He just wanted the demons removed. Eventually it became clear that he did not care to embrace Christ, he just wanted the consequences of his past choices to be over. He didn't care what religion or god would help him. He just didn't want the voices. We could not help him when he directly rejected Jesus Christ.

2. The exorcism methodology is open to deception.

The demons can, and often do, fake their exit in order to continue operating in the person. Wrenching and other signs of demonic departure may be nothing more than a show to impress the prayer team. If the goal of the prayer team or exorcist is for the demons to leave, then the demons are willing to leave momentarily so there is the appearance of victory. It is critical the goal be the full embrace of the person and work of Christ.

Any leaving must be the beginning of embracing Christ. Righteous living is the goal, not freedom from the voices or control of wicked spirits. Do not be deceived. When the demons leave, it should be easier to be righteous or there is deception present.

3. The exorcism methodology by definition is incomplete deliverance.

Exorcism is the removal of the demons. It is not to be equated with deliverance, which is the permanent liberation of the individual through fully embracing the truth of Christ. Exorcism provides freedom so that the real process of deliverance can take place. It is tragic when those helping the afflicted believe they have accomplished their job with merely the removal of the demons. There are reasons the demons were present. If those reasons are not explored and conquered, permanent freedom does not result. The removal of the demons was a temporary quiet.

It is possible prayer teams may be assembled which focus on the removal of the demonic spirits from places of influence and control in the individual. But there must also be prayer teams, discipleship teams, classes, mentors, and counselors who will need to work with a person into their new life in Christ.

SUMMARY

The exorcism model is a helpful and common way of dealing with demonic affliction. There is a need to discuss the biblical information on exorcism and reveal the myths and fairy tales in this area. There is also a need to combine this deliverance methodology with the other types. There are times when God will instantaneously deliver a person from the strain of demonic oppression through words of command and prayer. There are times when it is very helpful to play godly praise and worship music in one's home and office to create a spiritual space the Devil does not want to dwell in. There are times when reciting Scripture and playing tapes of Scripture being read has a powerful benefit. Deliverance usually requires intense discipleship, not just miracles. While we pray for miracles, we continue with intense discipleship.

4

POWER:

Flexing Your Spiritual Muscles

On a beautiful spring day I was invited over to Curt and Sandy's house after church. We sat in their living room and began to converse about their spiritual journey. They had just come to Christ a few months ago and seemed to be making significant progress in learning and living their faith. We talked about the need to pray and repent of the sins of the past. Sandy had been deeply involved in immorality and violence before she married Curt. She wanted to make a public break from those activities she now understood to be sin. She began reading a prayer of confession and renunciation. After a few paragraphs, she stiffened like a board and a deep guttural voice came from her mouth. Something that claimed ownership over her life was fighting this prayer. Immediately we called a prayer team from the church, and we began a pitched battle in the living room to let Sandy go. When the battle was done and her sins confessed, it looked like she had been involved in a ten-round prize fight even though no one had touched her and she had never left the couch.

This spiritual battle was different than others I had been involved in because we were dragging information out of the wicked spirits: What was their name, what were the sins they were claiming as their reason for being there and finally what was their work in Sandy? This type of deliverance is called Power deliverance. It has its positive and negative aspects. During Sandy's deliverance, we asked what specific unconfessed sins the demon was claiming for the right to be present. We wanted to know specific sins, when they occurred, and where they took place. We needed to confirm these things really took place. After the information was gathered, we would call Sandy back and talk with her about whether this incident or sin had taken place. If it was true, we had her confess this sin and renounce her involvement, and thank God for the cleansing that was in Christ Jesus. It seemed at times we were crawling over sin after sin and we would never finish, but we were making progress and slowly but surely the grip of the wicked spirit(s) was loosened until she was free. There was much prayer, rebuking of the demons, reading of Scripture, questioning of the demons and about their truthfulness, questioning of Sandy about her sins, and then periods of confession and renunciation.

This particular case illustrates what can be called the power model of deliverance. Power deliverance is a form of deliverance which seeks to demonstrate the power of Christ over the demonic realm in vivid and obvious fashion in the life of the afflicted. In some cultures and some cases it is important for the afflicted and others to see outward manifestations that Christ is more powerful than the wicked spirits. The power model can be divided into a three-part process: manifestation of the demons, information from the demons, and expulsion of the demons. Each phase needs to be explained in its operation and in the major techniques which are used. All three phases utilize the power and name of the Lord Jesus Christ. Before a more detailed explanation of the three phases can be undertaken, the use of the power and name of Christ must be examined.

The Name of the Lord Jesus Christ

The power model makes extensive use of the name of the Lord Jesus Christ. This is the Son of God's official title. All three parts of His name are important. Demons can take the name Jesus; they can take the name Christ; they can take the title Lord; but they cannot take the name the Lord Jesus Christ. This is a very powerful title for our Savior. In most encounters with wicked spirits, I will always refer to Christ as the Lord Jesus Christ because this so humbles the demonic realm and demonstrates their lack of power. First, let's deal with the title, Lord. He is the Lord or ultimate authority in the universe. He is not a lord but He is the Lord. There are bosses, kings, and presidents; but Jesus of Nazareth was and is the boss of bosses, the King of Kings, and the Lord of all Lords. There is not one higher ranking than Him. The wicked spirits know this and do not want to deal with Him or those who serve in authority and power of His name.

Secondly, He is Jesus, the God who saves. The name Jesus is a derivative of Joshua which means Jehovah saves. The name Jesus proclaims Jesus as the Savior of the World. There is only one Savior of the whole world. He is the only one who lived a perfect life and voluntarily sacrificed Himself to atone for everyone's sins. The demons know Jesus is the one who, through His sacrifice, completely defeated sin as a tool of condemnation. They want to cause people to feel guilt, shame, weakness, and denial about sin instead of embracing Jesus who has paid for all the punishment involved in sin. The demons hate the name Jesus when it refers directly to the Son of God. It declares their ultimate defeat and forgiveness by God offered to all who will believe.

Finally, He is Christ, the anointed Messiah, sent from God to bring us back to God. The name Christ means anointed one. God specifically anointed Jesus as His representative. He is the long-awaited Messiah who will lead us out of our bondage and into the freedom of the kingdom of God. The demons hate to hear that the Christ has come in the flesh because it means they are powerless to hold people in bondage and affliction. The Christ is and will lead them out of the bondage to sin and oppression and into His marvelous light. The only hold the demons can maintain is to keep people stupid about the leadership of Christ in their life. All three aspects of this name are important and powerful. When used together they address the Almighty God who is the Savior and Messiah for everyone. He is the leader, Savior, and boss of all those who will follow Him. He knows how to live a new life. He knows how to be free from the destruction and guilt of the past. He is the answer to the shame and punishment of the past. There is no other spiritual power or being that can claim this title. So be sure to use Jesus' full name: The Lord Jesus Christ.

Claiming and speaking the name of the Lord Jesus Christ is very powerful in spiritual encounters. Jesus Christ does have a name that is above every name and it requires submission. (Philippians 2:5-10) "Nothing fills demons with more fear than the name and the blood of Jesus. If a person dealing with demonically oppressed people fails to use the protection God has provided for him, he will achieve nothing."[1] The name of the Lord Jesus is so powerful that using it can cause dramatic effects. The leading secular authority on demonic possession says the name of the Lord Jesus Christ as used by the early church was the strongest "name magic" ever seen in the history of the world.[2] Utilizing the name of the Lord Jesus is, however, not magic but an appeal to the Son of God who died and gave Himself to be an atonement for the whole world. The early church had faith that whatever they asked in the name of the Lord Jesus Christ for righteous purposes would be done and it happened. (John 15:7) Calling upon His name produces results.

Christians in spiritual warfare should cloak themselves in Christ to survive the battle and to be able to strike a blow for righteousness. Christ already won the victory over sin and Satan, and it is our job to carry this victory to all those who will accept His benefits.

It is essential that anyone using the name of the Lord Jesus have a strong and vibrant faith in Christ. The case of the seven sons of Sceva in Acts 19 illustrates what takes place when Christ's name is used without faith. They were attacked because they were using the name of the Lord Jesus as a magic incantation without truly believing in Christ. It is one's personal faith in Christ's death, burial, and resurrection which activates the name of Christ to protect and empower.

The Power of the Lord Jesus Christ

The whole of the power model is built on the fact that Christ allows His children to exercise His power. The Scriptures say in Ephesians 1:18-20:

> *I pray also that the eyes of your heart may be enlightened in order that you may know the hope to which he has called you, the riches of his glorious inheritance in the saints, and <u>His incomparably great power for us who believe</u>. That power is like that working of His mighty strength, which he exerted in Christ when he raised him from the dead and seated him at his right hand in the heavenly realm*

This Scripture stresses how it is crucial for Christians to understand the surpassing greatness of the power available to them. Christ gave believers the use of His authority and His power. His power can be used in these battles against the spiritual forces of wickedness to liberate the oppressed and afflicted.

In order to use the power of Christ in spiritual warfare, two prerequisites are essential. First, one must be a Christian. Second, one needs to have surrendered control of their life to Jesus Christ, living in dependence and trust upon Him. These two are considered a living faith in Christ and are necessary for access to the power of Christ. There is a myth that holding up a cross or a Bible will offer protection from evil spirits and other supernatural ghouls. This is not the case and demons will push right through a religious symbol that is not backed up by vital faith. A living and active faith in Christ is very powerful in spiritual warfare.

Another essential element for utilizing the power of Christ is to understand it is available to the Christian. As previously stated, the Apostle Paul prayed that the Ephesians' eyes would be opened to the fact that they had access to surpassing power. The power model seeks to utilize this power by seeking direct interaction with demons and vanquishing them in the name and power of Christ. The spiritual world is real and it has rules and power sources just as the physical world. The greatest source of power is the Lord Jesus Christ – God Himself who came to earth, lived a perfect life, and sacrificed His perfect life to provide a way for sinful humanity to return to Christ. It is His Name that carries the power of His person.

Let's begin a more extensive examination of the power model of deliverance in all of its three phases: manifestation, information, and expulsion.

MANIFESTATION

Manifestation is one of the most controversial aspects of the power model because direct contact with the demons is sought. Jesus clearly used this approach at times when He encountered demons as he had them reveal their name, their work, and their number. He usually shut down this manifestation as quickly as possible. Manifestation is the first phase of the power model and involves making a demon or demons show their presence within or around an individual. This may be accidental or intentional in which a demon is believed to be present and is forced to show itself. Manifestation usually means having the demons speak through the vocal chords of the person they are afflicting. Some who use this model make the demons speak to the mind of the afflicted rather than allowing them to take control of the vocal chords. This speaking to the mind of the afflicted is thought to keep the afflicted person involved and conscious, allowing them to recognize the wicked spirits internal mental voices they have been using to tempt and control. Other forms of deliverance avoids direct contact with demons while this model invites it. Direct obvious interaction with the power of darkness only proves the power of Christ over the wicked spirits is the thought behind this model. The techniques to manifest a demon typically are the use of specific spiritual gifts, calling to attention, binding, various exorcistic techniques, and/or renunciation of sins. There are two ways to manifest demons: unintentionally and intentionally. This discussion involves the intentional or deliberate means for there are an almost limitless number of ways to manifest a demon unintentionally.

Spiritual Gifts

Of all the spiritual gifts listed in Scripture, the most clearly related to this process of demonic manifestation is the discernment of spirits. (1 Corinthians. 12:10) The discernment of spirits is "...the supernatural capacity to judge whether the motivational factor in a person is human, divine, or demonic. It is the supernatural insight into the source of spiritual activity."[2] God gave to certain people within the body of Christ the ability to know when a demonic spirit is present. In order to help understand who has this spiritual gift, I have occasionally asked my congregation and/or other Christian groups if there are any people there who see or hear demons or seem to be especially sensitive to the presence of wicked spirits. I ask them to come see me so we can talk about what this means. For many people who become Christians and are given this gift, they are vastly more sensitive to the spirit world than the average Christian and they do not know why. Those who fully develop this gift can often tell the name and work of a demon within a person, even at times when they are not present in the room with the person. Dr. Ed Murphy tells the story of working with afflicted people in Africa and being unable to discover the name of an obstinate demon. He placed a call to a pastor friend in the United States who had the gift of discernment of spirits. This pastor was able to discern the name of the demon and its work.[3] Technically what this person has been given is the ability to see or hear or sense the presence of demons and able to ask God about the name, work, and grounds of that particular demon. When God gives this spiritual gift to a person, He allows them to perceive the spiritual world as most others do not and have access to His database about the demon's involvement with that person so they may be removed. This type of experience is happening in churches across the country as believers develop their giftedness in this area.

When I ask people in Christian groups if there are any people who have the ability to see, sense, hear, or smell demons, I am trying to identify people with this spiritual gift of discernment of spirits. These folks will often come up to me and let me know they can do what I mentioned. I let them know it is very important for them to grow in the Lord Jesus Christ as Christians or they will be under significant attack because of this gift. The demons will realize they are being detected and will attack the person who can do this. I require each person to commit that they will grow in their faith and allow the gospel truths to become the way they live in each arena of their life. I ask the person when they received this gift. If a person says they have had this gift all their life, then I ask them about their background and conversion to Christianity. Spiritual gifts are not given to non-Christians and do not appear before one's conversion. If a person has had the ability to see, sense, or hear demons before they were a Christian, then that ability is a counterfeit gift. I have run across a number of people who have had this "gift" all their life and some even claim that it was passed on from a relative. This is wrong and is a spirit of divination or clairvoyance. This is where fortunetellers and mediums gain their abilities, and Christians should have nothing to do with these people. Any spiritual gift a person has before their conversion needs to be renounced as evil and coming from the wrong source. It is important to realize a lot of people are "spiritual" and can see demons, and they will even call this a "gift." **But Christians do not want to have anything to do with spiritual abilities that do not come from the Holy Spirit.**

It is time to talk about the righteous, Holy Spirit given gift of discernment of spirits. God does give this gift just as He gives the gift of teaching, mercy, helps and giving. As the person develops, after their conversion, a new awareness of angels, demons, and the spirit world, it usually means God is calling this person to help in spiritual warfare and prayer. They need to be told how to grow in the Lord Jesus and how to grow their spiritual gift. They are the radar and sonar for a spiritual war. Just as any physical war in modern times, station radar and sonar devices can tell of enemy troop movements, so in our spiritual war people with the gifts of discernment of spirits can detect the movement of wicked spirits. This information needs to be shared with the leaders of the church or para-church organization so appropriate plans can be made and orders can be given. Many times I have been alerted to the work of the enemies through these God-placed sonar operators. We have then been able to prepare our church, myself, and others for the particular attack that is coming. In an individual deliverance situation, people with the gift of discernment of spirits can provide the prayer team with incredible amounts of information without the tedious and exhausting work of dragging it out of the demon.

I have, at times, asked those with the gift of discernment of spirits to pray for the person and/or over the list of demonic sins. This tells me what God is saying about the places of demonic strongholds in this person's life. When I meet with them, we can move right into confirming these areas of sin and then confess and renounce them.

I have come to prefer this type of power deliverance over direct manifestation as it clearly proves the power of Christ over the Devil. God has access to the hard drives of the demons through these special gifted individuals and their pretentions and plans can be removed. An afflicted person can schedule a time with a prayer team and someone or a group has prayed for that person ahead of time with the sole purpose of uncovering the areas where the demons have strongholds. The accuracy of their report shows the power of God and the person can then get right to the business of confession and renunciation of their sins and the projects to strengthen their faith.

I have found people with the gift of discernment of spirits are often so sensitive to the spiritual world they should not be on a prayer team in a deliverance situation as this is exhausting and highly emotional for them. Unless the individual has gifts of leadership or mercy teamed with their spiritual gift of discernment of spirits, I will not allow them to be physically present at a deliverance. I will usually have folks who have this gift be a part of a secondary prayer team or pray alone some distance from the actual deliverance situation. Some who have this gift want to be in the fight with the prayer team, but it should only be allowed if they have grown in their faith to the place where they do not have any obvious vulnerabilities in their Christian life. I do not always allow people with this gift in direct contact with deliverance sessions, even though they want to be there because God gives me a caution or because I do not think they are strong enough spiritually, physically, emotionally, or mentally to handle what will most likely happen. Remember this is spiritual warfare and there can be casualties. If you are the leader of a prayer or deliverance team, then you bear the responsibility to prepare, train, and deploy the people God gives you with wisdom and skill.

Calling to Attention

A demon can be ordered to show itself by commanding it to come to attention. These commands are "Come to attention." "Manifest." "Show yourself."[4] This is then followed by the order to remain still and not tumble or split away. John Wimber discusses this process in detail in his book *Power Healing*.

"Frequently Christians misdiagnose psychological disorders as severe demonization. I make it a habit to never call anything a demon until I have actually talked with it. I use several criteria to assess whether I am talking with a demon. For example, demonized persons undergo major personality changes when the demon speaks through them (Mark 5:1-5) Their eyes also indicate the presence of a demon. They may roll back and flutter, or the whole pupil may disappear so all I can see is the white part of the eyes. Sometimes the eyes operate independently of one another or become very still and covered by what appears to be a film. They may also dilate to such an extent that all I can see is the pupil.

Other common physical manifestations suggest the presence of a demon. I have seen nostrils flair, lips purse, teeth appear to grow (though they were not actually growing), the throat enlarges, and the body puffs up. I have seen persons fall to the floor and slither and hiss like snakes. I have heard all kinds of animal noises—barking, bellowing, roaring. I have witnessed people excreting foul-smelling fluids out of openings in their bodies. Many of these manifestations happen only in the severely demonized, but when they happen there is not a question about the presence of a demon.

I then command its attention by looking straight into the demonized person's eyes and saying, "Look at me!" I then command the demons to tell me their names (see Mark 9:25). I say, "In the name of Jesus, I command you, spirit, tell me your name." Many people are not aware they have demons until I pray with them. Then they appear to become frightened, and the demons threaten them. "When I get you away from here," the demons say, "I am going to kill you." When I suspect this happening, I silence the demon and then gain the attention of the person for whom I am praying. When I am sure I am talking with the person and not the demon, I explain they have nothing to fear because Christ is stronger than any demon. I then ask them, to the best of their ability to cooperate with Jesus in casting out of the demon."[5]

As this extensive section from the book *Power Healing* notes, demons are real and they can be brought into manifestation so the person can be healed. This particular model of deliverance wants to have these kinds of confrontations in order to show the power of Christ is superior to demons.

I have often called a demon into manifestation when it became obvious I was not dealing with the person who was in front of me. The logic changed, the personality became unusually hostile, and there was a belligerence that was not there before. I will often ask if I can pray for the person right at that moment. Usually they will agree and in the prayer I will ask the Lord to bring to the surface any demons that are operating hidden in or around the person and cast them out of the person, releasing them from any hidden demonic bondage. I get very strong in those moments of prayer. Often a new voice or personality will scream out or begin demanding I stop this or declaring they do not have to leave. It is almost like fishing when one has a few bites on the line and you are wondering if what you are feeling is real, but then the fish really bites and goes for a run. When a demon manifests itself because of strong prayers, the name of the Lord Jesus Christ, or specific calling them to attention, it is evident one has something different than just an emotional person. At times it has been frightening for the person to realize they have had a demon operating in, around, or through them in some aspect of their life. They were not aware of how giving into some hidden sin or "secret" selfishness allowed a demon to have a stronghold in their life.

The manifestation of a demon or demons begins the process of moving toward deliverance. Not everyone is happy you broke the calmness of "its working" nature in their life. They don't want to deal with the sin and hidden secrets of their life. It's easier to return to the strange equilibrium they had before you jerked the demon to attention. Remember, ultimately it all revolves around their choice. They have chosen to allow the demon to be there even though they don't realize the sins they chose to do allowed these consequences. Until they rescind their choice to do the sin, the demon will claim it has the right to be there. People must believe in the Lord Jesus Christ to receive the benefits of His death, burial, and resurrection. The person must be obedient to the faith not just give mental ascent to it for it to become an active force in their life.

Binding

One of the ways to get a demon to manifest itself is to try to limit its control over the afflicted person's body and mind. If there is a suspected demonic affliction or oppression in, around, or through the person, pray a prayer to bind any demons that have been operating secretly in this person. Ask for it to be bound in the pit of the person's stomach so they cannot do their usual things. If there are no demons there then nothing will happen in the pit of their stomach. But if there are demons there, they will experience deep and constant stomach ailments until they choose to do something about this issue. I have asked to pray for people who I suspected were under spiritual oppression or they suspected they were under spiritual oppression and in the midst of the prayer, I have ordered in the "Name of the Lord Jesus Christ" any wicked spirits are operating in around or through this person to be bound in the pit of the person's stomach. This is a way to manifest them without necessarily starting a deliverance or exorcistic session right then. I will usually ask the Lord to bind the demons for a period of a month or two in order to begin a process that will lead to their expulsion.

When demons are brought into manifestation, they are often violent and seek to do harm to the person. I have seen a person's windpipe suddenly constrict, a person's body twist in excruciating pain, and a person get up against their will and begin to walk away. All of these harmful physical activities must be stopped. Take command over these physical manifestations and order them to stop. Bind the demons in the name of the Lord Jesus Christ. They are not allowed to choke, stab, hurt or damage the person. Some who have worked with demonic manifestations have had people try and physically restrain the person. This is counterproductive and not necessary. A simple command in the name of the Lord Jesus Christ will stop any physical harm. Someone in the presence of the afflicted needs to say something along these lines, "In the name of Jesus Christ you are bound and cannot afflict this person. You are not allowed any physical manifestation except to answer my questions." When there is obvious pain or demonic working in a part of the body, a special command may need to be given to release that part of the body.

Various Exorcistic Techniques

When one suspects a demon is active in another person's life, the techniques discussed in the previous chapter can be used to agitate the demons so they are closer to manifestation. The playing of godly music, times of praise and adoration, reading passages of Scripture, and proclamation of doctrines of Christ's person and work all can bring demons into manifestation. Then a call or command to manifest can bring them to the surface to deal with them if that is the direction that the Lord is directing in this deliverance.

It is important to note here that it is not always God's will that a demon be brought into manifestation. Some have assumed God always wants to use the power model of deliverance and, therefore, the manifestation of demons is essential. But God may be leading in a different direction. He may want a different method of deliverance used. In some cases the person is not ready to let go of their relationship with the wicked spirits. Throwing out wicked spirits a person still wants will guarantee more will return later and make things worse. Always be discerning when calling demons to attention and moving forward in deliverance. In almost every case of deliverance in the New Testament there was a request by the person in some fashion before deliverance was initiated.

INFORMATION

Information is the second phase of the power model process. It involves collecting all pertinent information regarding the demons, which will lead to their removal. The information which is sought includes the name of the demon, it's work within the person, how long it has been active in the person's life, and what reason it gives for still being in the person's life. It is this second aspect of the power model which sets it apart from the exorcistic model. The exorcistic model is not interested in why the demons are present, only that they leave. The power model, however, sees a key in understanding why the demons are present. It wants to close these doorways into the life which guarantee permanent freedom.

The Name of the Demon

The demon's name provides two key pieces of information. One, it provides a handle to retain this particular demon's attention. Without this handle, demons can switch, leaving the deliverer talking to a different spirit, thus receiving different answers. Secondly, the name of the demon can provide a clue as to the operation of the demon. Demons often take names which reflect what they do. They take the name lust or envy at times which reveals their purpose. They also take the names of mythological characters which reveal a dominant flaw or sin. I worked with a situation where the dominant demon took the name Achilles, who was an "invincible" warrior in Greek mythology. This demon worked to stir up people so they would war with each other and generate great anger.

The Demon's Work in the Person

In order for the power model to be effective, it is important the afflicted understand what the demon wants them to do. This "work" that the demon performs must be repudiated in the power of Christ. This is a power encounter where the afflicted chooses the power of Christ and the righteous behavior over the power of the Devil to accomplish wickedness. The demon is asked what its work is in the afflicted. It can take a few times of repeating the question to get an understandable answer. This work is then contrasted with its righteous opposite (what Christ wants instead). Then the afflicted person is asked to embrace Christ and the power He gives to perform the righteous act. In one case, a married woman was driven by the demons to frequent bars where she would socialize with immoral men. This wicked behavior needed to be repudiated through Christ. She was then asked to embrace the power of Christ to strengthen her family and marriage. This was a struggle for the woman as she was drawn to both power sources (Christ and demons). She eventually embraced Christ and His ability to save her marriage.

How Long the Demonic Influence Has Existed

Another critical piece of information is how long the demon has been associated with the person. The demon will often reveal the number of years it has been present in or around the person. The prayer team can then ask the person what took place seven years ago. Usually people can remember a particular event, relationship, or act which marked a turning point in their lives. Many times afflicted people try to bury this event without dealing with its effect. Demonized people must come to grips with the results of their sin. They need to repudiate the sin and its wickedness and embrace Christ's positive direction for their lives.

This is easier said than done! Some look back with pleasure on times of gross sin. Some still have pictures of themselves during these times. To repudiate these activities means repudiating some of their most "happy" times. They move toward freedom when, by faith, they embrace what happy times await them in the body of Christ.

A word of caution which all who use this method discover: demons are liars. Each of their answers must be checked for accuracy before the throne of God.[6]

The Sin, Ground, or Stronghold

The power model deals extensively with unconfessed sin. Unconfessed sin is often claimed as reasons why demons do not have to leave. The demons contend that if people have sin in their lives which they are unwilling to acknowledge, then they have the right to remain. The power model uncovers these sins. It does give the demon center stage in the people's lives for a short period in order to expose very private sins. These sins need to be uncovered and confessed to eliminate any demonic hold in a person's life.

Confession involves asking the afflicted person to proclaim the particular sin as wrong after the demon revealed it. It creates a back-and-forth process of dealing with the demon and then the afflicted. This process of confession forces people to face their sins. Remember, the only power the Christian has is because of Christ's life, death, resurrection, and ascension. It is the confession of sin to the Lord Jesus that brings new power and freedom to the person.

During the entire process of investigation and information, the demons must be commanded to remain at attention, and they must often be reminded they are bound and not allowed to physically harm the afflicted person.

EXPULSION

The third phase of the power model is expulsion. Expulsion means canceling out the attachment to sins by confessing those sins and repenting of them. Then it is possible to declare the ground or sin removed. It involves asserting Christ's power and authority over the demons and ordering the demons to leave. Finally it requires some demonstrated signs of the demons exit. The expulsion process can be quick or it can be incredibly long and tedious.

Confession and Renunciation of Sins

One of the most powerful ways to begin breaking the power of demons, moving toward deliverance, and bringing demons to manifestation is to begin confessing and renouncing sins. Confession and renunciation of sins destroys demons ability to be present in the life of a person. As long as they can get the person to hang onto the hatred, the bitterness, the lust, the pride, the occultic knowledge or practices, the demons can claim the right to remain. Demons will always protest the destruction of their foundation of oppression.

This technique of spiritual warfare does not have to be dramatic or bombastic. Within the power model, it almost always is dramatic. The idea of the power model is to have the demons tell the sins that have not been confessed and allow them to still be in the life of the person. I have led people through prayers of confession and renunciation involving parts of their actions in the past and had them tell me they felt strangely lighter when the prayer was finished. In those cases the demons were controlled from open hostile manifestation through our team's prayers. On the other hand, I have led people through prayers of confession and renunciation where demonic voices took control of the person's vocal cords and other parts of their body and violently protested any destruction of their demonic foundation in the person. An effective confession and renunciation prayer is a sincere willingness to agree with God that the actions, words, thoughts, and attitudes of the past were wrong with an invitation to the Lord Jesus Christ to be forgiven. (1 John 1:9) God promises that if a person looks to Jesus Christ in confession of their sins, they will be forgiven and cleansed of all unrighteousness that resulted from those sins. Some of the unrighteousness needs to be cleansed is the demonic stronghold and oppression. If a person has been engaged in significant levels of violations of the Ten Commandments, then a statement of renunciation of any power, place, or control that may have been given is appropriate.

The Christian practice of repentance has unfortunately been lost in the church. We have begun to believe as Christians that sin is not that bad; it is just a mistake and does not demand attention and forgiveness. It is entirely appropriate for Christians to repent of the things that they have done and to renounce their involvement in those things. Unfortunately, the church has moved away for this practice and its soul-cleansing power. Declaring a break with the past and forsaking the hidden practices of sin and darkness can be the beginning of deliverance and can bring the powers of darkness into manifestation. Although this technique is a part of the resistance method of deliverance, it can bring about a power encounter by manifesting wicked spirits.

Let me give you an example of this kind of prayer. The blanks in the prayer are for the person to put in the particular sin they are confessing. I will usually use this prayer only after having walked a person through some portion of the sins of their life: pride; bitterness; anger; lust; greed; occult involvement.

A Prayer of Confession

This is a suggested prayer of confession. You do not have to use these exact words, but these ideas of confession, repentance, renunciation, cleansing, and transfer should be present. This is not a magical formula; it is a suggested prayer. It is your sincerity and honesty before God that is important.

1. Confession and Repentance (1 John 1:9: 2 Tim. 2:24)

Lord Jesus, I agree with You that _____ is wrong. I turn away from it and ask for all the forgiveness that is in your death on Calvary be applied to my sin in this area. You say in your Word that _____ is wrong for you say _____. I realize that only in your power and energy and through your direction can I successfully turn away from this sin.

2. Renunciation (2 Corinthians 4:4)

I repudiate, reject, and renounce any ground, place, or power I gave to Satan in my life through my involvement in _____. I give to the Lord Jesus Christ all power over this area of my life. I willingly surrender this area to the Lord Jesus Christ and the Holy Spirit.

3. Cleansing and Expulsion (1 John 1:9; Ephesians 4:27)

I cancel any contract I may have made with Satan through _____. I ask you, Lord Jesus, to cleanse me of any and all unrighteousness (including demons and demonic strongholds) because you say in your Word in 1 John 1:9 that *if we confess our sins He is faithful and just to forgive us our sins and to cleanse us of all unrighteousness.*

4. Transfer of Ownership and Infusion of the Spirit of Truth (2 Cor. 10:3-5; Colossians 1:27, 28; Eph. 5:18)

I, right now, transfer ownership of _____ in my life to the Lord Jesus Christ. I choose to take every thought regarding _____ captive to Christ (2 Corinthians 10:3-5) and allow Him full lordship in this area. I ask you, Lord Jesus, that you would fill this area of my life with the Holy Spirit of truth, so I would be wise, thankful, and able to see your plan in this area in the future. Thank you, Lord Jesus, for dying on the Cross for me. I choose to cooperate with you in _____ area of my life so the process you began in me when I first trusted in You can continue. (Philippians 1:6). I realize you want to display through me the character qualities of the Lord Jesus (Colossians 1:27, 28; Galatians 2:20).

In the Name and for the Glory of the Lord Jesus Christ: Amen

In order for a prayer of confession to be maximally effective in breaking very powerful satanic strongholds and influence, it is best if this prayer is prayed out loud with a mature Christian brother or sister who is watching the prayer and is praying with and for you.

Declaring the Ground or Sin Removed

As a final act before ordering the demons to leave, the afflicted person or a member of the prayer team declares to the demons, "All your ground is gone. You have no more hold on _____ (name of afflicted)." It is common to ask the demon to admit this. This reinforces Christ's supremacy to the afflicted, to the members of the prayer team, and to the demons. This can be a critical event in the afflicted person's life when he/she is able to say, "I'm clean," and make the demon answer back in disgust, "Yes." This asserts Christ's power and authority over the demons.

The power methodology seeks to demonstrate Christ's power and authority over demons and proves He gave His power and authority to Christians. This technique highlights that spiritual reality. The demons are made to say Christ has authority and power over them. Sometimes demons procrastinate, but they can be made to admit Christ has authority and power over them. A way to relate this to the afflicted is for the demons to admit the afflicted person has power and authority over them. This can be of great encouragement to the afflicted person.

Ordering the Demons to Leave

The final act of ordering the demons to leave takes the form of a simple command, "In the Name of the Lord Jesus Christ, I command you to leave _____ and go to the place where Jesus Christ sends you." This command is the final order which asserts Christ's power and right to expel the demonic invaders. This statement must usually be repeated several times, while the rest of the prayer team is imploring God to send the wicked spirits from the person. This command is a crucial part of the power model. Some who work in this area think that if the reason for the demons' presence is removed, the demons will drift away to find other targets for their devices. This is not the case, as demons linger until they are ordered to leave. This thinking assumes the afflicted person will not succumb to temptation, creating no new ground. A strong declaration by the afflicted and those in the prayer team is essential to free the person.

A controversial type of expulsion used by some who advocate the power model is the transfer method or the intercessor method.[7] The transfer method commands the demons in the afflicted to be transferred to one of the members of the prayer team and then out to the pit of hell. It is suggested this type of expulsion is easier than direct expulsion with certain types of demonic bondage. It has been my observation that those with the gift of mercy (the desire to alleviate the pain of others) are the most ready to try this method. They are, however, often not mature enough to know when to use this method and when to avoid it. I was involved in one situation where a gentleman in the prayer team had the demons transferred to himself and then out to the pit. He had concluded that this was an easier way and tried to transfer the wicked spirits from a plagued family member to himself. This was too much for him to handle, and he began to drift from the Lord under the impulse of these familiar spirits.

The Signs of the Demons Leaving

Since the supernatural realm is invisible, those who use the power model often ask for a visible sign to demonstrate the demon is leaving. Visible evidence of a demon leaving is shown in Mark 9:26, the story of the demonized boy who went into convulsions as the demons left. Many different types of signs show the demon is leaving. I have seen horrible wrenching, vomiting, or bowel movements as evidence a demon is leaving.

It has been suggested the demons be made to expel a little air as they leave. The advantage of this is asserting control over the demons and thus allowing no harm to be done to the afflicted.

CRITIQUE

After having explained and explored the power model, a critique is helpful so the implications of this deliverance model can be understood.

Strengths

1. The power model has scriptural support and examples.

In Luke 8:26-37, Jesus encounters a demonized man and asks for the demon's name when it did not come out with a simple command. This episode, where the demon resisted the deliverance initiated by the Lord, implies His servants will also occasionally get involved in protracted power encounters. Ephesians 6:10 states the Christians wrestle with the spiritual forces of wickedness. Those involved in spiritual warfare realize this "wrestling" is real and intense, requiring all their energy. In Acts 13:4-12, the Apostles Paul and Barnabas are forced into a power encounter with the magician Bar-Jesus. They demonstrate through the blinding of the magician that Christ's power is greater than the Devil's. In this case, the power encounter allowed the proconsul Sergius Paulus to see a true picture of Christ. There is scriptural support for the power model's advocacy of pitched battles with the enemy.

2. The power model brings the unseen supernatural world into direct contact with the seen realm.

Many people are unaware of the raging war going on around them because they cannot see it. The power model manifests this warfare. One of the great strengths of the power model is it's pulling back the veil that hides the spiritual warfare. It shows people that there are snarling, evil beings seeking to control their behavior. I have witnessed revivals within people's hearts when they see the unseen battle. One young lady, who was asked to help on a prayer team, finished the session on her face before God repenting of her lack of commitment. People often believe spiritual realities are myths and fairy tales. Nothing is farther from the truth, and the power model shows the reality of spiritual warfare.

3. The power model dramatically displays Christ's superior power over demons.

Snarling, hateful demons are made to admit Christ is their conqueror even though they hate Him. This illustrates in a strong way Christ's superior power. The struggling, afflicted man or woman who is wondering whether to give in to the thoughts of suicide and perversion is given a powerful deterrent when the voice of the wicked spirit is made to admit the oppressed one in Christ is superior to the demon. In an age overcome by materialistic rationalism, having Christ's name and power produce immediate change in the oppressed is an incredible witness.

The church is being attacked from a multitude of sides: legally, morally, financially, and spiritually. The power of Christ must be demonstrated in response to each enemy. The time has passed when saying God is overcoming the Enemy is enough. It is time the church revealed the cultic bend of this society with open demonstrations of Christ's superiority over demons to speak to this generation.

4. The power model focuses the afflicted's attention on the connection between sin and demonic control.

There is an almost direct connection between sin and demonic control and oppression. This wicked link is not exposed in our present western culture, and there is less vigilance against sin. Evil of all types is allowed to increase with little thought to the satanic forces that are unleashed. Many think Christ's death on the Cross paid for all their sins, and they do not need to be attentive to holiness and righteousness. It is time for Christians to rally around the banner of HOLINESS. One of the ways to do this is to point out the effects of sinfulness. Allowing people to see how their lack of spiritual hunger, their unceasing depression, their fits of rage, etc., are rooted in particular sins in their lives gives them greater motivation to pursue holiness.

Having a demon list one's sins and telling how it gives them power opens many blind eyes to the biblical commands for holiness. The power model pulls the scales off of eyes, shows the devastating effects of sin, and reveals how sin begets more sin.

5. The power model utilizes the power and name of Christ in a practical way.

The truths of Scripture are meant to change the way a person lives. These biblical principles can be applied to life in numerous ways but are often not applied. The power model offers one way to apply the power of Christ. When Christians can see Christ's power does actually change things, then they can be encouraged to explore other applications of Christ's liberating person and work. Application of Scripture always encourages more application.

6. The power model sets up a power encounter where the afflicted must choose the power of Christ or the power of Satan.

Too often the church in our present day suggests one can embrace Christ and retain a sinful lifestyle. This leads to weak, nominal Christianity. Centuries of church history and the New Testament suggest that a true commitment to Christ is a choice between sinfulness or holiness, between selfishness or love, and between a demonic power or Christ's empowerment. The Christian life is one difficult choice after another. These choices to the demonically afflicted are almost impossible. The power model of deliverance offers to condense some of these choices into a power encounter. If two sources of power are seeking to control a person, the person must choose which power to follow. When confronted with the actual choice of Satan or God, some choose Satan. They would rather enjoy a particular sin than be free of the bondage by embracing Christ.

Missionaries tell stories of people praying to receive Christ but making little progress in their Christian lives until they burn their fetishes, charms, or idols. The power model focuses attention on the demonic arena of control and forces a choice.

7. The power model offers visible evidence for the presence of demons in or around a person and in their exit from the life of a person.

Many people are plagued with voices and unexplained physical and emotional pain. These problems may be demonic. It is helpful to show people some of their problems can be spiritual.

People want to know whether or not their problem is related to demons. The power model can demonstrate when a problem is related to demonic control or influence. The power model is helpful in that it displays evidences of demonic presence.

8. The power model exposes the work of the Devil in the lives of the unsuspecting.

John Wimber states in his book, *Power Healing*," In most instances, the demonized persons are not aware they have demons until I pray with them."[8] It has been said that the consequences of sin are not being clearly spelled out in this generation. People move into Satan's territory thinking they are protected, but then they come under satanic influence. There are numerous people who are bound from effective service because of oppression in their lives. The power model exposes the Devil's confidence game for what it is. People crippled spiritually for years realize the source of their problems and go to war with the Enemy.

9. The power model brings a level of honesty to a person's confession of sins.

It is true that people cannot always be counted on to comb through their lives with complete thoroughness. Some ignore sins that are rationalized. Others hide sins they do not want even God to know about. Some forget about or block out certain sins of their past. These hidden sins can give Satan and his hordes plenty of room to operate in the unexamined life. When the power model is used, the demons are usually eager to detail a person's sins. This can close a number of doorways for satanic attack as the oppressed person realizes and confesses these sins which gave the demons reason to be present.

Weaknesses

1. The power model promotes open and direct conversation with demons.

One of the most glaring weaknesses within the power model is it promotes conversations with spirits. This, in any other form, is called a séance and is forbidden in Scripture. Since the majority of the information is gained from demons, it brings a negative cast to the entire procedure. Those involved have a demonic focus instead of a focus on the Lord. Some are even led astray by curiosity and fascination with the spirit world. Although in Scripture Jesus and Paul had short conversations with demons, there does not seem to be extended interaction with them.

2. The power model is open to deception and inaccuracy because of the source of the information.

John 8:44 declares *"Satan is the Father of lies and a murderer from the beginning."* One must approach the power model knowing that the demons are liars. Each statement is made by a demonic source and should be approached skeptically. The demons must not be allowed to "teach" or tell stories about events or persons not in the room. Some involved in this type of work succumb to the lure of special information. This is a weakness with this method. Wimber seeks to overcome this problem by silencing the demons after he receives the information needed to throw them out.[9] Cotton Mather, the celebrated pastor involved in the Salem witch trials centuries ago, was deceived in numerous ways as his journal suggests. He believed the stories the demons told of others who were witches, therefore allowing the woman or the demons to accuse others in the community. These accusations were taken as true because they came from a supernatural source under the authority of a respected pastor. According to the records, the demons were able to convince Reverend Cotton Mather that the woman should be naked while the deliverance was performed and that his "holy" hand should be used to lightly stroke her body to drive the demons out. This, of course, led to a great scandal and ridicule of Reverend Cotton Mather by the secular media. All the while he was convinced the information he was receiving was true and accurate. [10] Some feel deception is such a difficulty with this method that the entire method must be discarded.

3. The power model can become an exercise in hunting demons.

This method can be accused of hunting demons, since the power method of demonic removal does not work unless there is manifestation of a demon. Wimber states he does not call anything a demon "unless I have talked with it."[11] This suggests that if a spiritual source is believed to be the problem, then a demon must be tracked down and manifested. The necessity of manifestation in this method is a limiting factor. The name and power of Christ can be used to release demonic strongholds without manifestation. Jesus and the apostle Paul never hunted demons but instead dealt with them in power when they were found.

4. The power model often gives more control to demons in the life of the afflicted than before.

The power model, by bringing a demon into open manifestation, can give more control to the demon than before the deliverance. This expanded demonic control can be doubly hard on the afflicted for two reasons. First, because the consciousness of the person is usually pushed into the background while the demon is manifesting. Second, if those that are afflicted are unprepared to deal with the sins in their lives, they can be faced with greater oppression than before. It is dangerous to, in any way, increase the control a spirit has over the body of a person.

5. The power model begins open and often violent conflict within a person who might not be able to handle this type of therapy.

When the Israelites fled Egypt, the Lord told Moses not to lead them directly into the land of Palestine lest they face the Philistines and lose heart with all the fighting. God calculated what type of conflict the newly delivered Israelis could handle and what would destroy their faith. The same idea must be examined when working among the demonic. I saw a number of people unprepared for this type of pitched battle. The whole encounter rocked their world and the "progress" that was made was often given back in a desire to deny the deliverance happened or was needed. Some of these people move backward in faith following their "'deliverance" instead of forward. Their faith is such that they respond better to less open conflict and more slow conquering of the satanic ground in their lives. They needed deliverance, but the power model was not the right choice.

6. The power model focuses on the exit of the demons rather than the embrace of Christian truth.

This particular method shares with the exorcistic method a natural focus on the exit or expulsion of the demonic. The climax of faith which results in the removal of the demons can blind the real work ahead. One does not remain free from satanic influence only by keeping the evil out but by embracing the positive truths of Christ. Unless there is a great emphasis on the person's position in Christ and how to use it in every day life, the afflicted can slip back into old ways. It is critical to realize deliverance is not attained when the demons leave. The focus of the growing Christian is learning more and more of the ways of Christ. The focus should be positive and on increasing surrender to the Lord Jesus Christ.

7. The power model promotes a picture of deliverance which the Devil utilizes to keep people from seeking help.

    The power model is one of the most frightening pictures of demonic removal. To be that a demon will speak from one's mouth, revealing all of one's secret sins is enough to cause most to avoid deliverance. Movies and books dramatize these types of spectacular demonic deliverances. This is a powerful deterrent for many spiritually plagued people. They listen to the voices in their heads and avoid this process. I dealt with one woman who was brought by her pastor to see me. She had horrible nightmares and visions of other people's death and dismemberment which in most cases came true. She had a spiritual problem and she knew it. However, she was very reticent to come and receive help because she did not want to end up writhing on the floor with a demon speaking out of her mouth. We made no progress in helping her until we convinced her we would not use that method.

8. The power model can promote a legalistic, fearful view of the Christian walk since people try to avoid sin, lest Satan again gain a foothold.

    When the sin and demonic connection is displayed as it is in the power model, some people become almost paranoid of sin, lest a demon come and attach because of the sin. Christians need to be holy but in a positive sense. Holiness is a positive. Holiness is purity of love, speech, and thought. One must not emphasize avoidance of sin to such an extent that one is unwilling to take the risks of love, joy, peace, patience, kindness, goodness, gentleness, faithfulness, and self-control.

Limitations

1. The power model is not the best method for every afflicted person.

   The point of this book is that there are numerous methods of Christian deliverance and the discerning helper will be prepared to use the method that achieves a godly result. The gut-wrenching power struggle between the forces of light and the forces of darkness is not always the most helpful for people afflicted with wicked spirits. Many times they are beaten down by the voices they hear and are in a weakened condition. This particular methodology can leave them further weakened and unable to grasp and live the positive aspects of the Christian life.

2. The power model depends upon the faith of the leader and team for the effectiveness of the deliverance.

   Power deliverance is dependent upon two critical factors: the willingness of the afflicted to confess their sin and second, the faith of the leader or team to believe Jesus can liberate the individual. It is often true the demons are able to slow down the liberation by their bravado and deception. If the demons can appear more powerful than the prayer team, by doubting the deliverance will take place, the team diminishes in faith. All Christians know that Christ has the power to cast out any demon, but it takes time to experience how the power of Christ works in different demonic situations.

3. **The power model requires great amounts of physical, emotional, and mental energy.**

One of the requirements in the early church for the office of exorcist was emotional and personal power. This method does not allow the weak person to be involved for a sustained period of time. The power method involves the whole person. It is very draining. Some now combine the power method with the resistance method to reduce the emotional and mental drain of this method. One of the dangers of this method is it encourages shouting and even yelling at demons. This emotional expenditure will eventually take a heavy toll on people.

SUMMARY

The power model is an excellent deliverance model for demonstrating the superior power of Jesus Christ over demons. There is a growing need for this particular model in this rationalistic age. The strengths and weaknesses of this model limit its application, but it must not be discarded or forgotten. The Holy Spirit has used this way of deliverance for centuries.

5

RESISTANCE:

Building the Impenetrable Fort

THE RESISTANCE MODEL

A lady cornered me after church and proclaimed, "It works, it works!" Innocently I asked, "What works?" She then proceeded to tell me the information I had taught about confession worked. She was concerned her husband was plagued by spirits. She knew he would never sit through a session in which the goal was to manifest a demon. So, she applied what I taught about the removal of demonic oppression through confession. She and her husband sat down one Saturday, listed their sins, and openly acknowledged them before God. They asked God on the basis of I John 1:9 to remove any uncleanness that might be present because of their sins. She said after specific sins were confessed, both of them felt lighter and freer as if something left their lives. When she came to tell me the good news, this was my introduction into a separate methodology called resistance methodology.

The resistance methodology finds a life verse in the scriptural admonition, "Resist the Devil and he will flee from you." This methodology suggests it is possible to free oneself from satanic bondage without directly contacting demons. The resistance model is a reaction against the direct contact with demons of the exorcist and power models. It is also the application of the truth that there are reasons for any demonic oppression in a person's life. The reason is either sin the person chose to do or sin that was done to this individual.

The resistance model is trying to build an impenetrable fort the Devil and his demons cannot enter into and or would not want to stay attached to if they did get in. The New Testament's major focus is on sin and all of the problems it causes: separation from God; alienation from ourselves; destruction of relationships; guilt; shame; the loss of God's blessings; physical, emotional, mental, sexual, and spiritual harm to others; destruction of societies; hell and even demons, the putrefaction committee of the spiritual world. Sin is the issue Christ came to deal with and sin is the reason for the ills of mankind. Too often we have the idea we have sin because we have demons, but the New Testament would declare we have demons because we have sins. (Ephesians 4:27) Demons are just one part of the uncleanness that can be cleared up with the forgiveness that is in Christ. When we clear up the sin problem, we clear up the demon problem.

Scanlan and Cimer describe this method as the second form of self-deliverance.:

> "This second means of dealing with demonic spirits is by making oneself less vulnerable to them. Christians often invite demonic attack by allowing themselves to be in unprotected positions. Without proper defenses, Christians become easy prey for the devices of evil spirits."

> "Sin places Christians on precarious ground. It drives a man away from the life of God and escorts him into the camp of the enemy. Satan knows about the effects of sin more clearly than man does. That is why his forces are constantly vigilant, looking for opportunities to tempt man to sin. John says,

"that it is the Devil's nature to sin and that whoever sins partakes of the Devil's own nature". (I John. 3:8) Through sin, the Christian gives the Devil access to his life. Paul warns Christians not to give the Devil an opportunity in their lives by sinning . (Ephesians 4:27) [1]

"The main point of this method is to have victory over the Devil without directly confronting him, simply by resisting him sufficiently until he goes away." [2]

The resistance model understands the issue is sin. It has been clear since the earliest days of the church that demonic oppression is directly related to sin in the life of the person. Either sin the person chose or sin that was done to them. The demons are attracted to moral filth and attach themselves to moral filth.

The resistance model is all about moral purity. Remember, the greatest protection against demonic infestation and attack is a holy, positive, loving, and righteous life. This creates a life where the demons can't get in and where they don't want to attach. This involves moral purity. Moral purity destroys demons' interest and their ability to attach. Too often a focus on holiness has been negative instead of positive. It is positive holiness that is attractive. It is positive holiness that is joyful. It is positive holiness that pulls us into a great future. It is not enough to eliminate the sin in our lives. We must embrace a positive holiness that radiates love and joy.

There are two forms of moral purity: Positive and Negative. Positive moral purity involves: living, loving, joy, peace, and righteous desire fulfilled. Jesus Christ lived the most enjoyable, full, life-giving, and positive life. He did not define His life by what He did not do but by what He did. The Scriptures tell us He went about doing good. If we are living a life of narrowness and constantly worried about contamination from the world, we are not experiencing positive moral purity. We should be living hilarious lives infecting the world with positive purity and rescuing people from the slave market of sin. Negative moral purity involves: confession of past sins; removal of occult and sinful objects; not doing immoral things. Positive moral purity involves: learning to LOVE in each area of life; positive righteous living.

Both of these forms of moral purity must be stressed at the same time. Too often the resistance model has emphasized only negative purity. This devolves into longer and longer lists of what you can't do. This becomes a legalistic maze, life denying, and restrictive way to live. In this caricature of the resistance model, the person who does the least is the most spiritual.

HISTORY OF THE RESISTANCE MODEL

The early church saw there was a direct connection between sin and demonic influence and control. Therefore if sin could be resisted, then any demonic attachment could be avoided. An early church document called the "Canon of the Apostles" develops this idea.

> Now the way of the evil spirit is the sin of the soul. And whenever he sees a little place of rest and goes in, he enlarges the way, and takes with him all other evil spirits, and goes unto that soul, and he lets not the man look up at all to see the right. Let your wrath have its measure, and check it after a little interval, and draw it back to you, lest it cast you into an evil deed. For wrath and evil pleasure, if they remain always continuing, become demons, and whenever

they have dominion over the man, they swell in the soul, and it becomes derision: and if they should bring him into deeds of wrong, they mock at him rejoicing over the destruction of that man.[3]

It has been clear since the earliest days of the church that demonic oppression is directly related to sin in the life of the person. Therefore, a type of deliverance was developed by doing the opposite of what brought the spirits into a person's life.

TECHNIQUES

The resistance model emphasizes moral purity – both positive and negative purity. Since it is the nature of deliverance work to focus on the negative side of moral purity (because of the presence of demons), let's begin the discussion of the resistance model's techniques with the positive side of moral purity. It is this positive moral purity that is the most powerful form of demonic deterrent. The resistance model usually gets so caught up in saying no to sin it never fully develops the truth and power of a righteous, loving life. So let's begin by getting a handle on the positive side of moral purity.

I have also found it is easier for a person to work through all the various rounds of prayer, confession, resisting temptation, and self-denial if they have a clearer picture of what they are trying to accomplish that is positive in their life. People can and will pursue their dream through all kinds of obstacles and difficulties, but they must have the dream of a better future.

Moral Purity: The Positive Side – The Soul Development Track

The greatest deterrent to demonic activity is loving righteous living. It is the positive righteousness that makes the greatest difference. Just as positive clean living is the greatest force against cockroaches and maggots, so living a life of godly love and joyful righteousness gives nothing for the enemy to get a doorway into the person's life. The power of positive joyful living blows back the enemies of our soul. Church history is full of the stories of men and women who lived for God and caused the demons to tremble because of their Christ-empowered joyful lives.

Since Satan has access to the life through sin, eliminating the sin eliminates the access. It is impossible to eliminate sin without replacing the behavior with something that is good and honoring to God. Righteous or holy living is the process of engaging in activities which God would do. It is important to not define righteous living in negative terms. Righteous living is a positive, God-honoring joyful life. Righteousness is a barrier to Satanic control because when doing what is right, then one cannot be doing what is wrong. When a person is not doing wrong, Satan does not gain access.

It is important to add that righteous living is the result of being filled with the Spirit of God and obedient to His promptings. There is no absolute list of good things. Righteous living is not following a list; rather, it is relating to Christ through the Holy Spirit and doing what is pleasing to Him. There is great power in righteous living. I worked with a man who was guilty of all types of sins and gross misconduct. Without ever discussing or approaching the demonic arena, he was set free by honest confession and by the substitution of righteousness for each area of sin. We spent considerable time talking and working through the righteous antidote to his previous sin. I received comments from his family and relatives stating, "I don't know what you did to him, but he is a completely different person!" It is amazing the transformation which God can perform on the willing person.

While it is true there is no absolute list of positive righteousness, I find it helpful to distribute a list of basic righteous actions in each area of a person's life. The person can then expect to be prompted by the Lord in these areas. As the Lord's promptings become familiar, the person should search the Scriptures and listen for the Lord's commands. I have regularly suggested people "listen" for God's promptings to do a fruit of the spirit. This means God is flowing through you like sap through a tree, seeking to produce one of the fruit of the spirit so others might benefit. The fruit of the spirit is love, joy, peace, patience, kindness, goodness, meekness, faithfulness, and self-control. God will nudge the person to live one of these qualities. It is at this point the Christian has a choice to make.

There are at least five key ideas from Scripture that mark out what positive moral purity actually is. Matthew 22:37; Ephesians 2:10; John 10:10b; Psalm 139:13-15; Matthew 5:3-12

What does God want us to do?

1. He wants us to **Love God, Others, and Ourselves** with strong righteous love Matthew 22:37

What does it mean to love in each of the major relationships?

It means to fulfill the Two Great Commandments. Matthew 22:37 We must find out what it means to actually do these commandments in our day-to-day lives. These are not religious platitudes but instead are commands that are for our good. When we follow the two great commandments, our lives are covered in a demon repellant. The Bible goes into quite a bit of detail about how to actually love God, Others, and Yourself. There are also lots of good Christian books that can help you develop a system of becoming a great righteous lover.

Spirituality – Loving God with all your heart soul, mind, and strength.

Self- Loving self (loving our mind, emotions, body, and spirit)

Marriage – Loving spouse

Family – Loving children and relatives

Work – Loving colleagues, boss, subordinates

Money – Respect and not Love

Church – Loving other Christians

Friends – Love at all levels

2. He wants us **to fulfill our destiny** by doing the good works He created specifically for us. Ephesians 2:10

God does love us and has planned a wonderful life for each of us. We all have a destiny to fulfill. We are to make a difference. We are to leave a mark on the world. We can turn away from the good works God has planned for us and waste our time in selfishness and sin, but that is not the great life God has prepared for us. Go out and grasp the life God has planned for you. He has not hidden it from you. It is in the righteous desires you have. It is in the righteous difference you want to make. It is in the righteous difference you can make.

Every day God has planned specific good works for us.

Every relationship He has planned specific good works for us.

Every project He has planned specific good works for us.

Find them and do them. Ask yourself what kind of difference do you want to make? What righteous dream do you have that you let die some time ago thinking you could never do it?

3. He wants **us to live a life of abundance sharing our overflow** with others. John 10:10

God wants us to pray for and experience a life of overflow in the major areas of life. Now it is important to realize that during the Bible a person who had abundance is one who had more than enough for that one day and with enough to share with others. Jesus was not saying He will supply enough for everyone so they will have more stored up so they will never need to depend upon Him. I do believe Jesus is inviting us into a life of overflowing love.

Ask yourself: What would a life of overflowing love look like in the major areas of life? (God, Self, Marriage, Family, Work, Friends, Church, Finances)

If God were to give you an overflowing life of love in your relationship with Him within five years, what would it be like? What would you know? What would you be doing? What would your interaction be like? What would your prayer life be like? What would your knowledge of the Bible be like? What would your service for God be like? What would your sensitivity to the Holy Spirit be like? Pray and start moving in those directions.

If God gave you a life of overflowing righteous love of self in the next five years, what would it be like? What schooling would you have started? What degrees would you have finished? What wounds and hurts would you have processed through? What is your weight, health, and hygiene like? What kind of food do you eat if you are righteously loving yourself? What type of exercise and sleep are you getting if you are righteously loving yourself?

If God were to give you an overflowing loving marriage within five years, what would it be like? Don't describe it negatively but positively. How would your spouse treat you? How would you treat your spouse? What would you say to your spouse to keep your spouse enjoying and loving being married to you? What would your spouse keep saying to you to keep you enjoying and loving being married? How do you overcome problems in your marriage of overflowing love?

If God were to give you a family life of overflowing love in the next five years, what would that be like? Again describe it positively, not negatively. Our prayers and goals must be positives. We can't move towards a negative. What does your family do for you in an overwhelmingly loving family? What do you do for your family if it is full of love? How do you speak to the members of your family if there is real love? How do you handle problems or disagreements in a family full of love?

If God were to give you an incredibly great loving work place within five years, what would you be doing? What kind of people would be at the work place? What would your attitude be to keep the loving atmosphere going? What would your boss be like at this loving work place? What would your colleagues be like? What would your job performance be like in this great work place?

If God were to give you an overwhelming loving group of friends what would that look like? How many would you have? What would you all do to hang out? What would you talk about? What would they say and do for you? What would you say and do for them?

If God were to give you an incredibly loving church within the next five years, what would it be like? How would they treat you? How would you treat the folks at the church? How would you serve? What would the worship services be like? What would the small groups be like?

If God were to give you an overflowing amount of money that was more than you needed to live on, who or what would you give that money to? What would your attitude be when you were being generous with the overflow? What would other people's attitude be towards you and your generosity? How do you think God might supply this overflow to you?

4. He wants us **fully use the skills, gifts, desires, abilities, experiences and passions** He has given us. Ps. 139:13-15

One of the crucial things God wants us to do is to fully explore and develop all the skills, gifts, desires, abilities, experiences, and passions He has given us. God says He was involved in giving us the physical, emotional, mental, and spiritual features that we have as individuals. There have been a number of different ways to classify all of the differences between people. It is these differences that make us unique and mark out how God made us. He made us this way so we would explore our love of working with our hands or our joy at public speaking; our need to organize our cabinets or be radically spontaneous. Ask yourself the following questions:

What skills do I have?

What spiritual gifts do I have?

What desires and dreams do I have?

What natural abilities do I have?

What significant experiences have I gone through?

What passions do I have?

The answers to these questions may surprise you. Sometimes it is very helpful to answer these questions in private and then share your answers with a trusted friend or mentor. Usually your answers will grow and expand as you come to see more of who God made you. God wants you to glorify Him by being fully who He made you to be.

5. He wants us **to develop the character of Christ** described in the Beatitudes **so we will have a blessed life**. Matthew 5:3-12

Jesus tells us there are eight key qualities that are key to our living a blessed life. He tells us what they are in the beginning of the greatest sermon He ever preached. The problem is we don't want these qualities because we don't see how these qualities are the key to anything. God knows we need these qualities if we are to make it in this world and really thrive and be blessed. These are the eight qualities:

Poor in Spirit – teachable, humble, self-esteem

Mourning – sorrow over sin, processing pain, loss and wounds

Meekness – flexible expectations, anger management

Desire for Righteousness – a righteous cause, ethical standards

Merciful – full of mercy and forgiveness

Pure in Heart – a mind full of positive righteous thoughts

Peacemakers – bringing peace to situations, peaceful

Persecuted for Righteousness – standing for what is right

Persecuted for Christ – being insulted and wounded for Christ

God wants us to have these qualities so badly – because He really does want us to be blessed -- that He signs us up for courses in these qualities without asking us. Whenever something happens that I didn't cause, I ask, "What quality is God trying to develop?"

Moral Purity: The Negative Side

It is important as we look specifically at the negative side of moral purity that we do not fixate there and become sin-focused or judgmental in our nature. Yes, we should eliminate sin; but all of us are sinners and we ultimately only have the grace of Christ to fall back upon to cleanse us from all sin.

Unfortunately many Christians can become focused on a particular sin. They can become judgmental about those who commit that sin and self-righteous that they don't commit that sin. We are all in the process of moving toward a holy life and we need to remove sin. Realize, it is the abundant life of loving relationships God wants to draw us into not a life of not sinning. Holiness is not about what we don't do but what we actually do. Holiness is about love, righteousness, positive benefit. There is a danger in some Christian circles about developing pride about what sins we don't commit. Do not take pride in how much sin you avoid but take pride in how much love, righteousness and positive benefit you can release into the world. Sin only holds us back from the incredibly great life God wants.

Confession of Sins

God's promise in 1 John 1:9 is incredible. He declares that if a person acknowledges breaking the standard of God and turns and does the opposite, God forgives the transgression and cleanses that person from any resulting unrighteousness. This promise is the basis for the resistance method. Unfortunately many do not understand the need to confess their sins nor how to confess their sins.

True confession of sin involves an honest evaluation of behavior against God's unchanging standard. It means acknowledging breaking God's standard and proclaiming the desire to live according to His standard. God's standard is explained in the Ten Commandments, in the Beatitudes, and Ephesians 4 as well as other scriptural passages. Many find it helpful to compare their actions with God's commands on paper rather than just mentally. This gave rise to pre-deliverance counseling where a person prayerfully works through a questionnaire regarding past behavior.

Pre-Deliverance Questionnaire and Confession worksheet.

It can be helpful to have the person fill out a simple table or questionnaire which would indicate potential involvement in sin and or to work through a basic confession of their sins. A more detailed questionnaire would come later when we add the insights from the counseling model.

Personal:

Pride: _____

Rebellion: _____

Adultery: _____

Bitterness: _____

Occult: _____

Practice: _____

Other Religions: _____

Abuse: _____

Relative:

Pride: _____

Rebellion: _____

Adultery: _____

Bitterness: _____

Occult: _____

Practice: _____

Other Religions: _____

Abuse: _____

I have included two spiritual workouts in confession from my book *Spiritual Disciplines of a C.H.R.I.S.T.I.A.N.* which walk people through basic confession workouts. These workouts can be assignments given in the days and weeks before a prayer session would begin.

Spiritual Workout: Disciplines of Confession
Extended Workout: The Seven Deadly Sins

1. Read each of the sins aloud slowly, including its definition.

Pride: Inordinate self-esteem; showing feelings of superiority; unwillingness to submit (rebellion); self-absorption; overbearing; lack of teach-ability; desire or demand for supremacy.

Envy: Desire for what belongs to another; being consumed by the unfairness of another's material possessions; desire to deprive others of what they have or could have; the feeling of displeasure at another's benefit; inability to rejoice with another's benefit without desiring it personally.

Anger: Selfishness expressed forcefully outward; being blocked from a goal; unwillingness to surrender a "right"; irritated; seething; vengeful; plotting against.

Lust: Strong/inordinate sexual desire; inability to interact with another person without sexual thoughts or innuendo; sexual desire for someone other than your spouse; constant sexual thoughts.

Sloth: Laziness; working with a minimum effort; procrastination; delaying crucial decisions; inordinate attention to insignificant things; unwillingness to do things completely.

Gluttony: Overindulgence in a physical pleasure; addictive behavior; seeking comfort, solace, escape in a physical pleasure; moving past moderation in anything.

Greed: Longing after money; evaluating all things in terms of the money that can be made or lost; pursuing money above other more important things; seeking in and through money the comfort, pleasure, security, and intimacy that comes from God.

2. Go back through each definition and dwell on its meaning. Jot down notes or key thoughts that come to mind.

3. Ask yourself the following questions. Is this true of me? In what ways have I committed this sin? Am I moving close to

committing this sin? Caution: Do not try to find violations just because you think you should.

4. When you begin to see ways you have transgressed the command of God, confess them to God, admitting it is wrong. It is not uncommon, and is usually desirable, to weep and mourn (James 4:7-10). It can be helpful to picture yourself doing the offense and watching God's reaction of grief, holy anger, sadness, etc.

5. Write down situations you need to clear up because of your involvement in one of the Seven Deadly Sins.

6. Accept God's forgiveness in Christ by acknowledging your need for Christ's payment on the cross for you. Thank Him for His forgiveness and love for you (Jeremiah 31:34; Zechariah 13:1; Isaiah 53:6; John 1:29; 1 Peter 2:24,25). It can be very helpful to picture yourself at the foot of the cross, admitting to Christ you are guilty of (name the sin).

7. Ask God the Holy Spirit to empower you to keep away from this sin. Picture yourself doing what would please God in each of the seven areas. Humility; Understanding; Caring; Flexibility; Meekness; Purity; Diligence; Moderation; Generosity. Think through every part of tomorrow in your mind and see yourself acting righteously, and not being prideful, envious, angry, lustful, slothful, gluttonous, greedy. Take your time and go through each sin individually and picture yourself acting in the opposite way. [4]

Spiritual Workout: Disciplines of Confession
Extended Workout: The Ten Commandments

1. Read through the Ten Commandments slowly three times out loud. (Exodus 20:3-17)

2. Go back through each major word of the command and dwell on its meaning and implications. You may want to circle key words or jot down notes or key thoughts.

3. Ask yourself these questions. Have I violated these commands? In what ways have I violated this command? Am I moving close to violating this command? Do not try to find violations. Write down what you have done.

   1. When you begin to see ways you have transgressed the command of God, confess them, admit they are wrong and an offense to God. It is not uncommon to weep and mourn (James 4:7-10). It can be helpful to picture yourself doing the offense and watching God's reaction of grief, holy anger, sadness, etc.

   2. Accept God's forgiveness in Christ by acknowledging your need for Christ's payment for your sins. Thank Him for His forgiveness and love for you (Jeremiah 31:34; Zechariah 13:1; John 1:29; 1 Peter 2:24).

   3. Ask God the Holy Spirit to empower you to keep this particular command of God. Picture yourself doing what would please God and give Him glory. Picture

yourself receiving and using the power of God to avoid the violation and accomplishing the will of God instead.[5]

Removal of Occultic Objects

Besides confession of sin and repentance (turning away from sin to positive behavior), removal of all occultic objects and literature is necessary. Demons, at times, utilize objects and other occultic paraphernalia as their reason for operation in the life of the person. Satanic affliction can be reduced or will go away when these objects are removed from the home. Experience has taught me it is helpful for people to go through their houses with a list of items which create problems (see Appendix 6). The process of going through a home usually requires three attempts before all the occultic or sinful objects are found. The scriptural method for disposing of occultic objects is to smash or burn them. The idea is to render the object unusable. Some suggest issuing a command after the object is destroyed that all wicked spirits connected with the object must leave in the name of the Lord Jesus Christ.[4]

It is unfortunate, but many people spend hundreds of dollars on statues or books and the monetary value of the objects keeps them from getting rid of these things. In this secularized society it is amazing what types of occultic objects make their way into Christian homes. Numerous stories are told of how even Christian workers bring home statues or masks from a foreign land, and the demons associated with them plague the Christian. I have instructed scores of people to destroy hundreds of items which they innocently brought into their homes but which helped hold them in bondage. Certain other objects also need to be removed from the home. All forms of pornography need to be destroyed. Heavy metal music and strongly sensual music should be removed from the home. Finally, all occultic books should be removed. The home of the Christians should be a sanctuary where peace and safety are insured.

The following few pages is an information sheet we give to people who are interested in making a break with the past and any involvement that may be drawing wicked spirits. Cleaning out our homes of those things that can attract the cockroaches of the spiritual world is a very good thing. Work through your home using this info.

Spiritual Workout: Cleaning Out Your Home

Exodus 20:3,4 *3 You shall have no other gods before Me. 4 You shall not make for yourself an idol, or any likeness of what is in heaven above or on the earth beneath or in the water under the earth. 5 You shall not worship them or serve them; for I, the LORD your God, am a jealous God, visiting the iniquity of the fathers on the children, on the third and the fourth generations of those who hate Me, 6 but showing lovingkindness to thousands, to those who love Me and keep My commandments.*

Psalm 16:4 *The sorrows of those who have bartered for another god will be multiplied.*

1 Corinthians 10:14,19,20 *Therefore, my beloved, flee from idolatry... 19 What do I mean then? That a thing sacrificed to idols is anything, or that an idol is anything? 20 No, but I say that the things which the Gentiles sacrifice, they sacrifice to demons, and not to God; and I do not want you to become sharers in demons.*

1 John 5:21 *Little children, guard yourselves from idols.*

The following is a suggested list of items that may be in your home, which can give the Devil an advantage in your life:

Idols

These are statutes of other religions for worship, veneration, or prayer. If an object has been or could be venerated, worshipped, or prayed to, it does not belong in a Christian home.

Examples: Totem poles, Buddhas, Demonic gods, Hindu gods, Native American gods or sacred objects, etc.

Occult Statutes

These would include the growing number of statues that are not idols but have strong occultic ties.

Examples: Wizards, dragons, trolls, demons, bats, serpents, witches, ghosts, gremlins, etc.

Occult Objects

These are objects used by those in the occult to practice their secret arts.

Examples: Channeling crystals, Ouija, astrology charts, tarot, amulets, charms, talisman, etc.

Any object from an occult ceremony or practice is also to be destroyed

Occult Jewelry

These are jewelry with devils, dragons, bats, skulls, Egyptian gods and goddess symbols, etc.

Occult Books and Movies

These are books and movies that detail the practices of the witchcraft, Satanism, false religion, etc.

These are written at various levels from children to adult level.

Examples: Many horror films; *Poltergeist*, *The Exorcist*, magical cartoons, Satanic Bible, Dungeons and Dragons manuals, *Harry Potter*, etc.

Pornography

All types of pornography should be destroyed, as it stirs up levels of lust and immorality. The making of this material involves the destruction of the people who are shown in them. By consuming this material you are encouraging people who destroy others.

This would include pictures, films, posters, paintings, novels, stories, and literature.

Cult Books

There are many books that promote a corruption of the glorious gospel of our Lord Jesus Christ. These should not be in the home of a Christian unless God has specifically called you to a ministry dealing with these groups.

Examples: Book of Mormon, JW Bible and literature, Christian Science literature, Unitarian, etc.

Satanic or Occult Music

Any music which details Satanic practices or offers praise to Satan or demons is to be discarded. Any music which arouses immoral, violent, or sinful desires is to be discarded. Different people will draw the lines here differently. But get rid of the clearly occult or demonic.

Prayer of Confession

This is a suggested prayer of confession. You do not have to use these exact words, but these ideas of confession, repentance, renunciation, cleansing, and transfer should be present. This is not a magical formula; it is a suggested prayer. It is your sincerity and honesty before God that is important.

Confession and Repentance -1 John 1:9; 2 Timothy 2:24

Lord Jesus, I agree with you that _____ is wrong. I turn away from it and ask that all the forgiveness that is in your death on Calvary be applied to my sin in this area. You say in the Scriptures that _____ is wrong. I realize only in your power and energy and through your direction can I successfully turn away from this sin.

Renunciation - 2 Corinthians 4:4

I repudiate, reject, and renounce any ground, place, or power I gave to Satan in my life through my involvement in _____. I give to the Lord Jesus Christ all power over this area of my life. I willingly surrender this area to the Lord Jesus Christ and the Holy Spirit.

Cleansing and Expulsion - 1 John 1:9; Eph 4:27

I ask you, Lord Jesus to cleanse me of any and all unrighteousness that may have attached to my life because of my sin. For You say in Your word, *"If we confess our sins He is faithful and just to forgive us our sins and to cleanse us of all unrighteousness.*

Transfer of Ownership - 2 Corinthians 10:3-5; Colossians 1:27,28; Ephesians 5:18

I right now transfer ownership of _____ in my life to the Lord Jesus Christ. I choose to take every thought regarding _____ captive to Christ (2 Corinthians 10:3-5) and allow Him full Lordship in this area. I ask you, Lord Jesus, to fill this area of my life with the Holy Spirit of truth so that I would be wise, thankful, and able to see your plan in this area in the future. Thank you, Lord Jesus, for dying on the Cross for me. I choose to cooperate with you in _____ area of my life so the process you began in me when I first trusted in you can continue. (Philippians 1:6) I realize you want to display through me the character qualities of the Lord Jesus. (Colossians 1:27,28; Galatians 2:20)

Night Time Prayer

Dear Heavenly Father, I come in the name of Your Son the Lord Jesus Christ. I bow before You in worship, submission, and praise. I ask You to protect me and every member of my family tonight while we sleep and tomorrow while we are busy with the day's activities. Guard us in our *spirit, soul and body, in our dreams, in our subconscious and in every part of who we are. I ask You, Almighty God, to place the totality of who we are under the protection of the name and blood of the Lord Jesus Christ and the power of the Holy Spirit. Keep the enemy from attacking, oppressing, harassing us in any manner. I ask You to build a hedge of protection around us so the Devil could not penetrate and we might clearly be a trophy of Your grace. I pray You would station Your holy angels all around us so that we might fight the good fight of faith. I ask that You would make us sensitive to the ministry of the Holy Spirit in our life so we would demonstrate the character of the Lord Jesus Christ. Do not allow the enemy to in any way deceive, distract, or destroy us.*

It can also be helpful to pray for areas of needed growth (spiritual, mental, physical, emotional, and volitional, etc.) for each member of the family during this time of prayer.

If the Devil is scheming against you or your family, then it is helpful to pray against these schemes. It is also helpful to pray for specific Fruit of the Spirit or specific Beatitudes for each individual in the family as you would discern the character qualities Christ is seeking to develop in each person.

The Demonic Sins

The demonic realm has its favorite sins—sins which consistently appear in those who suffer under the oppression of Satan. Some call these sins doorways for demons through which they enter the life of the person. When the resistance model is used, stopping these sins is strongly stressed. It is usually helpful to have a questionnaire or piece of paper where individuals can privately work through the following areas of sin.

After each of the demonic sins I have included a simple little table that will allow you to quickly work through you or your family's involvement in these sins that open doorways to wicked spirits. You may be shocked at what you or your family have done when you look at it listed in this type of table form. Realize these sins need to be voluntarily confessed by you and brought under the blood of Christ to cut off any attachment that demonic spirits may have in your life because of these issues.

1. Pride

Satan's first sin was pride. He wanted to be equal or above God. (Isaiah 14:12-14) Those who are arrogant, proud, or haughty open a door to the demonic realm with their desire to focus on themselves or be above others. These sinful qualities should be replaced by humility, submission, and a servant's heart. I remember working with a man who needed preeminence in everything. He could not just attend a Bible study; he had to lead it. For every story that was told, he told one that topped it. He needed the attention focused on himself. Although his pride seemed unconnected with a number of gross sins in his life, it was not until he began esteeming others more highly than himself that he was freed from enslaving sin.

Check	Involvement in Pride	Who Practiced? You / Relative
	Pride – Inordinate self-focus	
	Poor Me – Constant negative self-focus	
	Arrogance – Overbearing superiority	
	Bigotry – Prejudice	
	Criticism – Overbearing negativity	
	Unteachable spirit	
	Lack of self-acceptance	

2. Rebellion

This day and age is one where few want to submit to authority. Most want exceptions from the established policies or standards. Rebellion is rampant. Rebellion from God-given authorities opens a door for demonic influence and control. Submission to authority is a quality all Christians must express.

There can often be a place for appeal, but submission must be the standard. Rebellion is seen as a teenage plague, yet it is not only their problem. There are scores of people who are ensnared in the Devil's trap because they refuse to submit. These people choose to be uninvolved in a church unless they can be the undisputed leader. They are often self-employed because they cannot stand to work for someone else. The church must again teach the power and need of biblical submission and the consequences of rebellion.

Check	Involvement in Rebellion	Who Practiced? You / Relative
	Unrighteous rebellion	
	Lack of submission	
	Rebellious attitude – negative attitude toward authority	
	Lack of teamwork	
	Lack of a servant's heart	

3. Bitterness

Every single person I ever counseled for demonic affliction has been bitter. There is an absolute connection between bitterness and the Devil's influence in a person's life. Many do not know how to forgive, so they continue growing bitter. In many cases the bitterness is allowed to fester and become a malignant cancer spreading its poison to other events and people. In these cases, the person needs to make a list of who deeply wounded them. Then they need to make the choice to forgive.

It is at this point that crucial, liberating projects can be introduced. The Bible suggests seven key projects in regards to overcoming bitterness and replacing it with forgiveness: Luke 23:34, Matthew 18:21-35, Romans 8:28, Matthew 6:14,15, 1 Peter 2:19-25, Matthew 5:38-42, and Matthew 6:7. I find specialized projects based on these verses can liberate bitterness and demonic bondage.

Check	Involvement in Bitterness, Revenge and Forgiveness	Who Practiced? You / Relative
	Bitterness: grudges, hatred, unresolved wounds	
	Revenge: plots, schemes, actions	
	Lack of forgiveness	
	Rejoicing in harm to others	
	Refusal to move on: past person who hurt you; past event that damaged	

4. Anger

The Bible gives prescribed limits to the anger of man. (Ephesians. 4:26-28) People are not to end a day without resolving what angers them. Usually anger is a result of selfishness. People do not get their own way, so frustration is expressed. This selfishness must be confessed and replaced by meekness and a servant's heart or Satan will retain a hold on the individual. I can remember one individual who refused to see the Devil's work in his almost murderous tirades. When he did not get his own way, he flew into a destructive rage. He wanted to go into Christian ministry, but his Christian growth was always destroyed by an episode of rage. The Devil was using this man's selfishness to destroy his dream.

Christian's must learn how to be flexible with their expectations. Meekness is this quality of adaptability which is the opposite of anger. Anger usually grows out of unreasonable expectations. Most angry people allow every desire to harden into an expectation. Then they get upset when their expectations are not met. More mature people temper their desires and do not allow them to harden into expectations. In this way they are saved the ravages of rage.

Check	Involvement with Anger, Violence and Murder	Who Practiced? You / Relative
	Outbursts of anger	
	Rage	
	Wrath – seething when in that person's presence	
	Burning resentment – inability to escape thinking about what they did and what you would like to do back	
	Malice – delighting in planning harm to the person; doing harm to them	
	Violence against others: often to get your own way	
	Assault: physical, sexual, financial	
	Murder: mental/emotional, racial, abortion, physical, spiritual, sexual	

5. Lust

The Greek word for lust means *a strong desire of any kind*. A lustful person allows a desire for a particular thing to become inordinately strong. The first tenet of Satanism is "indulgence with no moderation." It is easy to see why inordinate desire (food, sex, drugs, etc.) can lead to demonic bondage. Strong desire must be replaced by temperance and moderation. The Scripture says all things are lawful, but not all things edify. All things are lawful, but the Christian should not be mastered by anything other than God. One woman was under tremendous oppression because she would not say no to food. It was not until she closed this Satanic pathway that she was able to move towards freedom.

Christians in our present culture are not used to hearing they need to moderate their desires so we hear of believers arguing for pornography, gluttony, drug use, and other toxic desires. Our present culture is awash in sexual desire, and it is providing destructive temptation for many young men and women.

Check	Involvement with Lust and Various Forms of Adultery	Who Practiced? You / Relative
	Pornography	
	Mental adultery	
	Transvestitism: cross dressing, gender confusion, and rejection	

Check	Involvement with Lust and Various Forms of Adultery	Who Practiced? You / Relative
	Immoral conduct: indecent exposure; voyeurism; masturbation; sexual harassment	
	Premarital sexual encounters	
	Extramarital sexual encounters	
	Prostitution	
	Same-sex sexual encounters	
	Familial sexual encounters	
	Sexual encounters with animals	
	Sexual encounters with spirits	
	Ritualistic (Satanic) sexual encounters	

6. Occult Involvement

It should be clear, if you have read this far in the book, that involvement with occult practices is opening a large door and inviting Satan into one's life. All these practices should be confessed and renounced. Any related paraphernalia should be destroyed. One fellow I knew began dabbling with Satanism as a means of getting back at his Christian parents. He wanted to shame them, so he put curses on them. They remained unharmed by his actions, but he became bound hand and foot by the Enemy. He was driven by impulses which scared him, but he was powerless to stop. At this writing he continues to shun Christ, for it is the religion of his parents.

Christians must clearly and openly speak of the dangers involved in all the various occult religions that are seeking adherents. The church has gone silent on this subject when these secret ritualistic groups destroy people's lives.

Check	Involvement in Occult Practices	Who Practiced? You / Relative
	Satanism	
	Astrology	
	Witchcraft	
	White Magic	

Check	Involvement in Occult Practices	Who Practiced? You / Relative
	Black Magic	
	Séances	
	Magical role-playing games	
	Extrasensory perception	
	Clairvoyance	
	Medium	
	Spiritism	
	Calling to the spirit in the mirror	
	Second Sight	
	Mind reading	
	Fortunetelling	

Check	Involvement in Occult Practices	Who Practiced? You / Relative
	Palm reading	
	Tealeaf reading	
	Crystal ball	
	Tarot cards	
	Horoscopes	
	Reincarnation	
	Metaphysical healings	
	Deep hypnosis	
	Curses, hexes, vexes	
	Spells: casting, receiving	
	Oaths: death, blood, generation, etc	

Check	Involvement in Occult Practices	Who Practiced? You / Relative
	Voodoo	
	Santeria	
	Levitation	
	Psychometry	
	Automatic Writing	
	Channeling	
	Numerology	
	Astral Projection	
	Occult literature	
	Psychic phenomena	
	Crystals	

Check	Involvement in Occult Practices	Who Practiced? You / Relative
	Pyramid power	
	Pacts with the Devil	
	Sacrifices (ritual and actual)	
	Bride of Satan	
	Parapsychology	
	Religious yoga	
	Transcendental meditation	
	Spirit guides	
	Ascended masters	
	Ecstatic utterance	
	Prophecy	

Check	Involvement in Occult Practices	Who Practiced? You / Relative
	Religious acupuncture	
	Conversation with spirits	
	Black Mass	
	Mind control	
	Death magic	
	Free Masonry	
	Poltergeists	
	Psychic abilities	
	Queen of Darkness; Queen of Black Witches	
	Table lifting	
	Trances, speaking in a trance	

Check	Involvement in Occult Practices	Who Practiced? You / Relative
	Spiritistic prophecy, soothsaying	
	Spiritistic magic	
	Transfiguration, translocation, materialization, apports, deports	
	Symbols of occult peace: Egyptian Fertility, Pentagram, Nazi Cross, etc	
	Vampires, vampire practice and ceremonies	
	Weleda medicines	

7. Other religions other than Christian.

One of the other areas where spiritual doorways can be opened is involvement in other religions. If a person has been deeply involved in religious traditions other than Christian, there can be spiritual doorways and attachments that have been set up in their life. These would need to be closed through confession of the truth of Christianity and the open acknowledgement of the error of the other religions. I can remember working with a man who had strong demonic oppression because of his involvement in Buddhism in his past. We prayed and worked but every time it came to his making a complete break with Buddhism by confessing the truth of Christianity and destroying the altar that was a part of his worship in Buddhism, he would not do it. He refused to come out fully for Christ and shrank back at a number of crucial moments. He turned away from the peace and forgiveness that was in Christ because of the spiritual torment he had opened himself to through his worship in Buddhism.

Check	Involvement in Other Religions	Who Practiced? You / Relative
	Unity	
	Jean Dixon	
	Scientology	
	Mormonism	
	Jehovah Witness	
	Unification Church	
	Meher Baba	

Check	Involvement in Other Religions	Who Practiced? You / Relative
	Edgar Cayce	
	Masons	
	EST	
	Scientology	
	Silva Mind Control	
	Eckanar	
	Hinduism	
	Buddhism	
	Isalam	
	Rosicruscianism	

Check	Involvement in Other Religions	Who Practiced? You / Relative
	Hare Krishna	
	Masonry	
	Dianetics	
	Satanism	
	Science of the Mind	
	Bahaism	
	Other	
	Other	
	Other	
	Other	

8. Transference

One of the most unusual areas in working with deliverance is the problem of transference and victimization. Demons stay where sin is chosen or done by others and/or spiritually transferred onto others. In this way families can become completely infested with demonic spirits through the sins of the parents and the sins of the individuals. (Exodus 34:7b) It is important to acknowledge the sins of one's ancestors and be spiritually cut off from the sins of one's natural family.

This is especially true where there are occult practices in a family line. It is not uncommon for all types of hexes, charms, spells, curses, etc., to be placed in a family tree and released on a later generation. I worked with one lady whose grandmother was involved with the occult and pledged every other generation's first born daughter to Satan. This curse exercised a strong influence on the woman's life until it was exposed and broken.

Another transference problem occurs when a victim of a violent or Satanic crime is oppressed by the demons that assisted the attacker. Victims often do not know how to deal with the swirling and raging emotions they feel. Unless they receive counseling and prayerful support, they can give into demonic ways of dealing with the pain. I remember working with one man whose father was murdered when he was younger. He did not know how to deal with this incredible trauma and his personal anger. The Satanic suggestions of hatred were slowly built layer upon layer until there was a sufficient pathway for Satan to work in his life.

This first chart looks at the area of being a perpetrator of abuse. This may be a difficult list to look at but realize even these things Christ can and does forgive when a person is willing to acknowledge and turn away from the works of their past. If you have been a part of any of these forms of abuse, confess your sins to the Lord Jesus Christ and draw near to God for His forgiveness, mercy, new direction, and holiness.

Check	Involvement in Abuse (Perpetrator)	Who Practiced? You / Relative
	Spiritual abuse – transference, dedication, oaths, curses, etc	
	Animal mutilation / Animal sacrifice	
	Physical abuse/violence/murder	
	Cannibalism	
	Self abuse - alcoholism	
	Self abuse – drug abuse	
	Self abuse - other	
	Imprisonment	

Check	Involvement in Abuse (Perpetrator)	Who Practiced? You / Relative
	Emotional abuse	
	Mental abuse	
	Sexual abuse: assault /rape	
	Financial abuse: fraud, stealing, etc.	
	Spiritual abuse – transference, dedication, oaths, curses, etc	
	Animal mutilation / Animal sacrifice	
	Physical abuse/violence/murder	
	Cannibalism	
	Self abuse - alcoholism	
	Self abuse – drug abuse	

Check	Involvement in Abuse (Victim)	Who Practiced? You / Relative
	Self abuse - other	
	Imprisonment	
	Emotional abuse	
	Mental abuse	
	Sexual abuse: assault /rape	

CRITIQUE

The following are the essential critiques of the resistance model. Although this model has high recommendations, it also has some glaring weaknesses.

Strengths

1. The resistance model has evident scriptural support.

The Bible is clear in James 4:17, *Resist the Devil and he will flee from you.* The attack and work of the Devil must be met head on with resistance by the individual who is under attack. The biblical mandate of resistance is illustrated in Jesus' stunning rebuke of Peter in Matthew 17:23, when Jesus forcefully resists the advice of the Devil. It is negatively illustrated in the story of Judas and Peter on the night of Jesus' betrayal. Both of these men were seduced by Satan and did his work that night because they did not resist him.

The resistance model takes full advantage of the truth of 1 John 1:9 that all unrighteousness will be swept away by God as a result of true confession. It is the resistance of true confession before a Holy God that causes the Devil to flee. When a person is humbled under the mighty hand of God, the plan of Satan can be resisted.

The great passage on spiritual warfare in Ephesians 6:10-18 emphasizes resistance. The apostle writes that we wrestle with spiritual forces. We must stand firm against the schemes of the Devil. The Scriptures plainly speak of the need for resistance in the Christian's battle with the Enemy. The resistance model reveals this aspect of the spiritual warfare and offers practical scriptural techniques on how to resist.

2. The resistance model focuses attention on the vital link between sin and demonization.

There is an absolute link between sin and demonic oppression. The resistance model makes the afflicted see this connection. The other methodologies do not place primary emphasis on this connection. It is liberating to realize my actions can stop demonic invasion.

3. The resistance model stresses the elimination of the underlying cause of demonic invasion through the God-ordained method: confession.

Confession is the biblical method for cleansing a life from sin and its effects. In numerous counseling sessions, I have stopped people while confessing their sins because they were not actually confessing. Many people assume they are confessing when they pray, "Lord, help me not to do this sin anymore," or "Lord, forgive me for this sin. I need Your help." The resistance model shows the afflicted person the parts and process of confession. It is only when confession is real that the power of Christ is released. The correct declaration is, "Lord, I was wrong about _____. I do not want to do that anymore. Please cleanse me and forgive me."

4. The resistance model does not involve direct communication with wicked spirits.

Most people do not want to directly confront demons. There is an innate fear of that procedure. Even if they are clearly plagued by demonic problems there is a desire to avoid open and direct encounters with demons. The resistance model tends to free more people of demonic control because more people are willing to submit to its procedures.

5. The resistance model is not a frightening method.

Since there is no direct demonic manifestation, there is no element of fear in the process of deliverance. Many biblically-based recovery programs use this methodology in their treatment program. Having people come face to face with their sins is not easy, but it is easier than showing them they have surrendered ground to spiritual forces of wickedness.

6. The resistance model – when properly balanced between confession and righteousness – does promote a balanced Christian life.

The resistance model used to be called Holy Living. It is the ultimate plan for every Christian. God wants us to live holy lives because He is Holy. (1 Peter 1:15,16) There is incredible power in the life, death, resurrection, and ascension of Jesus Christ and holy living takes advantage of it. Too often in deliverance ministry the focus has been on the demons and on the sin instead of the goal of a Christ-honoring holy life. When a person surrenders to Christ, they do not give their life to exist in a prison camp; but they want to experience the wonder of life in Christ. They want to have a life full of love and joy in the Holy Spirit. This wonderful life full of good works, full of love, and full of abundance is what we should be helping people gain. Dealing with demons is just an obstacle to get there.

The great danger in working with deliverance is to begin to see a demon in every circumstance. Even when some people are delivered, they can develop a mindset that sees wicked spirits causing every problem in their world. The resistance model, when properly taught, shows demonic bondage is a consequence of sinful behavior. After dealing with numerous types of deliverance methods and scores of people, I have found if only one method is used and no combinations are involved, the resistance model produces the most healthy Christians.

7. The resistance model involves the afflicted person in the deliverance process.

As stated before in other models, the greatest danger in demonic involvement is passivity. In fact, demonic oppression demands passivity to the promptings and control of wicked spirits. If the afflicted person is not completely involved in their deliverance, the life of liberty is not usually seized. The resistance model allows full involvement in the deliverance from start to finish.

8. The resistance model does not require an expert or a team to supervise the process.

The resistance model can be a self-deliverance model. The resistance model can be self-guided. This has tremendous appeal for those suffering affliction and for those involved in counseling the oppressed. Many who come for help can be given a tape or pamphlet explaining the resistance model. They can be set free without lengthy counseling. Since most people who work in this field are overloaded, this information can be a helpful tool.

Weaknesses

1. The resistance model often becomes negative and legalistic.

The resistance model tends to stress what to avoid more than what to do. Because of the detailing of sin and open confession, the resistance model lends itself to a sterile list of rules and regulations to govern the Christian life. Those using the resistance model keep adding lists of sins and activities that initiated demonic oppression and are therefore verbotten. Without proper research, any kind of fun or relaxing activity will be outlawed.

2. The resistance model is reluctant to directly confront the demonic arena.

Those using the resistance model almost never initiate or continue a power encounter with wicked spirits. This reluctance limits the offer of help to those who can keep the spirits from manifesting. There are many who are under such spiritual oppression that any talk of Christ, the Bible, or confession of sin brings the demons into manifestation. When this happens, many who advocate the resistance model no longer want to help the individual.

3. The resistance model can cheapen confession just because of the volume of things needing to be confessed.

Often when a person is properly taught on the nature of confession, the task seems overwhelming. The number of things which need to be confessed seems too great and a rushed or shortened confession takes place. In a number of cases, people have rushed and short-circuited the process of confession in order to get through their list. In these cases they need to go back through the list slowly and thoroughly when confessing their sins. I am aware of a particular denomination that uses the resistance model and requires those diagnosed as demonized to attend a weekend retreat so there are no interruptions in the confession process.

4. The resistance model tends to exaggerate Satanic power which results in fear instead of security.

In order to cause people to stay away from demonic sins, the power of Satan is magnified. This exaggeration which is designed to cause avoidance puts great stress on how particular sins can lead to Satanic bondage. This spotlight on the demonic connection of certain sins does produce avoidance but also can result in a magnification of Satanic power. The Christian must realize Satan is powerful but Christ has power over the Devil. Two women I know became so concerned about "demonic" sins, their whole lives revolved around these sins. They would openly confront anyone they felt were committing these sins without thought as to how to approach them or if they were accurately perceiving the situation. This also caused a great disruption in the church. Sometimes Satan is the only one who is promoted as powerful. To be godly means not doing the sinful things. There are segments of Christianity which so stress avoidance of sin that the positive aspects of Christianity are excluded and forgotten.

Limitations

1. The resistance model is unusable if one is in the midst of a demonic manifestation.

The benefit and power of the resistance model can only work with a lucid and conscious person. The nature of the method limits it so that direct confrontation must be excluded. A number of those involved in deliverance suggest at times great strides can be made only when the demon is directly confronted. The indirect method does not always move the process along.

2. The resistance model does not work well in cases of severe demonization.

Jesus did not stop the Gaderene demonic and ask him to confess his sins and live a righteous life. The resistance model was inappropriate in that case when the severe demonic was approaching. The Apostle Paul does ask the slave girl in Acts 16 to stop, confess her sins, and make positive choices. He commands with the voice of authority that the demons leave. Severe demonization requires more dynamic intervention than the slow, methodical resistance model.

3. The resistance model does not always deal with the psychology of sin and its effects upon the thought patterns.

While confession and positive choices are essential to clearing away the rubble of demonic destruction, there are often uncharted mental patterns which direct a person to sinful behavior without demonic activity. These mental patterns must be examined or permanent freedom is not possible. The destruction of sin is not just demonic, it is the mental pathways that produce habitual choices. It is these choices, and the psychological effects of repeated sin, that can be ignored in this model. All that is desired is the behavior be stopped. Outward conformity is the goal.

SUMMARY

The resistance model is invaluable in framing the basic discussion of spiritual warfare. Without the proper emphasis on sin and its consequences deliverance moves throughout the supernatural arena producing heat but very little light. The Christian must understand the commands of Scripture demand action on their part. Resistance is not easy nor passive. Resistance is actively using the simple weapons Christ gives to keep the Devil at bay. This emphasis is needed in the church today. Parts of the church have been fed positional truth in such a way they believe the Christian life is done for them.

6

COUNSELING:

Focusing on the Battle for the Mind

Cindy definitely had demonic problems. She had been to numerous deliverance sessions and had been miraculously delivered on more than one occasion. However, two to three months after each session, the problems and the voices returned. Cindy needed to be delivered, but she also needed something beyond deliverance—a new way to think. The forces inside her had developed well-worn, destructive patterns of thought. These patterns of thought told her what to do when she was depressed. They told her what to do when she wanted to have fun. They told her how to get over her feelings of rejection. They told her to see herself as worthless. For almost every situation, the demons and her previous choices had developed destructive patterns that would keep her imprisoned in a false world. Even when the wicked spirits were thrown out, she still thought in the same patterns. Those destructive patterns caused Cindy to think in a demonic way even when no spirits were present. It was not long after each deliverance until her thought patterns and actions invited new invaders, and she was bound again. Scientists now tell us we develop habit loops that become imbedded in our subconscious. These habit patterns feel right because we have done them so many times even though the results are not what we want. Cindy needed to examine her mental habit patterns and learn new ways of thinking before she could be completely free. Cindy was directed to a Christian counselor who would uncover these habit patterns which kept turning her towards sin and bondage. Together they were able to change the way Cindy thought about herself and others so she could be free. Cindy did not really win until she began changing the underlying thinking that was so comfortable in the past.

Cindy's story underscores the need in many cases for more than just straight deliverance. The counseling model of deliverance is a subtle form of deliverance which attempts to expose and free the person from destructive patterns of thought, speech, and action. Within this model there is little or no attempt to contact the demonic. If wicked spirits manifest, they are shut down and the root causes of their control are examined. If demonic forces control the way a person thinks, then they control the person. It is clear the battle with Satanic forces is a battle for the mind. The counseling model can expose the lies of Satan without doing battle directly with wicked spirits. It is often the patterns of thought, speech, and behavior which keep a person bound and not experiencing the fullness of the Christian life.

HISTORY

The counseling model began as a reaction to the other demonic deliverance models. Prior to the advent of modern psychology, much of man's behavior was explained in terms of supernatural forces outside of the control of individual volition. People were at the mercy of forces beyond our control: the fates, the stars, God, angels, the Devil, and demons. To some, these explanations were excessive and unwarranted. An attempt was made to explain behavior strictly in terms of environmental, emotional, and mental factors.[1] As a starting point supernatural forces were ruled out as direct causes for behavior. The individual has choices, and it is those choices that determine why things happen. It is this naturalistic starting point that has caused some Christians to reject all of the techniques and methods of psychology. This non-supernatural starting point however allowed psychologists to develop specific techniques which isolated and explained behavior based solely on choices and environment.

While the anti-supernatural worldview is not valid, the counseling approach, when done well, does put the focus on the biblical principle of responsibility. Galatians 6:7 says, "*Do not be deceived, God is not mocked whatsoever a man sows that shall he also reap.*" This verse tells us the life we are living is the result of our choices. We are responsible for the choices we make. Yes, there are environmental and human factors that shrink or expand our choices. But each person is responsible for the choices they make. A number of the techniques that were developed in the counseling model to find the choices, influences, emotions, and root actions are very helpful for moving a person toward a productive life. Remember the goal of any demonic powers is to occlude, distract, or control a person's choices. If a person has invited demons in, then it is important to examine how the person thinks in order to uncover the destructive patterns and any righteous choices that are being missed. More and more Christian counselors (and even some secular psychologists) are considering demons as a working hypothesis to explain influences on some behavior. In the extreme cases, it is usually put under the rubric of a dissociative disorder.

The counselor's job is to help identify faulty thinking, destructive patterns of behavior, reactive speech and behavior, as well as demonic logic. The counselor must also show and train their clients what normal and even godly behavior is like. It is not enough to just show how the person is being programmed to repeat the mistakes and destructive actions of the past. There must be exercises and new programming that establishes righteous ways of thinking and acting. The counselor can be very helpful in identifying the lies of the Devil and repairing the destruction of the wicked spirits.

If we think of the work of wicked spirits as the spiritual maggots and cockroaches, then the counselor is the person who will help the afflicted person clean up their life. The counselor is not the exterminator but rather the expert showing how to live a "normal" life. It is the moral filth that draws the demons and the lack of pure patterns of life that keeps drawing them and allowing them to influence behavior. People who have embraced (or been forced to embrace) a filthy lifestyle need to be shown how to live differently. They need to be shown how to think differently. This is the very important work of the counselor and the counseling model. This is one-on-one discipleship. This is training in godly living. Finally, as the person walks in more and more purity and depth with the Lord Jesus, they will be free and protected from being re-infested. We are talking about learning and practicing tools for developing a joyfully pure life. This process needs to be seen as taking time in just the same way as helping a person clean up their house and then keep it clean. A year to two years is quite common.

The counselor must understand what the person does in a number of situations and moods. The counselor knows the person is being programmed to act and react in certain ways that will never let them be free to enjoy the success they really want. The counselor must help the client see these patterns in what they produce. We know everyone is like an iceberg with a little bit above the surface for all to see and much more below the surface that supports it all. We know that our parents or guardians imprinted us with a system on how to live life in almost every area. It is these imprints or systems many of us are still following. If the system is bad, then it will consistently bring about a bad result. If the system was good, then we will have a good result. Until we examine that system, we will not be able to understand why we keep getting the results we are getting. The Scriptures tell us God visits the iniquity of the fathers on the third and fourth generation of those who hate Him but has lovingkindness to thousands who love Him and follow His commandments.

In many cases counseling is re-parenting a person into a different way of dealing with the areas of life. If a person has a faulty financial system, then they need to be shown and try a more effective system. If a person has a faulty romantic system, they need to understand a more correct one and practice it. If a person does not know how to handle their anger, then they need new ways of dealing with their rage and significant practice until this new way becomes their way. If a person consistently finds they are tempted to do things that are destructive to their life, then they need to be shown other things to do rather than giving in and significant training and accountability to make sure this new system is imbedded.

Sometimes counseling has been seen as just understanding the pain and experiences of another person. This is a crucial aspect of counseling, but it must go way beyond just listening. Counseling, if it is going to be truly effective, must show the way to a healthy way of living that does not rely on the inadequate systems of the past.

The following are questions that can be used to establish mental patterns and behavior routines that may or may not be destructive to the person.

Examples:

What do you usually do when you get depressed?

1.

2.

3.

What could you do instead of what you do now?

1.

2.

3.

When you want to have a "good time," what three things come to mind?

1.

2.

3.

What could you do instead of what you do now?

1.

2.

3.

How do you respond when you don't get your way?

1.

2.

3.

What could you do instead of what you do now?

1.

2.

3.

What do you do when you start feeling lonely?

1.

2.

3.

What could you do instead of what you do now?

1.

2.

3.

If someone is mad at you, screaming, or yelling what do you do?

1.

2.

3.

What could you do instead of what you do now?

1.

2.

3.

When you feel attracted to another person romantically, what do you do?

1.

2.

3.

What could you do instead of what you do now?

1.

2.

3.

When you have the chance to make a lot of money, what do you do?

1.

2.

3.

What could you do instead of what you do now?

1.

2.

3.

Right after an argument, what do you usually do?

1.

2.

3.

What could you do instead of what you do now?

1.

2.

3.

If someone has manipulated you, what do you feel like doing?

1.

2.

3.

What could you do instead of what you do now?

1.

2.

3.

What is the most important person or thing in your life?

1.

2.

3.

What could you do instead of what you do now?

1.

2.

3.

When you don't know what to do, what do you do? Who do you ask?

1.

2.

3.

What could you do instead of what you do now?

1.

2.

3.

What do you do when you run out of money?

1.

2.

3.

What could you do instead of what you do now?

1.

2.

3.

What are three ways you earn money?

1.

2.

3.

What could you do instead of what you do now?

1.

2.

3.

Who are you trying to please the most?

1.

2.

3.

What could you do instead of what you do now?

1.

2.

3.

What do you do when you like someone?

1.

2.

3.

What could you do instead of what you do now?

1.

2.

3.

How would you let a person know that you are grateful to them?

1.

2.

3.

What could you do instead of what you do now?

1.

2.

3.

We need to answer the following questions if we are to get a handle on what is in the way of a joyful life. It is entirely possible the following questions may need to be answered numerous times over the course of the sessions as the afflicted person opens up more and becomes more aware of themselves and their past.

1. What traumas, losses, wounds, difficulties, and hurts have I suffered through and how might they be affecting my life?

2. What is your family programming about how to deal with the problems and issues of life?

3. What is your current culture (friends, community, media, authorities) directing you to do, say, and think like with the issues and problems of life?

4. What actions have you taken and/or words have you used that you are deeply ashamed of and wish you could take back?

I have worked with a number of counselors and psychologists in healing people who have been oppressed by wicked spirits. It is the tandem of spiritual healing and psychological healing that provides a sure foundation for the person. The way a person thinks about themselves, their past, their destiny, and the people around them is crucial to an abundant Christian life. It is not enough to throw out the demons and then expect the person to start living in a completely different way. They need to establish new ways of thinking and living. This is the discipleship process. The way a person responds to a number of situations, feelings, people and obstacles will determine how life goes for them in many instances. If they have embraced a programmed response to various life situations that is wrong, destructive, or demonic, then they are doomed until they change those responses.

TECHNIQUES

Listening Skills

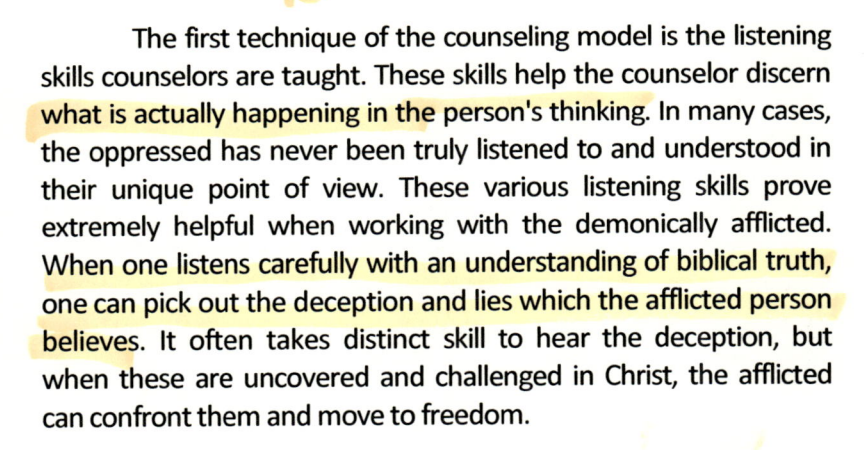

The first technique of the counseling model is the listening skills counselors are taught. These skills help the counselor discern what is actually happening in the person's thinking. In many cases, the oppressed has never been truly listened to and understood in their unique point of view. These various listening skills prove extremely helpful when working with the demonically afflicted. When one listens carefully with an understanding of biblical truth, one can pick out the deception and lies which the afflicted person believes. It often takes distinct skill to hear the deception, but when these are uncovered and challenged in Christ, the afflicted can confront them and move to freedom.

In one case, I was dealing with a woman who regularly pursued sexual adventures that were destructive. It was clear there was demonic power behind these sexual desires, but deliverance eluded us. Listening over an extended period of time, I learned that when she was ten or eleven years of age, she was abandoned by her mother. This early trauma caused her to believe she was of no value to anyone. Having believed the lie of being worthless, she succumbed to the temptation of sexually destructive behavior. It was not until the original lie of her self-worth was exposed and challenged that she could reject the demonic suggestions to destroy herself through risky sexual liaisons.

The value of careful, penetrating, and probing listening cannot be overestimated. This process can expose ways of thinking and suggest adjustment for destructive thoughts or ideas. It is often a person's thought process or pattern of thinking that causes a tendency toward destructive activities. Suicide is often the result of a sustained incremental process and not a rash individual act. Sexual perversion is also the result of a process of thought and not a leap into deviant behavior. Teenage rebellion is often the result of conclusions drawn over a number of years. If these thought patterns can be understood and exposed, then the individual can detect the lying and twisting of reality. This detection allows the power of the thought process to be broken, no matter what power source is behind it.

It is important to walk through the basic active listening skills. When someone is trusting you with their intimate secrets and deepest pains, the counselor needs to be fully engaged in the listening. While these techniques would seem to be extremely basic, these basics allow the formation of deep communication.

Eye Contact: Look at the person while they are talking. Let your eyes communicate interest and even curiosity about them and their story.

Body Lean: When we are interested in what another person is saying, we naturally lean towards the person. Therefore, this becomes a cue to the other person about how interested people are in their story. Therefore it is important the counselor lean in and show they care with their body language as the conversation goes along.

Minimal Encourages: These are the little grunts, noises, facial expressions that tell the other person to keep talking. These could be phrases or words such as "Well" or "No" or "Really." All of these little ways of saying to the person, "Tell me more." It is very hard to keep talking to a person who doesn't give these encouragements.

Verbal Following: This is where the listener follows the topic of the speaker and does not try and change the subject to something that interests them more. One of the greatest gifts people can receive from a friend, a relative, or a counselor is to follow their thread of conversation all the way to the end of its path. Very few people are given this gift. The counselor must fight the tendency to turn the conversation down the myriad of side topics that would seem more interesting.

Yes, there are times when the counselor must turn the conversational topic to an insight that needs to be noticed but be careful of doing this constantly or the counselee will not feel heard.

Mirroring/Paraphrasing: This is technique where the listener reflects back the exact emotional word of the counselee or a similar word. This technique tells the listener that they are being heard. This usually will cause the counselee to excitedly agree and tell more of the situation, emotion, or circumstance. It is important to note it is the emotional word that is mirrored or paraphrased, not just the ideas.

Summarize: This is where the counselor repeats back the general ideas that they have heard the counselee speak of in the last little bit to see if they have heard the person correctly. This process of having a person repeat back your ideas and thoughts causes you to feel like the center of attention and focus. This will usually allow you to go further in the development of your ideas. This is a very good way for counselors to really love their counselees.

It is amazing what can happen when a person is listened to about their life. There is a huge need to be listened to and understood. These basic elements of listening well can make a huge difference.

Detailed Family Histories

Another helpful technique of the counseling model is to research a person's past and family background. This detailed analysis allows the counselor, as well as the afflicted, to examine the roots of aberrant thoughts. Sometimes a genogram and other forms of looking at a person's family lineage can expose the devastation of sinful choices and the destructive reoccurring patterns in the family. Detailed histories can uncover traumas which occurred years before. These traumas often play a significant part in the person's thinking patterns. Intense emotional experiences can be used by demonic spirits to warp the person's thinking. Many times a memory of the past has been warped by fear, lust, anger, bitterness, or ego to cause a person to come to a faulty conclusion. Asking a person about their earliest memories of money, sex, approval, condemnation, abuse, etc., can reveal the places where their thinking about themselves and others was warped. The critical events of a person's past may need to be reexamined and new conclusions formed based upon an adult understanding and a biblical foundation. It can be helpful to pray specifically for God to heal certain memories and transform them into positive memories which reinforce God's love and truth. God is faithful to answer these prayers for inner healing. When I have prayed for the healing of a particular memory, God often helps the person see that event in a completely different way. As the memory is relived with God involved, the person's perspective changes to see the positive which God produced from the situation. This is only possible after understanding the person's detailed family history.

A detailed family history can also expose involvement with demonic sins by the family as well as by the individual themselves. If the individual is living in a whole environment of sin and demonic involvement, this information is vital for their deliverance. On a number of occasions a detailed family survey has revealed demonic problems that need to be cleared up.

It is extremely helpful for individuals to have discussions about how their families shaped them in crucial areas. All of a sudden there may be an "AH HA" moment when the person says, "I am doing the same things that my dad did." Or "I am just doing what I saw my parents do." These points are when people can realize the strategies their parents employed for dealing with these various issues didn't work.

It is at these points a person can consciously begin to change. We don't have to replay our parent's (foster parents, first boyfriends, teen groups) solutions. We don't have to allow the default settings we were programmed with to be the way we will handle our life. It takes a lot of work to choose to act, speak, react, and think differently; but it can be done. We can choose to be different. We can choose the new behaviors that actually produce the results we desire. It is amazing how often we know what we are doing is not working, but we keep doing it anyway because it is just easier and well known.

Early Childhood Programming

What did your family teach you about _____?

All of us have been programmed by our families and/or growing-up experiences. Remember, your family may have given you a wonderful system of handling these various areas or they may have given you a completely dysfunctional system for dealing with these issues. You, however, need to examine what system they gave you so you can see if the system needs to be replaced. This process is always enlightening and sometimes life-changing.

Sometimes the initial work here can be done alone or with a counselor. Bringing light on the hidden operating system which has directed your behavior is one of the keys to developing a successful life.

For some people, their parents were non-existent so it is best to answer these questions about the people who raised you. If you ran away from home, you may need to look at the way the people you stayed with did the following things. The idea here is that you are a compilation of the systems you saw modeled and experienced. You can change, but you must become aware of what you are doing and then make a decision about whether you should change it. It will then take practice to actually put a new habit pattern over the old one. It may seem impossible, but it is possible. However, it takes consistency.

You may want to answer these questions in the book or on a separate piece of paper or talk your way through them with a friend or counselor.

1. **Money**

How did your parents handle money?

What were your parent's sayings and attitudes toward money?

What did your parents model in regards to making, managing, or giving money?

Did your parents teach you anything about making, managing, or giving money?

In what ways are you handling money the same way your parents did?

What do you believe is God's way of handling this area?

2. **Success**

What did your parents say or believe made a successful life?

What messages did your parents give you about success in life?

How did your parents try to become successful?

What was your parent's success plan?

What do you believe is God's way of handling this area?

3. Feelings

How did your family deal with feelings and/or expressed emotions; i.e., crying, shouting, screaming, anger, hatred, etc.?

What did your parents say about people who expressed their feelings or emotions?

How do you handle feelings? Is it like your parents?

What do you believe is God's way of handling this area?

4. Roles of Men and Women

How did your parents model the roles for men and women?

How would you like your mate to act?

How close does your ideal mate conform to the actions of your parents?

What did your parents model about how a man should behave?

What did your parents model about how a woman should behave?

What do you believe is God's way of handling this area?

5. Physical Affection

How physically affectionate were your parents?

Did they say anything about public displays of affection?

What do you believe is God's way of handling this area?

6. Compliments and Praise

When would you receive compliments or praise from your parents?

What did your parents model to you about compliments or praise?

What was the greatest compliment or praise you ever received from your parents?

What do you believe is God's way of handling this area?

7. Sexual Relations

How did your parents deal with sexual relations?

What did they say or do to teach you about sexual relations?

What do you believe is God's way of handling this area?

8. Loss and Grief

How did your family handle grief and significant loss?

What did your parents say or teach you during times of significant loss?

How long did your parents allow themselves or you to process significant loss?

What do you believe is God's way of handling this area?

9. Expressing Anger

How did your parents express anger?

What did your parents do when someone was angry?

What did your parents say or teach about anger?

What do you believe is God's way of handling this area?

10. Parenting and Children

What did your parents do to train or control their children?

What did your parents say about their role as parents or your role as children?

What was communicated about having children? Joy, duty, drudgery, etc.

What do you believe is God's way of handling this area?

11. God and Religion

What did your parents model about God and religion?

What type of spirituality or religion did your parents practice?

What did your parents teach or say about God and religion?

What was confusing about their approach to God and religion?

What do you believe is God's way of handling this area?

12. Conflict

How did your family deal with conflict?

How was conflict resolved?

What did your family do if someone remained in conflict?

What do you believe is God's way of handling this area?

13. Marriage and Singleness

What did your family say about being married or being single?

How did your family treat married couples and single people?

Was singleness an acceptable goal?

Was marriage the ultimate goal?

What do you believe is God's way of handling this area?

14. Pleasure, Recreation, and Fun

What did your family do for fun?

What did your family allow the individuals to do for fun?

How much money and time was given to recreation or fun?

What do you believe is God's way of handling this area?

15. Race, Culture, Class

What did your family communicate about your race, culture, or class?

What did your family communicate about others of a different race, culture, or class?

What do you believe is God's way of handling this area?

16. Authorities and Power

What did your parents model in relation to authorities?

What did your parents teach or say about authorities?

How did your parents react to an authority stopping them from doing something?

17. Politics

What was your parents attitude toward politics?

What did your parents say about politics?

What were your parents political views?

What do you believe is God's way of handling this area?

The key question in this arena is: Are you following your parent's way of relating and interacting in a given area or are you following God's way of relating and interacting?

Detailed Mental Analysis

Another helpful tool in uncovering the deception and lies of Satan is to listen to the way a person thinks. This requires listening and cataloging the patterns of thought that emerge when the person talks about why they took a particular action or said a particular thing. If a man thinks of women only in a sexual way, then there is an abnormal pattern of thought. If a person always reacts to obstacles or disappointment with anger and rage, then they have embraced a destructive way of thinking. These patterns may be reinforced by inner demonic voices or they may just be a pattern that seemed to work at one time in their life. If a person speaks with derision of every authority figure, then this thinking pattern of rebellion must be confronted. If the person is hyper critical and/or hyper sensitive to all offenses, then this destructive bitterness pattern blocks their freedom. All of the above patterns are aberrations of the normal Christian mind and give Satan room to develop or reinforce a destructive behavior. The Devil does not need to constantly speak or punish a person in order to control a person. If he merely excites an aberrant mental pattern on occasion, he can keep the person in bondage. I have watched people with wonderful opportunities to change their life make the same destructive choices with their money, their relationships, their education, and their authorities that they have made in the past. In many cases of deliverance, the person is not free until the pattern of thought is exposed and changed.

Realize a person is not really free to make a different choice until they know about the choice, can see themselves making this different choice, and have actually made the different choice a number of times. It is not enough to describe a different future if the person does not understand the individual choices that are required to achieve their new future reality. If the destructive patterns of thought and reaction are left in place, then it is only a matter of time before all the destructive and demonic results will reappear in a person's life.

How does this person think about and react to the following areas of their life? Is there any dysfunctional, destructive, or demonic reactions to any of these areas? Many of these damaging ways of thinking may come from their parents or they could come from experiences they have had; but this thought and/or behavior pattern sits in this person's life and consistently switches them from the track for success, joy, and love to a destructive track. The counselor can help them find these destructive patterns and begin putting new choices, new behaviors, and new habits in their place. This is crucial.

1. **Money**

2. **Success**

3. **Feelings**

4. **Roles of men and women**

5. **Physical affection**

6. **Compliments and praise**

7. **Sexual relations**

8. **Loss and grief**

9. **Expressing anger**

10. **Parenting and children**

11. **God and religion**

12. **Conflict**

13. **Marriage and singleness**

14. **Pleasure, recreation, and fun**

15. **Race, culture, class**

16. **Authorities and power**

17. **Politics**

It is important to add again at this point, it is not enough to just identify the destructive pattern, how it got there, and what it is doing. The counselee needs the pattern to be replaced with a positive one that will produce healthy life giving results in their life.

Alternate Mental Perspectives

The counseling model of deliverance can and should suggest a number of new ways of reacting and living. These new healthy ways of thinking, speaking, and behaving allow the afflicted one to break free from the patterns of the past. In many cases the afflicted person does not have any examples or personal knowledge of positive ways of living. So telling someone to live differently does not work. The counselor must provide exercises, teaching, examples, and training to show a person how to live in a different way.

The major relationships of life have basic actions that make them work. These basic actions are the definition of love in their relationships. The New Testament spends considerable time instructing Christian disciples about how to act in each relationship of life. These new actions must be tried and practiced before they will yield the results of a blessed and pure life. These major relationships would include our relationship with God; our relationship with ourselves; our relationship with our spouse; our relationship with our family; our relationship with our work; our relationship with our church; our relationship with our friends; and our relationship with our money. It is in this practice of a solid Christian life a person enjoys the abundance that God provides and defeats the Devil in the best possible way. A well lived life.

When a counseling model is functioning properly, there is considerable time spent on teaching, training, modeling, and practicing the new behaviors needed for abundant living in Christ. This is as important, if not more important, than talking about what the person did wrong in the past or had done to them in the past. There is no future if the powerful new actions of love are not incorporated into the afflicted person's life. They must be able to look forward to a bright future where they will be acting in new ways, thinking differently, and seeing very positive results that are different than what they have seen in the past.

One of the dangers of the counseling model is it can spend so much time listening and exploring the problems, difficulties, and pain of a person's life that it does not train a person how to have a positive, joyful life. The New Testament instructs us, in significant detail, in each of our relationships so we would begin acting differently than we have in the past. If all we do is rehearse our brokenness and do not work through what would healthy relationships look like, then we never escape the gravity of our brokenness.

There are numerous books and workbooks in the Christian world that can help with the development of new actions and reactions in each relationship. I have written a few books on these topics myself. I have also written a companion book to this book called **Breaking Free** which gives multiple different exercises for developing humility, forgiveness, submission, purity, meekness, righteous desire, patience, and peace in the midst of turmoil. Having a person actually begin thinking in a different way is extremely powerful. Helping a person realize there are alternative ways of thinking and acting instead of the well-worn destructive patterns of their past is liberating. Then the counselee can make a real choice to live differently because they have practiced a pure way of living. The counselee can make responsible monetary decisions rather than reckless and foolish monetary decisions. The counselee will have practiced submitting and gaining the affirmation of that choice rather than automatically moving in the direction of rebellion.

Alternative mental perspectives can break the tight hold of the patterns of the past. For instance, if something bad happens, some insist this means God does not love them. This perspective can be held with incredible certainty. It is the counselor's job to suggest other perspectives which could also be true. For instance, a difficulty or obstacle in some area of the person's life might be God beginning a new round of training for greater blessings rather than fresh evidence that God doesn't love them. A second positive thought might be trials and difficulties which might help in understanding and comforting someone else's pain. Third, a trial might keep a person from particular sins which could otherwise be seductive.

Emotional Attachment

One of the most important aspects of the counseling model is the connection between the counselee and the counselor. The relationship of trust and candor between the counselor and the client often transfers energy from the counselor to the counselee to change their counselee's life. Interestingly enough, studies have suggested the type of counseling practiced is not as important as the relationship of trust between counselor and counselee. This trust relationship provides the opportunity to uncover and redirect thinking patterns in a non-threatening environment. Counselors are trained on how they relate to the individual is just as important as what they say. This powerful bond between counselor and counselee can put a wedge between the afflicted and a demonic influence.

The radical importance of the bond between the counselor and the counselee can hardly be overstated. This is one of the strongest elements in recovery and development toward a new reality in the person's life. "In a review of variables contributing to therapy outcomes, Beutler (1989) concluded that the therapist–client match is the strongest predictor of outcome."[3] This is why I usually suggest a counselor/mentor role would last many times over a year. There must be time to develop a bond. There must be a relationship of trust built up so the counselee can try new actions and behaviors based almost completely on their trust for the counselor.

The counselor role is one of surrogate parent or trusted mentor. The counselee may have had multiple destructive relationships with adults in the past which have helped embed wrong ways of thinking in the person. A new relationship of trust and encouragement can often allow a client to make significant changes in their life and strike out in new directions that would simply not be possible without the encouragement and relationship of the counselor.

CRITIQUE

While the counseling model can be useful in dealing with all types of behavior problems, it is important to critique its strengths and weaknesses in regard to deliverance and the demonic arena.

Strengths

1. The counseling model has distinct biblical underpinnings.

In 2 Corinthians 10:3-5, the apostle speaks of the intense spiritual battles taking place in the mind of every individual. The goal of the Christian is to take every thought captive to the obedience of Christ. The apostle demands we submit our thoughts to Christ for evaluation. He states it is possible to be held prisoner in our own minds in fortresses made by demons. It is not until false concepts are destroyed that the Christian will be able to fully obey the Savior.

In Romans 12:1, 2, the apostle declares the need to transform our lives and present ourselves to the Lord as living sacrifices. This takes place when we renew our minds. No details on how to renew the mind are given in this section, but it is clear how and what we think controls how we act. A Christian can never expect to escape the corruption in the world and serve the Savior in freedom unless his/her mind is free from the sinful patterns and misplaced values.

Galatians 6:7 states whatsoever a man sows that shall he also reap. A person's choices are his/her own. This is the bedrock of Christian deliverance. While spiritual and physical forces may exert strong influence on a person they still have the ability to choose. It is this ability to choose that is under attack in spiritual warfare. When the counseling model seeks to expose the choices a person made to bring about the current situation, it is very helpful. When the counseling model shows a person they have established a pattern of destructive behaviors, it is powerfully helpful. When the counseling model shows the person alternative choices and alternative paths a person can take, they are showing the way to deliverance.

Numerous examples in the New Testament can be explored which suggest the key role for the mind in victorious Christian living (Romans 8, Philippians 4, Matthew 6, etc.). It is obvious that authentic Christianity involves right thinking. While the excesses and anti-supernatural conclusions of psychology cannot be embraced, the emphasis on clear, cogent, and known mental processes is supported in the Scripture. These techniques form one more application of the riches of Christ Jesus to those held in bondage in the kingdom of darkness.

2. The counseling model focuses on the battle for the mind

The battle in spiritual warfare is for the mind. If wicked spirits can control the mind, they can control the person. In 1 Chronicles 21:1, David is moved by Satan to number the children of Israel. If David was aware of the thoughts he was having were not from him but came from Satan, it is doubtful he would have gone ahead with the sin.

It is a truth of Christianity that not all of the thoughts that flow through our minds come from us. The Devil, the world system, and our own selfish sinful desires can and do put ideas and temptations in our minds contrary to God's Word. The strength of the counseling model is its focus on what is happening in the mind. People do not have to accept every thought that flows through their mind. Every thought should be examined to see if it should be accepted or rejected. In the counseling model, people are directed to examine what and how they think. When the proper amount of emphasis is given to showing biblical thinking versus abnormal thinking, great progress can be made.

3. The counseling model can make the critical distinction between the thoughts of the individual and the suggestions of the demonic agent.

When used properly in the hands of a skilled Christian counselor, the counseling model helps the afflicted identify thoughts that come from a satanic source. Since the demonic thoughts always seek to sell themselves as the normal thinking of the person, this distinction is critical. When the truth that not all of the thoughts in their mind are their own, it can be liberating, shattering, and a flood of questions follow.

How do I know which voice or thought is which?

Which thoughts are the demons, which are mine, and which are the Lord's?

How do I know the promptings or voice of God?

Why do the wrong thoughts feel so right many of the times?

These questions can be answered by the counselor and by a thorough search of the Word of God. The Lord never authors a prompting which is contrary to His own Word. Our minds never willingly think destructive thoughts. The Devil, however, deceptively authors that which is perverse, seeking to twist our minds into accepting his type of thinking (Matthew 4). Distinctions between types and sources of thought have brought many to freedom. Once the distinction is made and personally accepted, then wrong thoughts can be rejected in Christ's power.

4. The counseling model keeps the afflicted person active in the healing process.

One of the dangers in certain types of deliverance is a passive client. This passivity can create an avenue for re-oppression and re-affliction. The essence of spiritual warfare is a battle to claim the abundant life God has planned for us. God requires involvement, action, training, growth, and faith to achieve the life He meant for us. Some forms of deliverance do not require the afflicted person to do anything to be delivered. This can give the person a false sense of how life in Christ is to be lived. The life of God is a life of active choosing, not a life of being a passive robot while God does it all for us and through us.

The counseling model is healthy in that the person must cooperate with the counselor and seize control of his/her mind. The Christian life is a life full of choices. We must be effective in exercising our will or we will never enjoy the benefits Christ offers. One man I worked with was filled with joy and hope as he saw how he could avoid the thinking process which resulted in his nearly destroying his marriage. He became increasingly excited as the weeks progressed, and he applied the new thinking and new actions to his marriage. He was becoming free, and he was fully involved in the process of his freedom. He understood his marriage was a cause-and-effect relationship. If he did certain things, then it resulted in certain damage in the relationship. The Devil was not trying to liberate him by suggesting he spend hours involved with porn and pursuing immoral relationships, the Devil was trying to help the man destroy the one precious relationship in his life – his marriage. He could fight back by making different choices.

5. The counseling model exposes the thought patterns that allow continued demonic control.

Like post-hypnotic suggestion, demonic thoughts explode with destructive frequency in the mind of the afflicted without the wicked spirit even being present. These types of destructive mental bombs must be exposed and removed from the psyche of the person. The counseling model, by focusing on the thinking of the person, is narrow enough in its vision that it can deal effectively with these wrong thoughts. The counseling model exposes these thoughts as foreign agents and builds new ideas in their place.

In 2 Corinthians 10:3-5, the apostle outlines the battle for the mind as a warfare in which no thought or thought process can be allowed to construct a fortress in the mind but that every thought should be brought before the Lord Jesus Christ. Deliverance counseling does not often focus enough on how the Devil uses unexamined thought processes (self-worth, paranoia, or bitterness) to destroy or damage the believer without ever taking possession. In a number of cases it was not until the thought or thought process was uncovered that the oppression was destroyed. Thoughts like:

"I deserve a miserable life."

"God has it in for me."

"I'm just a person who is environmentally, genetically, emotionally, or educationally drawn to this particular sin."

"I've been too bad for God ever to love me now!"

"I hate all men, women, poor, rich, blacks, whites, Asians, or Mexicans. They can't be trusted."

These types of thoughts must be exposed and displayed in all their destructive power.

It is important for one not believe the process of changing old mental patterns is quick and easy. It takes time and patience to expose this thought pattern in all areas of life and in the many disguises in which it comes. The counseling model can accomplish this process extremely well.

6. The counseling model uncovers the significant traumas which become pivotal points for thinking and demonic control.

Significant pathways for destruction are the traumas and abuses of the past. Because of the nature of the listening, analyzing skills, and studying family histories of the counseling model, the major traumas in a person's life stand out in stark relief. These traumas often need to be explored in depth in order to expose the Devil's interpretation of these traumas. Wicked spirits offer their own "comfort" to the victims of abuse. This "comfort" is designed to twist the thinking until certain destructive and sinful ideas are more palatable years later. The demonic interpretation often correlates quite well with the victim's own immature understanding of the incident. A major strength of the counseling model is the trusting environment and careful listening which allows the details of past traumas to be exposed and discussed.

7. The counseling model can repair the scars of demonic occupation.

New understanding of the past from a more mature position can allow the healing process to occur. Few people, especially children, can accurately evaluate tragedy or trauma when it first occurs. The counseling model allows a more mature attitude to be brought to the examination of the trauma. New perspectives, new understanding, and new reasons can speed healing and complete health. A woman I worked with was sexually molested by a relative when she was a young girl. She was liberated from nightmarish memories when she examined the perpetrator and circumstances as an adult. As she saw those dark years from a new perspective, she could even see the benefits from God that resulted from this evil deed.

8. The counseling model can identify demonic patterns and demonic agency without raising the subject of the demonic.

A helpful technique in dealing with those who are oppressed is to have them identify the sinful pattern and give it a name. If your anger had a name, what would it be? What would it do if you gave it full control? In this way the person can begin to see it as something foreign and alien without raising the specter of the demonic. In a few cases this has introduced the severity of the need in those reluctant to face the problem. Many are willing to deal with the anger that lives within them but are unwilling to deal with a demon working in them. Many are ready to learn how to free themselves from the lusts which take over at times but are offended if deliverance from wicked spirits were offered as a solution. The strength of the counseling model is that the source and the action can be dealt with and then explained as to the potential demonic connection. The counseling model allows the cure to be affected without frightening labels being attached to the problem.

Weaknesses

1. The counseling model can encourage the idea that one's thoughts, not sin, are the key to demonic control.

Since the counseling model focuses on the battle for the mind, it can magnify the importance of thinking to the point where actions are not sufficiently weighed into the equation. The counseling model reinforces that the mind is the target Satan is seeking to control. The mind is the goal of Satan's stratagems, but there are many battlefields besides the mind on which Satan must be defeated. The counseling model also needs to emphasize that the actions which were done in the past are power plants of Satanic influence in the life of the person. One teenager tried, without much success, to change his mental set about lust and wounds of the past. His lack of success was the result of his focus only on his thinking. He was unwilling to build real world consequences, real world accountability, and real world changes to his routines. Only when he expanded his solution to include confession and repentance and real world changes in action did his new mental perspective begin to work.

2. The counseling model has the tendency to be a self-contained universe, excluding the supernatural

A major flaw in the counseling model is its naturalistic and rationalistic tendencies. Psychology began with the desire to eliminate all supernatural causes for behavior, and it still suffers from this tendency. Even among those counselors who admit the existence and influence of the supernatural, there is a desire to downplay its impact. There can be a tendency to see the world only as a place of naturalistic influences and environments where prayer, God, and demonic spirits are not real. The world is seen naturalistically with demons rarely invading a mechanistic universe with clearly visible signs. It is more biblical to see the universe as a swirl of interactive parts with all events being a cadre of influences.

One should not discount God's ability to act into our universe and into our lives. We should not pretend that the Devil is not scheming against us and that the circumstances that bring us close to our greatest temptations are actually coincidences. God can and does send help to us. Things can change in miraculous ways.

3. The counseling model often does not confront sin.

Because of the emphasis on the way people think and what took place in their lives to shape who they are, the counseling model can leave a subtle impression that past sins do not need to be cleared up. Many leave a counselor's office with a focus on what others did to them and little understanding of the impact of the choices they made. Sin must be dealt with; guilt and blame accepted; sinful choices and actions clearly turned away from. Sin is the doorway Satan walks through to influence and control people. In counseling, the emphasis on understanding and sympathizing does not always lend itself to labeling certain actions as wrong. This can often lead to the person seeking to build a new life upon the toxic waste of the past. Until there is recognition of the sin, there can be no permanent freedom.

4. The counseling model offers no tools for dealing with direct demonic manifestation.

The counseling model uses archaic methods of restraint or drugs to subdue open demonic manifestation. Since the counseling model focuses on the mind, there is usually an inability to deal with the direct manifestation of the demonic. The counseling process requires a calm, coherent counselee so the process can continue. Once the demons are in manifestation, it is impossible to make progress in this model. One does not counsel a demon. The counseling model is an incomplete model in that it offers no way to deal with open supernatural manifestation.

5. The counseling model often does not recognize the personal responses and stories of the individual could be lies or deception.

Counselors who are not spiritually sensitive can be deceived as to the nature of the problem and the true feelings of the afflicted person. The counselor is responsible to be biblically aware and open to the insights of the Holy Spirit. In one case, the counselee's version of critical events of her life were significantly different than what actually occurred. The counselor had worked for years with inaccurate information most likely supplied by inaccurate mental perspectives and wicked spirits. The woman believed the demonic interpretation of her past and altered the memory of the events to fit these conclusions. Some may suggest these changes were a defense mechanism designed to protect the woman's psyche from the pain of the actual events. It is possible the fabrications were the result of defense mechanisms, but it is amazing how those fabrications yielded themselves to destructive and sinful actions which totally changed the woman's life. Only when reality is dealt with and truth embraced do people find lasting freedom (John 8:31,32). The counseling model has the inherent weakness of believing the counselee's statements in order to establish a trusting environment.

6. The counseling model is dependent upon the mental discipline of the afflicted.

The greatest weakness of the counseling model is the dependence on the ability of the counselee to retain the new mental framework constructed in the counselor's office. After years of wrong thinking, it is not easy to think totally differently about oneself and one's situation. One demonically oppressed person sought help from a spiritual warfare counselor who used the counseling model with a special emphasis on teaching the person their position in Christ. This person went through the procedure in the office and was freed from the troubling voices and spiritual oppression. Upon leaving the office, however, he was unable to sustain the biblical thinking and regressed back under demonic oppression. The mental discipline of the person must be nurtured and strengthened or the help from the counseling model will turn into a quick fix which quickly goes away.

Jesus states, *"You shall know the truth and the truth shall set you free."* We often put the emphasis on the truth and its liberating power. This is all true, but what we often do not acknowledge is the knowing of the truth. If the counselee is unable to hold on to the truth, then the truth will not set them free. They will be bound up under a lie. The mental patterns have become habits which are not easily overcome. Too often in deliverance – and even in counseling – there is the thought that because an area was talked about or corrected once, then it is fixed. The counselor must help the person develop new mental disciplines.

Limitations

1. The counseling model requires a great deal of time.

Because the counseling model depends upon listening carefully to the counselee and then constructing a plan for improvement and change, the freedom sought takes a long time. Many who are afflicted by the Devil want and need some immediate help. The counseling model is not designed to give this type of immediate relief. The prayer and declarative techniques of the other deliverance models can be very helpful for providing short-term relief. In a number of cases, drug therapy is used to mask the symptoms of demonic oppression without truly dealing with the issue. In many cases where the major problem is actually demonic, drug therapy only reduces the individual's ability to fight off the demonic suggestions. This is not a healthy side effect of drug therapy.

The lengthy time frame involved in the counseling model limits its effectiveness while at the same time recommends it for post-deliverance procedures. In our day of instant everything, there is the expectation that any problem can be fixed quickly and painlessly. This quick-fix mentality can move many to abandon the counseling model and keep seeking the other deliverance models which may not touch the destructive mental patterns of their lives. Often a combination of appropriate deliverance techniques from the other models and then post-deliverance counseling allows the best result.

2. The counseling model is a dependent model especially in the early stages of counseling.

The counselor can become the only source of warmth, love, hope, and new thought patterns. This dependency, which is essential, can cripple the afflicted if the counselor does not connect the person to the Lord and the Scriptures. The counselor must embrace personally the power of the Lord and the Scriptures to be active in the lives of people. Unfortunately, some counselors are more convinced about the power of counseling techniques than the power of the Scriptures or the power of the Living God to speak into a person's life. The counselor must cause the afflicted person to see in the Scriptures a separate source of help for them. The counselor must direct the afflicted person to the Lord so He is a living relationship in their lives. If the afflicted believes the weekly meeting with the counselor is the only hope for freedom, then the dependency relationship of the counseling model becomes a limitation on freedom rather than a doorway to greater freedom.

The counseling model must help a person become an independent person who can access the Lord and the Scriptures on their own for the answers they need. When this triad of help (God, Scripture, and Counselor) is fully cemented in the afflicted person's mind, the possibility of a fully realized, positive life is possible.

3. **The counseling model can shackle the severely oppressed by demanding new thinking without removing the sources of the destructive thoughts.**

The counseling model exposes wrong thought patterns and destructive thinking and moves the individual toward new thinking. The severely oppressed surrender the ability to think for themselves so often they are convinced they cannot think in different ways. This passive acceptance of destructive thought patterns cannot be reasoned out of existence. Some type of power encounter or other God-ordained event is often needed to release the person so clear thinking can begin. These power encounters and God-ordained events are outside the perimeters of the counseling model. Therefore, this model is self-limiting, especially in severe cases of demonic oppression.

There are wicked spirits who really do "speak" to the afflicted. There are temptations that do not grow out of our upbringing, circumstances, and/or situations. There are emotional, psychological, and even physical punishments that source in evil supernatural agents. These supernatural voices must be dealt with in Christ-honoring supernatural ways. The power of the life, death, and resurrection of Jesus Christ are sufficient for liberating people from the bondage of the Devil. Christ's power can cut through the work of the Devil, and it must be used on spiritual bondage.

SUMMARY

The counseling model is a helpful collection of tools which can assist Christians in spiritual warfare. It can be very helpful in the beginning stages of deliverance and in post-deliverance work. This model alone is often incomplete and needs the impact and strength of the other models to balance its weaknesses and limitations. The counseling model places strong emphasis on the mind. The Christian church needs this model to help it set people free. The counseling model has brought a needed corrective to an overly supernatural emphasis in certain parts of the church. The counseling model is very helpful for specific training in righteousness by those who have been the most destroyed by victimization and high levels of wickedness. Some people are not ready to listen to lectures on Christian living and Christian doctrine and incorporate them into their lives until the specific destructive elements of their past have been dealt with and new Christian patterns are put in place.

I have noticed in many parts of Western Civilization – with its current naturalistic worldview – the counseling model is preferred as a deliverance process. It is common for people to see a counselor or a psychologist in much of the Western world and so deliverance can be pursued if it is contained in the perimeters of this type of model. The use of other deliverance techniques can be incorporated into this model and new levels of freedom are achieved.

7

TRUTH:
Exposing the Truth and the Lies

Esther could not believe what she was hearing. She attended one of my lectures on God, angels, demons, and every Christian's involvement in spiritual warfare. She was astounded when I stated matter of factly that,

"There is a personal being called the Devil and Satan and he is scheming against you."

"The Devil is not omnipresent but has thousands of angels who rebelled from God and choose to follow the Devil instead of God."

"These rebel angels are now called demons or wicked spirits."

"There are invisible spirits that incite sin and wickedness."

"These invisible spirits whisper temptation, doubt, and fear into your inner being."

The desires, feelings, and the voices I was describing as a part of the Satanic realm all were familiar to her. She came up after the Bible study and insisted we get together and discuss the information I had shared. I scheduled an appointment with her two evenings later.

When I arrived at her home, she and her husband began to describe the incredible events of the last few days. Since the class, she had been besieged by voices and objects moving in the house. Based upon the information she had received in the class, she destroyed everything in her home with an obvious occultic connection and tried to ignore the voices. Esther told me the story of her and her husband's involvement in fortune telling and numerous other occultic activities. They wanted to become Christians and were wondering if I could help them. That night I had the privilege of leading this husband and wife to Jesus Christ as Savior. This was the start of cleansing themselves of the oppression, temptations, and fear that came from the voices.

The above example demonstrates the power of the biblical truth taught plainly and directly. The biblical truth about the spiritual world was taught clearly, and it was received with great results. This is called the truth model or the teaching model of deliverance. The stress in this form of deliverance is placed on the truth that is communicated. It is assumed that if the truth from the Word of God is explained in regard to the supernatural realm, the individual hearer will be able to apply that truth. This form of deliverance is not interested in manifesting demons or coming against the demonic hosts during the meeting. All action and/or application is assumed to take place after the meeting as a result of the truth that was taught. The most effective information the truth or teaching model injects into the believer's life is titled under seven topics: Truth, Righteousness, Peace, Faith, Salvation, Scripture, and Prayer. These topics are given to us in Scripture as the Armor of God. When an afflicted person has a firm grasp on these areas of Christian truth, it changes the battle with the enemy. Obviously lots of information can come under these rubric, but God has declared these truths and their application into the believers life is essential for victory.

1) Satan's origins and future

2) Satan's ways

3) The Armor of God

4) The doctrine of salvation; specifically the position of the believer in Christ

TECHNIQUES

The truth or teaching model essentially wants people to put on the Armor of God in a functional way. In this section I will detail some of the various topics, truths and applications that are necessary for really putting on the Armor of God. These seven topics have lots of different truths and applications beyond what I am able to discuss in this book. This particular model appeals to teachers and preachers because it utilizes their gifts to help everyday Christian's fight Satan and expose his deceptive work.

The Armor of God

The truth or teaching model almost always involves an explanation of Ephesians 6:10-20. This passage when properly exposited, explained, and applied makes a significant difference in the life of the believer. God gave extremely powerful weapons to Christians. These weapons provide protection in the midst of satanic pressure. The picture of the modern church is one of a huge, defenseless army dodging one incoming shell after another. Yet, it is standing right next to an incredibly powerful arsenal. The weapons of God lay in an unused heap at the feet of the retreating army of God.

Unfortunately, when Ephesians 6:10-20 is taught, much of the exposition of this passage does not reveal the weapons God has provided. Instead, there is much talk about Roman soldiers and their military hardware. The Apostle Paul under the inspiration of the Holy Spirit is trying to tell Christians about the weapons and protection God has given to them. He names seven spiritual weapons: TRUTH, RIGHTEOUSNESS, PEACE with God, FAITH, SALVATION, THE WORD OF GOD, and PRAYER The Apostle uses Roman military hardware to help people see the usability of the spiritual weapons God has given. But the illustrations used to clarify must not get in the way of understanding the weapons. If the teacher spends more time on Roman military history than the basic weapon itself, the believer is left confused and defenseless. It is critical that expositors bring to light the weapons God has provided. Again let me say the spiritual weapons are: TRUTH, RIGHTEOUSNESS, PEACE with God, FAITH, SALVATION, THE WORD OF GOD, and PRAYER. God's weapons for fighting Satan are not belts, breastplates, sandals, helmets, shields and swords. God is trying to tell us about a spiritual war with spiritual weapons.

The Apostle Paul divides the list of spiritual weapons into two different types of armor. First, he describes those pieces of armor which must always be worn. These are TRUTH, RIGHTEOUSNESS, and PEACE WITH GOD. Christians should always have with them truth, righteousness and peace with God. They can't take these protective weapons off. There is never a time when they should embrace the lies of the world. There is never a time when they should abandon their dependence on Christ as their only way to heaven and their should never be a time when they just revel in actions they know are sinful and rebellious to God's ways. There should never be a time when a Christian maintains open rebellion against God and/or needless enmity with others. Every day we should strengthen ourselves in the understanding of and use of these spiritual weapons. In other words every day we should learn more truth. Every day we should rely upon Christ's righteousness more and grow in our own righteousness. Every day we should make sure we are in harmony with God and the people in our life. If a person strips off these spiritually protective weapons they are exposed to the attacks, temptations and oppression of the devil and they will pay a price.

Secondly, in Ephesians 6:10-18, the Apostle Paul describes those pieces of armor to be picked up and be ready to use at a moment's notice. This second type of armor includes SALVATION, FAITH, WORD OF GOD, and PRAYER. This second grouping is to be utilized in specific engagements with the Enemy. They may not be used any particular day, but they are to stand ready. The Christian is to be familiar with their use. When we are facing fear, doubt, obstacles we need to make sure we take up our understanding of and use of SALVATION, FAITH, WORD OF GOD, and PRAYER. When we are facing temptation, attack or spiritual oppression we need to be ready to take up our understanding of and use of SALVATION, FAITH, WORD OF GOD, and PRAYER.

These are not toys or abstract ideas, but they are real weapons for slaying, resisting and winning against the devil and his schemes. It is therefore radically helpful to understand these pieces of armor and how to use them.

1. Truth

The basic protection of the Christian is the truth. Jesus said, "You shall know the truth and the truth shall set you free." Down through the centuries since Jesus came it has been the Christian's ability to dig for truth and push away at superstition that has led to incredible breakthroughs in knowledge. This includes all facets of truth starting with the truth about God. It is the Christian's unflinching desire for truth that protects him even if the truth is not what they expected.

Right now the world around you, Satan, and your own desires are trying to get you to embrace lies. Realize Satan is the Father of Liars and wants you to believe lies so you will make bad decisions. He may be lying to you about God. (Exodus 34:7) He may be lying to you about yourself (Psalm 139:13-15); your potential; your abilities; your future (Ephesians 2:10); your friends; your family. He may be lying to you about salvation (John 10:10) or about the Bible (John 17:17; 2 Timothy 3:16). He may be lying to you about how the world works. If he can get you to believe a lie, then he can keep you from reaching your potential. You must fight for truth.

The Christian is given undiluted truth in every area. Truth should be the foundation of a Christian's life. In almost every case of demonic bondage there are lies which a person believes and acts upon. These can be in a number of areas: doctrine, self-concept, family, relatives, and/or the world in general. These lies form the basis of the satanic attack. Until these lies are challenged and corrected, there will be little or no permanent improvement in the person. The Bible offers truth in every area of life, and must form the backbone of every teaching program within the church. Lack of strong teaching in many churches makes way for demonic forces to hide the truths of God from His people. When the truth about God, about self, about the world in general is taught, it has a liberating effect upon those who hear and understand. Without ever confronting a demon or engaging in a protracted battle, truth believed liberates from bondage. It is common to hear the following comments after a seminar: These truths have cleared up many things in my life." "I have been set free by the things that you taught."

In order for the truth to be an adequate protection against the onslaughts of Satan, the following areas of truth must be taught: truth about God (including His nature and Trinity), His attributes, and His decrees; truth about salvation, including justification, sanctification, and glorification; truth about the Christian, including his/her position in Christ; and truth about the universe, including creation and apologetics (reasons for faith). It is a shame the average Christian does not receive solid doctrinal truth of this sort. I have written a basic doctrinal workbook called Developing a Christian Worldview that helps a person work through the ten basic Christian doctrines from Scripture. In this way they can grow in their grasp of the truth of the Universe in which they live.

The Truth about Satan's Origins and Future

Another area of needed truth for the growing believer is the doctrine of Satan and his schemes1. Let me go into a little bit more detail about this area of truth to arm believers against Satan's schemes. Three key passages explain Satan's origin and future. This particular biblical information is of critical importance to the growing Christian. The first passage is Ezekiel 28:12-19 as it explains the origin of evil and Satan's internal desires.

Ezekiel 28:12-19 refers directly to the King of Tyre; but he is understood to be a symbolic reference to Satan, the power behind the earthly ruler of Tyre. The descriptions are too extreme to refer to a human and are, therefore, understood to apply to Satan. Taken from this perspective, Satan is described as possessing the seal of perfection, full of wisdom, and perfect in beauty. He is declared to have been in Eden and was covered with every precious stone. He is described as the anointed cherub who covers. He was on the holy mountain of God and walked in the midst of the stones of fire. He was declared blameless in his ways until unrighteousness was found in him. His sin is described as being internally filled with violence through the abundance of his trade. It is suggested this means Satan's original job was to reflect the glory of the other angels toward God, and yet he felt he was himself worthy of the praise. Milton, in Paradise Lost suggests Satan sinned when he heard of God's plan to provide a Savior for mankind and to make the angels the servants of men. Satan's downfall is further described in the passage in Ezekiel 28 as his heart being lifted up because of his beauty. Then God threw him to the ground. This passage uncovers the origins of evil and how a perfect being could become corrupt.

This next passage which draws our attention concerning Satan's sin and original position is in Isaiah 14:12-15. This passage is speaking of the King of Babylon but begins to describe in verses 12-15 a person of much greater proportions. Satan is referred to as the star of the morning (Lucifer) and the one who has fallen a great distance. Satan's thoughts are described as he leads the assault on God's throne. Satan declares he will ascend to heaven. He plans to raise his throne above the stars of God. This is thought to be a reference to the angels. He desires to be above the angels; their lord and master. He desires to sit on the mount of the assembly. This is thought to refer to the throne of God, judging all things. He also plans to ascend above the heights of the clouds. This is thought to be a reference to being the one who rules all the world. He finally desires to make himself like the Most High. He wants to be God. Each of these desires can be echoed in the lives of those who allow Satan to control them. They may dream on a different scale, but they have desires to be like God, to rule angels, and to replace God with themselves.

The final passage of significance in exposing the origin of Satan and evil is Genesis 3:1-7. In this passage the Devil is disguised as the serpent. He injects his own temptations into the human race so they fall from their state of grace. This famous passage declares how sin entered into mankind. Sin is not a necessary result of the material world but rather a result of the selfishness of one woman and one man. The serpent was able to deceive the woman into believing God was withholding a good thing from her and her husband. He got her to believe if she partook of the fruit, she would become like God. In one sense what Satan said is true. If they ate of the tree of the knowledge of good and evil, they would be like God in that they would know good and evil. However, they would not be equal to God. Satan remains consistent with his deceptive stratagems since this first temptation. He focuses people's attention on that which is beautiful and questions why God has not allowed it. He suggests the desired thing is good and will be helpful. He makes promises which are not true. He suggests if we commit a particular sin, we will be masters of our own fate. If the believer can see the stratagem of Satan and how Satan is still using this same methodology, then the believer can be alert and resist the logic of the Devil.

All of these passages shed considerable light on the designs and plans of Satan. Armed with this knowledge, the thinking Christian can identify the wrong or improper thoughts of the Enemy.

The Truth about Satan's Schemes

The truth or teaching model seeks to expose the ways of Satan so the believer can be aware of what he is attempting to do. Therefore, there is some stress in this model (much like the resistance model) on the types of sin and the way Satan lures people into his trap. In 2 Corinthians 2, the Apostle Paul says, "We are not ignorant of the Devil's strategies." Sadly, in the modern church this is not the case.

A good deal of time must be spent educating believers on how the Devil seeks to trip them up. The Scriptures are clear that the schemes of Satan are the various titles and names given to this once powerful angelic being. Since his actual name was Lucifer the other titles and names are descriptors of what He does or wants to do to people.

The following is an abbreviated list of the titles and names of Lucifer and the schemes this title suggests he will use on people. As you read this list, put a checkmark by those ways Satan has schemed against you in the last month. He will keep using the same schemes until you successfully resist.

Lucifer (Isaiah 14:12): He is Brilliant and Beautiful. He will try to seduce you to ignore your salvation through what is beautiful or appealing to the eyes.

Satan (Job 1): He is the Adversary. He will come against you to keep you from progressing in your faith.

The Devil (1 Peter 5:8): He is the Accuser. He accuses Christians to God. 1 John 2:1,2: He whispers accusations to the Christian. He get Christians fighting each other. He has people accuse us; spread rumors. He seeks to depress, discourage, distract, or enrage you so Christ is not glorified.

Tempter (Matthew 4:3): He tempts people to sin. He entices you to be selfish and pleasure-seeking. He finds sins you are naturally drawn to and then sets up those exact sinful conditions so you can give in conveniently.

Roaring Lion (1 Peter 5:8): He seeks to scare, intimidate, and bring fear. He wants you to give up, stand still, stop fighting, and be devoured. He seeks to get you running away from him instead of being led by the Holy Spirit. He tries to produce fear in you to stop you from doing something.

Belial (2 Corinthians 6:15): He is the worthless one. He wants you to spend all your time and get tremendously excited about worthless things. He wants you to feel worthless/unusable. He wants to yoke, marry, and partner the good with the worthless or evil to dilute or hide the evil.

Deceiver (Revelation 12:9): He is the master at deception. He will get you to place all your hope for happiness and satisfaction in what can never satisfy. If he can get you to take your eyes off Christ, he wins. He will promise or show you anything so he can keep you from doing the main thing you are called to do.

Father of Lies (John 8:44): He originated falsehood and lying. He uses lies to get us to believe his "truth." He convinces us to lie to keep from being punished. He confuses and disappoints us with a whole web of lies. If he can confuse you with lies or put you into a position where you lie, he wins.

Murder (John 8:44): He incites to anger, violence, intimidation, and murder. He incites people to hate so much they contemplate, plan, and murder. He incites to suicide.

Sinner (1 John 3:8): He encourages a greater level of selfishness and sin. He is the one who is rejoicing with you when you indulge in sin. He encourages the partying and the feeling that sin is right and positive righteousness is boring.

Beelzub (Matthew 12:24): He is the Lord of the flies. He is the king of the refuse pile. He hangs around the low-life places seeking to turn the patrons into flies for his manure; feeding off the refuse of life.

Enemy (Matthew 13:39): He is the one who is against whatever we want to do for God and seeks to block it. He will try and oppose and stifle anything that could really make a difference for God.

Evil One (Matthew 13:39): He loves evil -- that which harms others. He takes good things and twists them until they harm others and turns it into evil.

Angel of Light (2 Corinthians 11:13): He can look like he is from God. He loves to bring false messages about religion and God so a person is deceived and later destroyed.

God of the World (2 Corinthians 4:4): He is the author of false values. He encourages each culture to value something other than God.

The Dragon (Revelation 13): He seeks to create terror. He seeks to make others afraid and even paralyzed of some coming catastrophe. If he can get you to be afraid and keep you from doing God's will out of fear of what will happen, he has won.

The Snake (Genesis 3): This is a sly and devious creature. He will usually slither into your life with an accusation or proposal. He prefers not to be noticed or to approach the person he is working on directly. He seeks to have the person believe these new ideas are theirs.

Prince of the Power of the Air (Ephesians 2): He is the controller of unseen angelic forces. Just as the air we breathe is invisible yet has tremendous power, so Satan has tremendous power through his minions. He is above us and around us all the time through his demons.

Ruler of this World: (John 17): He uses governments to promote sin and evil as well as to persecute Christians. He seeks to keep nations as a whole from recognizing the truth of the gospel.

The Wicked One (Matthew 13:19; Ephesians 6:16): He lives outside of God's moral code and encourages others to do the same. He seeks to draw whole nations over to the place where they believe that violating God's laws are normal and healthy.

All of these passages shed considerable light on the designs and plans of Satan. Armed with this knowledge, the thinking Christian can identify the wrong or improper thoughts of the Enemy.

2. Righteousness

It is clear when a Christian sins, Satan is attacking. This forms the basis for the second piece of armor which Christ gives to the Christian. Righteousness of life is indispensable to liberty and freedom in life. There has been a needless controversy over whether the righteousness talked about in Ephesians 6:13 was Christ's imputed righteousness or the individual righteousness of the person. Arguing over which type or kind of righteousness misses the point. Both are included in the offer of righteousness. Christ died on the Cross and His righteousness was imputed to our account so we might become the righteousness of God in Him. (2 Corinthians 5:21) Without Christ's righteousness we could not produce true righteousness in our lives, and if we do not produce true righteousness of life, then it is clear we are not taking advantage of Christ's imputed righteousness. Bubeck takes us back to the Puritans who also refused to see these two forms of righteousness as separated. They called them imputed righteousness and imparted righteousness. Both are dependent upon Christ, and the one gets its life from the other.2

It is critical to teach the believer of the impeccable righteousness of Christ and how we stand in His work and His perfection. Every detail of God's wonderful provision in Christ must be explained and relied on by the believer. These truths allow surety of salvation and ensure the believer understands his protection does not rest on his righteousness. It is equally important the believer be challenged to live righteously in every area of life. Righteous living must be spelled out in its negative terms and its positive terms. The term righteous must be more than just a word; it must be alive in a person's mind. We must be able to see ourselves living out the imputed righteousness of Christ in our lives. As we live righteously we take the imputed righteousness of Christ and impart it into our lives.

The question might arise as to how righteousness offers protection from the onslaughts of Satan. Christ's righteousness paid for our sins but it also marked out the moral boundaries of a righteous life. His life was a life of love within the boundaries of the Ten Commandments. This is the kind of life we should lead. If we want Christ's forgiveness and grace but we refuse to be loving or live within the boundaries of the Commands of God then we deny what we say we want.

We have to see Christ's righteousness and salvation offering benefits to us within a certain arena. If we want Christ's blessings and grace but we refuse to repent of our evil desires, selfish actions, and harmful behavior, we will not receive Christ's protection or His provision. Let's use an illustration here to help us. If you were given a special suit that would increase your strength, wisdom, and compassion and this suit had a constant supply of energy for beneficial things, you would probably be tempted to put it on. This suit protects you from those who would harm you and allows you to help others who need your help but you cannot help on your own. The suit also will not allow you to be selfish or to violate God's laws. In order to indulge in selfish pursuits or sinful activities, you have to take the suit off. When you are out of the suit, you are not as strong, wise, or compassionate and you are not protected from temptation, attack, fear, and doubt. This is what the righteousness of Christ is like. Christ and His death on the cross provided the suit of righteousness you don't deserve. When you put it on you are able to do things you cannot do on your own. You naturally are interested in doing loving and beneficial things for others. There are times when you are in the suit that you are tempted to do something totally selfish or in complete rebellion against God who gave you the suit. The only way you can do these things is to take the suit off. When you take the suit off because the pleasure, the selfishness, the desire is too strong, you are vulnerable to mental, emotional, spiritual, and relational attack. Keep the suit on. Learn to love at a new level. Keep living in Christ's righteousness. When God prompts you to love others, He will provide the strength to do the job.

It is clear from Scripture God preserves His servants through their righteous choices. Righteousness means that one is often not in the pathway of evil. (Matthew 2:13-18, Proverbs 22:3) Righteousness means one is not aware of how to accomplish evil. (Matthew 10:16) Righteousness means one can endure the evil day. (Job 1-3) Christ's righteousness protects the believer through His unassailable perfection. The Devil, as the accuser, seeks to condemn the believer before the throne of God. Wrapped in the robe of Christ's righteousness, we are welded to His perfection. The accusations which could cause us to believe we are separated from the love of Christ fall harmlessly at our feet. The imputed and imparted righteousness which God offers in Christ is a potent weapon in spiritual warfare. The Christian church as a whole is ignorant of Christ's imputed righteousness and is also shredding its defenses by a lack of living righteously.

To love righteously -- according to Jesus -- to love God, others, and myself in a holy way. (Mark 12:29-31) If we are going to win in our battle with Satan, then we must embrace the love of Jesus and give it out effectively and powerfully in all the relationships of our life. What Satan wants is for us to be selfish, sinful, and negative. What Christ wants is for us to be loving, joyful, peaceful, and patient. The more biblically loving I am towards all the people in my life, the more righteous my life is. Let me ask you a series of questions to get you thinking how you can use more of the righteousness of Christ in your life and gain a new level of victory over the devil.

Let me help you understand love does not mean to have a feeling for someone; it means to meet their needs, to pursue them, and to please them. Love is a verb, biblically, and demands some type of action. I have loved someone when I have met a real need they have or when I have pursued their soul or when I have pleased them. I don't have to feel anything about them. My love is not dependent upon my feelings. It is dependent upon the grace of Christ. If you do not know the answers to these questions, then ask a mentor, a pastor, or spiritually mature person to help you. There are numerous Bible studies and biblically-based workbooks that will help you understand how to grow in this area. The Scriptures have sections on each of these relationships that spell out how to love these people.

What does it mean to love the people in your life with a Christlike love? The following questions will help you begin walking out the truths and actions of a righteous life. A righteous life is the life you have truly dreamed of. It is a great life of love and without the constant worry and fear.

Do you know how to love God deeply?

Theologically God has no needs I can meet so I cannot love Him in this way. He accepts my pursuit of Him and my seeking to please Him as love.

Write down three ways to love God biblically.

Do you know how to love yourself spiritually, mentally, emotionally, physically, relationally?

Write down three ways to righteously love yourself in each area.

Do you know how to love your spouse effectively?

Write down three ways to love your spouse biblically.

Do you know how to love your family?

Write down three ways to love your family biblically?

Do you know how to love your friends?

Write down three ways to love your friends biblically?

Do you know how to love your boss at work, your colleagues, and your subordinates?

Write down three ways to love the people at your work biblically?

Do you know how to respect your money and not love it?

Write down three ways to make sure your respect the power of money but that you do not love it.

Do you know how to love your enemies?

Write down three ways to love your enemies biblically.

Do you know how to love your community, region, nation, and world?

Write down three ways to love your community, region, nation, and world.

Another key area of practical growth in righteousness is to live within the boundaries of the Ten Commandments. It is important to take a quick survey to see if there are any areas of your life where you are consistently living outside the boundaries of the Ten Commandments.

    1. Do you have any people, places, activities, or things that are more important to you than God?

    2. Do you have any physical objects or items that have become so important they are more important than God or more important than they should be?

    3. Do you live your life or use words that deny you are a servant of God Almighty and His Son the Lord Jesus Christ?

4. Do you dedicate each day to the Lord Jesus Christ and gather at least once a week with other Christians to worship and serve Him.

5. Do you have any areas of your life where you are resisting, refusing, or rebelling from proper authorities in your life?

6. Do you use anger, violence, or intimidation to get your way?

7. Do you have any relationships outside of your marriage relationship that have become sexual in some way?

8. Do you have in your possession someone else's property without their approval?

9. Do you lie for personal benefit or avoidance of punishment?

10. Do you dream, plan, or scheme to take away the property or relationships of someone else?

The above questions are what it means to stay within the boundaries of the Ten Commandments in our behavior. It is within these boundaries we have freedom from worry and fear. There is liberty when love is launched from this place.

3. Peace with God

The Christian has a third powerful weapon in the battle against spiritual warfare which must be carried at all times: the preparation of the Gospel of Peace. This is a matter of much debate as to its meaning, but it clearly involves standing within the grace of God in a state of peace. Christ secured this peace through His victory on Calvary, and it is applied through believing the Gospel. It is clear, if the Christian is going to fight spiritual forces of wickedness, he/she must not be at war with God. It is also clear a number of Christians are at war instead of peace with God. Christians move back into peace with God the same way they became a Christian – through confession and repentance. The Christian must not retain known sin in his/her life. A war cannot be fought on two fronts – one with God and one with the Devil. Confession and repentance are essential ingredients for a truly successful life. The teaching model explains these daily needs and shows the believer how to take advantage of daily peace with God. It is a shame that much of the Christian church languishes outside the grace of God waiting for a traveling evangelist or conference speaker to call them to this basic truth of confession and repentance.

The following are a few thought-provoking questions that will move you more into the center of peace with God:

Are there any areas or relationships where you know you are at war with what God wants you to do? Stop!!!

If you were to truly be in harmony with what God wants in your life, what would be different in your life? Talk over this list with a mentor or pastor to make sure you are accurately hearing from God.

Are there any areas or relationships in your life where you are having a battle?

What would it look like for you to be harmony with those you are currently at odds with? In other words, if the other person were totally pleased with you, what would you be doing, saying, and/or emoting?

God does not expect us to make peace with the wicked -- those who are living outside of God's moral boundary structures. To be in harmony with the wicked means we have been pulled into their sinful lifestyle, and God does not want you to be doing sin in order to have peace.

4. Salvation

With the fourth piece of armor, God begins discussing a type of weapon which does not need to be worn at all times but which must be available for use in "the evil day." The Apostle Paul declares that salvation is the first weapon which must be taken up when the battle begins. This suggests Satan seeks to attack a clear understanding and exercise of salvation. The mental war over salvation will eventually swing to the questions of assurance, present fellowship, and future hope. The Christian must understand his/her salvation in all the wonder of its parts – past, present, and future. The Devil will attack the concept of God, the possibility of salvation, whether the individual is worthy of saving, and the assurance of salvation. It is at this point the Christian teacher must make clear the nature of justification. Salvation is not dependent upon the works or righteousness of the individual but upon the finished work of Christ on the Cross. It is at this point the doctrine of eternal security provides a great advantage in our warfare with Satan. As Spurgeon said, "At times I have such great bouts with depression that I assume that I am not saved, but my salvation does not depend upon me but on Christ's work on the Cross."[3] When we are in a battle with Satan, we must not hand him the mental weapon of hammering us over our assurance of salvation.

By salvation the Christian must understand Paul means sanctification – the present outworking of salvation. The Christian needs to know of the sealing, guiding, and convicting ministry of the Holy Spirit. The Christian must not live as though God does not exist in the present. He must have a vital, living relationship with Him through the Holy Spirit. One of the interesting aspects about involvement in spiritual warfare is some Christians who have ignored the present ministry of salvation become suddenly aware of the Holy Spirit's promptings and conviction. One woman, who was raised in a conservative church, came to a deliverance session at the insistence of her husband. After the session she was shocked and stunned at the movement of the Holy Spirit during the meeting. After the session she had an entirely new understanding of the present ministry of the Holy Spirit. She began to discern the promptings of the Holy Spirit, and it revolutionized her life. In fact, the next day her Spirit-led prayers became instrumental in setting another believer free. The present ministry of the Holy Spirit is essential to living the victorious Christian life.

The third aspect of salvation is glorification. There is a future for the Christian. Jesus is coming back for His own. Regardless of what millennial or rapture position one holds, the Scripture says Jesus is coming back. Satan and his hordes are constantly trying to destroy a person's future. The demons suggest that there is no reason to go on living, so suicide should be pursued. They suggest that circumstances will not change, so why not commit a particular sin to redirect one's life. They promote a distorted and depressing picture of the future to defeat the Christian. All this can be resisted by a clear understanding of the future abode of the Christian. If we love the world too much and seek to make our fortune here, then we will be disappointed. In the midst of the most tremendous suffering and deepest personal pain, when sin or suicide seems the only way out, a firm grip on our final abode will preserve us and defeat the designs of Satan.

Exposing the Position of the Believer

It is critical for believers to realize God already gave them everything needed to defeat Satan through the work of Christ on the cross. Our salvation is sufficient and gives us all we need to be free. All the power and position to live a life free of demonic control is provided.

A new wrinkle in the war with Satan involves teaching believers who they are in Christ and having them reject any other thoughts about themselves. This has proven very powerful in helping Christians take their stand against Satan. It allows the lies of Satan to stand out in stark relief against the backdrop of the Christian's position in Christ. In this technique, the truths of the believer's position in Christ are taught and clearly explained. Then the believer is assured that any feeling or thought that runs contrary to these truths is a Satanic lie or a result of parental or socio-environmental conditioning. The person is then asked to confess all known sin and completely turn his/her life over to Christ. The believer is then asked to challenge these thoughts and feelings in the power of the Lord Jesus Christ by turning his/her mind and emotions over to the Lord Jesus Christ. The resulting quiet and internal peace is astounding to many.

This exciting new technique in our warfare with Satan has helped liberate many who battle with subtle, deceptive demonic forces. This new technique is an example of applying the teaching to the life of the individual. This process is working because the ideas are taken from the printed page (Scripture) and pulled through the person's life. It is the unique application of these truths which transforms the positional truths of the believer into life-changing, battle-tested weapons of liberation. The position of the believer is only one part of one weapon. It is unwise to make the whole of the spiritual warfare dependent upon this one aspect of one weapon. This should serve as a starting ground and a model for utilizing the other weapons God supplies. It is hoped the strength of this new technique will challenge many to discover other new and unique ways to utilize the weapons God supplies.

The Christian's Position in Christ

One of the most helpful exercises the disciple can do is to look up the verse, write out the verse on a separate piece of paper, and then study it, memorize it, or meditate on it. These truths will change us if they are allowed to sink deep into our soul. It can also be very helpful to write down your observations about the various things in the verses that have to do with your position in Christ.

I can remember one woman who was tremendously helped by writing out the following Scriptures and imbedding the truths of Christ's love for her. She had opened numerous doorways through sin and occultic involvement, but this allowed her to close those doors and stop hearing the voices.

I am God's child. John 1:12
> Having believed in Jesus as God, He accepts me as His child.

I am Christ's friend. John 15:15
> He calls me His friend because He is willing to reveal His plans to me.

I have been justified. Romans 5:1
> I have been declared righteous through my faith in Christ's death on the Cross

I am united with the Lord, and 1 am one spirit with Him.
1 Corinthians 6:7
> I have been bonded to Christ in a spiritual union which is indissoluble.

I have been bought with a price. 1 Corinthians 6:20
> I have been purchased at very great cost to God; so God sees me as valuable.

I belong to God. 1 Corinthians 6:19,20
> God claims ownership over me so He can set me free to live abundantly.

I am a member of Christ's body. 1 Corinthians 12:27
> God has incorporated me into the mystical body of Christ presently operative on earth.

I am a saint. Ephesians 1:1
> Because of my trust in Christ, God sees me as holy and set apart for Him.

I have been adopted as God's child. Ephesians 1:5
> I have been brought into the place of full privilege in God's family.

I have direct access to God through the Holy Spirit. Ephesians 2:18
> I can pray and know my prayers get through because of the Holy Spirit.

I have been redeemed and forgiven of all my sins. Col. 1:14
> I have been bought out of the slave market of sin and released from the ultimate penalty of my sins.

I am complete in Christ. Colossians 2:10
> I have all I need because I need Christ. He and I are a perfectly sufficient unit.

I am free forever from condemnation. Romans 8:1,2
> God does not condemn me anymore because of my embrace of Christ.

I am assured that all things work together for good. Romans 8:28
> God is so powerful and brings good out of all the evil that comes into my life.

I am free from any condemning charges against me. Romans 8:31
> The Devil cannot bring an accusation against me that God will listen to.

I cannot be separated from the love of God. Romans 8:35
> Nothing can separate me from the love of God that is Christ Jesus. NOTHING.

I have been established, anointed, and sealed by God. 2 Corinthians 1:21,22
> God has planted me firmly to grow in Him. He has especially blessed me and marked me for heaven.

I am hidden with Christ in God. Colossians 3:3
> My real life is hidden with Christ, and all I really am in Christ will be fully displayed when Christ returns.

I am confident the good work God has begun in me will be perfected. Philippians 1:6
> God has begun the process to make me like Christ, and He will not stop.

I am a citizen of heaven. Philippians 3:20
> My true home is in heaven with Christ. I am out of place down here.

I was not given a spirit of fear but of power, love, and a sound mind. 2 Timothy 1:7
> God has given me His Spirit to strengthen my spirit and give me new abilities.

I can find grace and mercy in time of need. Hebrews 4:16
> Every time I need God's power, His favor, His forgiveness, and encouragement, it is mine in Christ through prayer.

I am born of God, and the Evil One cannot touch me. 1 John 5:18
> God gave birth to a new creature when I trusted Christ, and the Devil cannot touch that new creation.

I am the salt and light of the earth. Matthew 5:13,14
> God has called me to help preserve what is right and good in this world, as well as to show the glory of Christ and how life should really be lived.

I am a branch of the true vine, a channel of His life.
John 15:1,5
> God has connected me to His inexhaustible storehouse of energy, creativity, and power. All I have to do is stay plugged in to God, and all I need for any assignment will be available to me.

I have been chosen and appointed to bear fruit. John 15:16
> God chose me to be one of His children. I did not get in by mistake. He wants me to show the fruit of the Spirit in my life.

I am a personal witness of Christ's. Acts 1:8
> God has empowered me to tell others what Christ has done for me.

I am God's temple. 1 Corinthians 6:19 .
> God has established His eternal presence in my body.

I am a minister of reconciliation for God. 2 Corinthians 5:17
> I have been asked by God to tell others that He is not holding their sins against them because Christ died for all their sins. They must accept Christ's payment.

I am God's co-worker. 1 Corinthians 3:9; 2 Corinthians 6:1
> God has been willing to work with me to accomplish His will. He has in some sense restricted a part of His will to my cooperation. I am working with God.

I am seated with Christ in the heavenly realm. Ephesians 2:6
> In terms of my position, Christ says I carry the same authority He has as the one seated at the right hand of the Father -- the highest position of authority in the universe. Every other being is under that authority, including the Devil.

I am God's workmanship. Ephesians 2:10
> God is working on me to bring me to completion and will not stop until He is completely satisfied and ready to enjoy eternity with me in heaven.

I may approach God with freedom and confidence. Ephesians 3:12
> My ability to approach God is not dependent on my perfection but on Christ's finished work on the Cross. I have freedom and confidence in Christ to come to God.

I can do all things through Christ who strengthens me. Philippians 4:13
> There is not a job God will ever give me where He has not also supplied all the power I need to complete that job.

Personal Application of Christ's Salvation

Let me give you an applicational understanding of the nature of our salvation and then the more technical theological understanding.

1. GOD'S FOREKNOWLEDGE: Romans 8:29; 1 Peter 2:1,2

God planned the universe from the beginning to the end and all the possibilities in between. He saw everyone and everything before it ever took place.

Before God created anything, He knew me and every choice I could and would make. He supplied the conditions and the grace I needed so I could freely chose Him and receive salvation, heaven, and a relationship with Him. He loved me before He ever created anything. He knew I was coming into this universe. He has kept the universe and this rebellious planet going so I could be born and receive His love.

This is the penetrating gaze of God's all-knowing mind which sees whether a person will voluntarily come to Christ with the prevenient grace under any circumstances (Romans 8:29). (It is possible God's foreknowledge is based upon something else in the mind of God; but voluntary acceptance of Christ seems to be the only thing that fits the confines of justice, biblical injunctions, and human responsibility.)

2. ELECTION: Romans 8:28-29; 1 Peter 1:1, 2; Romans 9:14-18

God made the decision to chose us and set His love upon us. He wanted you and made sure you would find Him. Based upon all that God knew about His plan and about you, He decided you would exist and be one of His chosen people. He made sure all the conditions I needed to have happen to bring me to my realization of my need for Him took place so that I would find God and embrace Him in love. He has been waiting for me to be born so that He could rescue me from my place of rebellion, sin, and misery into His arms of love.

The sovereign act of God in grace whereby He selected certain persons to receive salvation in Christ Jesus. (Romans 8:28-29; 1 Peter 1:1, 2; Romans 9:14-18) This election means God has selected the person or salvation no matter how unlikely a candidate they may seem. His election is based upon His foreknowledge.

3. CREATION OF THE WORLD: Genesis 1 and 2

God created the world that He had planned so carefully so those who would worship and love Him would come to exist. He did this in spite of the mountains of rebellion, sin, and selfishness that would also come into His universe.

In order to have people who were going to freely love and worship God, He needed to actually create the universe and the planet they would live on. Even though it would be thousands of years before some of the people who He was looking for would be born, He still created and began the long wait for the birth and life of those who would accept His love and return it voluntarily. He has been very patiently waiting for me so He could set His love upon me.

The sovereign act of God whereby He brought into being all the things that exist (Genesis 1:1). He spoke and the universe came into being; before He spoke there was nothing but God. Before there could be salvation, there needed to be a world and people needed saving.

4. THE FALL OF LUCIFER, THE SON OF THE MORNING: Ezekiel 28:11-19; Isaiah 14:12-16

God allowed His most perfect creation to rebel and set the whole universe on a path of rebellion, pain, selfishness, and hurt so love would be real and not forced.

Sin entered into God's perfect creation through the perversion of the highest created being, Lucifer, the anointed cherub that covers. He decided he wanted to be God and rebelled from his appointed position. When he turned from God's rulership in his life, he perverted the goodness (true freedom to love God) that God designed in the universe. The cancer of selfishness and rebellion has spread through the whole world.

5. THE FALL OF MAN: Genesis 3:1-24

God allowed Adam and Eve to rebel from Him and express their own independence in defiance to Him just as He allows you to defy Him to your own hurt.

In an act of supreme love, God allowed Adam and Eve to rebel from His love and plunge humanity and planet earth into rebellion against God. God then began the process of drawing individual men and women back to a loving relationship with Him.

God knew angels and humanity must be given a real choice to love God or their worship would be meaningless. He knew Adam and Eve would rebel and spread the angelic contagion to all humanity. Just as Adam and Eve rebelled against God, so every human also turns away from God and has no way back unless God provides it. The whole human race was plunged into spiritual death because of Adam's choice. God had already designed a plan to redeem humanity that was put in place before the world was created. Everyone who has faith in the Supreme God to supply the answer for their sins and rebellion has a way back to God through Him.

The action of Adam and Eve to reject the direction of God and to seek to be gods themselves. They rebelled from the God-designed submission which would have brought everlasting life and harmony and chose to go their own independent ways. (Genesis 3:1-24).

6. THE ESTABLISHMENT OF ORIGINAL SIN: Rom 5:12-21

What Adam and Eve did condemned all of humanity to life without automatic connection to God. We were born dead in our trespasses and sins.

Adam's rebellion robbed all future generations of automatic relationship with God and spiritual life. Every person would now be born spiritually dead and need to be born again to enjoy life with God.

The sin of Adam and Eve robbed all future generations after them of perfect submission and communication with God. It was therefore inevitable that individual men and women would commit acts of sin and rebellion against God because they are born spiritually dead without the life of God. Before God began to work on you and with you, you were spiritually dead and unable to interact with Him.

7. THE INCARNATION OF THE GOD-MAN: JESUS CHRIST: 1 Corinthians 5:19-21; John 1:12

In order to actually save some humans, God Himself had to become a man and live a perfect life and then voluntarily give up His perfect human life and take on Himself the sins of the whole world. He did that for you.

God personally invaded human history in order to redeem mankind. He, God, must become a man, live a perfect life, give up that perfect life for the sins of others, rise from the dead to prove His power over death, and ascend to Heaven. Without the perfect life, voluntary death, resurrection, and ascension of Jesus the Christ, salvation is not possible.

In God's infinite wisdom, God saw there were countless people who would love God but that He must provide a way to bring them back to Him and give them the ability to choose Him. God miraculously provided both so you and thousands of others could reconnect with Him. In order for God to provide salvation for mankind, He had to have a sinless man and an endless life. This could only be accomplished by the second person of the Godhead becoming permanently welded to humanity through an incarnation. This God-man then lived a perfect life to meet the requirement of perfection to enter God's heaven. The God-man then must be willing to voluntarily give up His personal claim on eternal life and take on the sin of the world. (1 Corinthians 5:19-21) His endless life as God then allowed Him to offer the sinless perfection of His perfect life to as many as would receive Him. (John 1:12)

8. THE RESTRAINING MINISTRY OF THE HOLY SPIRIT: Genesis 6:3; 2 Thessalonians 2:7

God worked on you, those around you, and the world at large to not do all the evil they could have done so some could hear His voice and turn to Him.

After God created the world capable of sin, He was actively involved in suppressing the full measure of selfishness and sin of the world through the Holy Spirit operating on and in people. Without this restraining ministry, evil would completely overwhelm the human race. This does not mean God keeps evil from happening but He constantly puts a strain on Christians and non-Christians to not do all the evil that is possible in a given situation. (Genesis 6:3; 2 Thessalonians 2:7)

9. THE MINISTRY OF CONVICTION (REPROOF)
Matthew 12:31, 32

God, through a number of different circumstances, situations, and inner promptings, brought you to the place where you knew you needed to be forgiven of your sins and you needed God.

One of the key ways God gets people to realize they need to love Him to have a blessed life is to bring conviction, reproof, and rebuke. God specifically brings conviction of sin, selfishness, and evil onto people so they will recognize their need of a Savior and God. The Holy Spirit presents the claims of Christ in an unmistakable and powerful way. God presents the love, forgiveness, and hope that is in Christ to you in a way that brings you forward to receive it and to realize you would be guilty if you rejected it. When a person turns away and blasphemes the work of the Holy Spirit demonstrated before them and working on them, they remain in their sins -- the unpardonable sin. (Matthew 12:31, 32)

The ministry of the Holy Spirit in the world -- in and through the Christians -- of bringing conviction of sin, righteousness, and judgment. (John 16:7-11. This means the Holy Spirit works on the non-believer to bring conviction before salvation.

10. GOD'S CALL: John 3:16; Matthew 11:28; Rev. 22:17

God called you to repentance and faith. He gave you the grace to respond to Him. He wanted to redeem you.

God specifically called to you to repent and follow Him. Christ invites men and women to accept by faith the salvation that Christ provided in His life, death, and resurrection.

When a person responds to the work of God on their heart about their sin, rebellion, and lack of love, God calls them and energies them to accept his love and repent from their sins. He energizes the person to respond to God's call. If you are a Christian, then you responded and the flow of God's power accomplished in you what you could not do on your own. The act of grace in which He invites men to accept by faith the salvation provided by Christ. (Luke 5:32; Matthew 22:3-10)

11. CONVERSION: Matthew 18:3

God changed you from one who went your own selfish way to one who had His interests at heart.

God acted when you accepted His grace and turned to Him in true repentance and faith and He converted you from a sinner to believing saint. He put into you a new center and focus of your life. Something actually changed in the center of your being.

The act of God and man in which the man turns to God in true repentance and faith. (Matthew 18:3) This is where salvation first becomes fully visible and operative in the life of the person. The person is converted to accept a new center of their life. They are converted to become a worshipper of God and their new love life starts

12. JUSTIFICATION: Romans 3:23

We have been declared forgiven and fit for heaven because of our faith in what Jesus Christ did for us on the cross.

When you responded to the grace of God and repented, God declared you forgiven of all your past sins and righteous under Jesus Christ's life and death.

When we were given the ability by God to respond and then we responded, God legally changed our status from sinner deserving of death and condemnation to forgiven. We were declared righteous by the life, death, and resurrection of Christ. While this is a legal transaction in the courts of heaven, it carries significant benefits and advantages. We have passed out of judgment and death and are now in the category of life and forgiveness.

The act of God where He declares righteous the individual who believes (puts his full trust) in Jesus Christ for salvation. (Romans 3:23) This is purely a legal transaction which takes place in God's records.

13. REGENERATION: Titus 3:5; John 3:16

We have been injected with the life of God in our spirit. We were disconnected from God and now we can listen, respond, and be directed by Him.

God pours into us life, energy, desires, and passions we did not have before we were Christians. This new life will change us if we allow it to work its wonder in us. We have been given new life. It will move us to decide new things, love new people, forgive others, overlook the slights and selfishness of others, and, most importantly, love God and desire to please Him.

The act of God where He gives a new life, a new creation into the believer in the Lord Jesus Christ. (Titus 3:5; John 3:16) The believer is born again and has a whole new life which wants to take complete control over his daily actions, thoughts, words, attitudes, and motives. (2 Corinthians 5:17)

14. UNION WITH CHRIST: Romans 6:1-5

We became one with Christ and able to change our orientation to this world. We died with Christ to the temptations of this world, and we rose from the dead with Christ to the joy of serving God.

When a person becomes a Christian, they are united with Christ in a spiritual way which allows them to enjoy the actions, position, and benefits of Christ. These benefits of our spiritual union with Christ can be used to resist temptation, claim a new future, live an overflowing life, see God's assignments, and enjoy relationships at new levels.

The act of God where the individual believer is united with Christ and shares in the actions, position, and benefits of Christ. (Romans 6:1-5) This powerful aspect of salvation is declared to be intimately connected to baptism and the Christian's ability to resist temptation.

15. ADOPTION: Galatians 4:3-5; Romans 8:15; John 1:12

We are a part of God's forever family, with the rights and privileges to act in His name for His purposes.

God has specifically set His love on those who respond to His overtures. He goes beyond just restoring them to what they could fully be as humans; He brings them into their forever family and connects them to Himself and His eternal inheritance and the spiritual blessings that go with it.

The act of God where He releases us from our tutelage under the law and proclaims us a full member of His family under the law of the Spirit of life. (Galatians 4:3-5; Romans 8:15; John 1:12) When we enter into the power of this adoption, all the problems inherited from our ancestors are erased.

16. SPIRIT BAPTISM: 1 Corinthians 12:13, Mark 1:8

God has made us a part of the overall body of Christ by injecting into the core of who we are the Spirit of Christ. We are now a part of Christ's activity in the world; marked as one of His and carrying the Holy Spirit as the link to the whole body of Christ.

God knows we will never be able to live the Christian life on our own energy, so He has drenched us and imbedded the Holy Spirit and His energy in us. It is this common element of the presence of the Holy Spirit that makes all Christians a part of the body of Christ. We have the same DNA. Christians are now capable of actions, speech, motives, and attitudes they were never capable of before. They should no longer see themselves as what they were before but as forgiven. They are new creatures, endowed with new life and a new agent in the very midst of who they are.

The ministry of the Holy Spirit to Christians of placing them in the body of Christ. (1 Corinthians 12:13, Mark 1:8) There seems to be a double action here: The Lord Jesus baptizing us in the Holy Spirit (causing us to drink of one Spirit) and the Holy Spirit baptizing us into the body of Christ.

17. THE INDWELLING OF THE HOLY SPIRIT: Rom. 8:8-11

God not only forgave us and destined us for heaven, He also gave us His Holy Spirit to live within us, directing us, teaching us, and encouraging us.

An extension of the Holy Spirit's baptism of every believer is that He now indwells in each true believer speaking, directing, guiding, and encouraging them about what to do to please God. His presence is reassurance, wisdom, and direction.

The ministry of the Holy Spirit in which His presence abides in each believer confirming their salvation, giving comfort, and direction. (Romans 8:8-11) The fact that He is present means you are truly saved and bound for heaven.

18. THE SEALING OF THE HOLY SPIRIT: Ephesians 1:13

God puts His seal on us and proclaims we are His. He marks us as His. By putting the Holy Spirit in us, God ensures He will continue to work on us as we go through this life bound for heaven. What God began, He will complete. Cooperate with the indwelling Holy Spirit and enjoy the wonder of a full Christian life.

The ministry of the Holy Spirit whereby He ensures the completion of salvation. (Ephesians 1:13) God puts His mark on His people and they are secure (like in Revelation 7:4, 14:1). God Himself ensures that believers will be kept from stumbling in a permanent total fashion. (Jude 24)

19. SANCTIFICATION: Romans 6:19

God wants me to enjoy more and more of His kind of life. He prompts, guides, teaches, reproves, and corrects me as I become more and more like He wants me to be.

God wants us to fully enjoy the Christian life and all the assignments, holiness, blessings, and good works that go along with this kind of life. This is a process which means we must cooperate with God as He brings us forward into all He has planned for our life. God does not want to settle for you being less than all you can be so he uses circumstances, the Holy Spirit, church, non-believers, family, angels, Bible, authorities, etc.

The process which brings the believer into conformity to Christ and holiness. (Romans 6:19) God uses all available means to conform us to the image of His Son -- circumstances, the Holy Spirit, church, non-believers, family, angels, Bible, authorities, etc.

20. THE FILLING MINISTRY OF THE HOLY SPIRIT: Ephesians 5:18

God the Holy Spirit wants to flow out of the innermost parts of my spirit into my mind, will, emotions, body, words, actions, and attitudes so everyone can see Him in me.

In the heart of every believer is the Holy Spirit dwelling and whispering. God wants this indwelling presence of the Holy Spirit to spill out into our mind, will emotions, and actions. This is called the filling of the Holy Spirit. This is where you say things you didn't know you knew. This is where you act in ways that are uncharacteristic of you but not uncharacteristic of God. This is where you decide to move in directions consistent with God's plans and pleasure even though they may be opposite of your past plans and pleasure.

The ministry of the Holy Spirit in which He takes over control of actions, words, and attitudes of the believer. (Ephesians 5:18) He is implanted in your spirit and seeks to move out through your mind, will, emotions, and body.

21. SPIRITUAL GIFTS: 1 Corinthians 12:4-7

I have been given special spiritual abilities so I can benefit others and bless God. These form a core of what God is asking me to do for Him.

Not only has God saved us from His wrath, forgiven us, made a place in heaven for us, and energized us with His Holy Spirit, He has also given us special abilities we did not have before. Often these gifts become a major part of our lives because of the good they do for others and the joy in using them. Many Christian's find their life calling in the use of these spiritual gifts even though before they were a Christian, they would have been completely unable to do these things.

There are three different kinds of gifts: the gift itself, the ministry it is used, and finally the level of its effect. Each of these are controlled and given by God.

The ministry of the Holy Spirit in which He gives a special ability to each believer to benefit the cause of Christ. (1 Corinthians 12:4-7) Each believer has at least one. It is impossible to figure out one's life purpose without incorporating your spiritual gift as a major component of your life and work.

PERSEVERANCE: John 10:27-30

I am being given the power to persevere until the end.

God ensures that those who are elect will endure until the end of their lives as believers and forgiven. He is active in their lives and makes sure they do not finally or fully fall away from the faith and love of God.

The actions of God which ensure that those who have truly been born again will not totally or finally fall away from the faith. (John 10:27-30) God Himself becomes active in the life of the believer ensuring the completion of the journey of faith.

GLORIFICATION: Romans 8:29-30; 1 John 3:2, 3

I will be perfected and made ready to dwell with angels, redeemed humans, and God in the perfection of eternity.

There comes a day in the life of every believer that they are graduated to heaven and the difference between what they are and what they can be is erased. They are transformed by God. They are glorified by God into the fullness of what they are supposed to be in Christ. They are made into a person who can live in God's presence and not be consumed by His Holiness.

The action of God where He glorifies and purifies the believer so they can live in the presence of God. (Romans 8:29-30; 1 John 3:2, 3) This begins at death or rapture. This seems to be an instantaneous process which makes one fit for heaven.

REDEMPTION OF THE BODY: 1 Thessalonians 4:1-8;
1 Corinthians 15:50-58; Romans 8:11

I will be given a new resurrected body that is far superior to my present earthly body and able to dwell in the perfection of eternity.

God will redeem your body and give you a new glorified body that will be able to house your soul and accomplish the spiritual and physical assignments God wants you to do. Your new body will be way beyond your present one, but the seed of the next one is in the present one.

The action of God where He comes back for the body of those who have died and gives them a new body so they might be body, soul, and spirit. (1 Thessalonians 4:1-8; 1 Corinthians 15:50-58; Romans 8:11)

MARRIAGE SUPPER OF THE LAMB: 2 Thess. 1:10; Rev. 19:7

I will be invited to be one of the special guests at the great party and celebration where Jesus the Christ permanently welcomes, connects with, and begins living among those humans who are redeemed

You will be invited to a great feast in which all those who have been redeemed through the ages will be invited. They will all marvel at the Savior and His work. The invited guest will also converse and enjoy the company of the other faithful through the ages. It will be quite a feast to celebrate the beginning of forever loving, serving, and worshipping God.

The period of time when the saints shall enjoy the Savior and come to fully appreciate Him. (2 Thessalonians 1:10; Revelation 19:7) Some associate this with the time in heaven during the tribulation; others the millennium.

NEW HEAVENS AND NEW EARTH Revelation 21,22

I have a place in heaven waiting for me. Eternity is my destiny and my future; what can they do to me on this planet?

After all the wars, sin, and selfishness of our present planet, God will establish His permanent kingdom in the new heavens and new earth where He will place us. We will live in Holy City. It will be a city full of peace and gratefulness to God. It will remember the lives and sacrifices that were made to accomplish the wonder of our life in the presence of God. You will dwell in the presence of God who is life Himself.

This is the time to settle into the eternal state, serving the Lord in final glorification in the new heavens and new earth. (Revelation 21-22) We shall live in the holy city, the new Jerusalem, with all its blessings and wonders -- the greatest of which is the Lamb of God, which is its light.

5. Faith

The second of the battle-ready pieces of armor is Faith. It is so often called the shield of faith that many cannot think of it without the metaphor. There are two possibilities for this word faith. It can mean the objective doctrines called the faith once delivered to the saints by Jude. It can also be the subjective trust in God in spite of contrary circumstances, e.g., Job. Since the power and nature of the objective doctrines are covered under the piece of armor called truth, it is better to see this weapon as subjective trust in God. Right now God is asking you to trust Him for something. It could be in any one of the relationships of life, but faith is always a component of a healthy Christian life. It is also truth Satan will at times attack your trust in Christ and in what Christ wants you to do to live out your Christian life. He attacks with doubts, fear, obstacles, temptation, enemies, and/or opposition. He is trying to get you to give up on the dream God has given you. He is trying to get you to give up on ever conquering the temptation that is destroying your life. He is trying to have you pull back from trusting Christ and moving forward with loving at new levels. What is God asking you to trust Him for? What attack, temptation, doubt, fear, or obstacle is Satan throwing in the way so you will not trust?

When Satan attacks, it is critical one possess a strong trust in the basic goodness of God. The message of Scripture must be believed even in the face of difficult, if not impossible, circumstances. Faith is the result of keen observation in Scripture and experiencing God's goodness in life. Simple trust in God is necessary and must be developed in order to sustain the Christian life. This weapon is available to new believers, but it should be deepened as time is spent walking with God. Answers to prayer, diligent study of Scripture, and careful observation of nature and circumstances all help to strengthen faith. The book of Job describes a man who utilized all these methods to develop an unshakable faith in God.

The teaching model must show believers how to develop and express faith rather than just talk about the need for it. Too often, those who follow the teaching model spend time explaining faith but do not demonstrate how to develop faith or how to express it in the midst of Satanic attack. Like Peter walking on the water, Christians under attack must learn to keep their eyes focused on the Lord Jesus and not the circumstances around them. The Christian must come to believe and live by Job's credo, *"Though He slay me, yet will I trust Him."* (Job 13:15) Faith is the ability to "hang on until morning." Jeremiah, in the book of Lamentations, says in the midst of the darkest circumstances, *"Great is Thy faithfulness, they are new every morning."* (Lamentations 3:23) It is the ability to believe God in spite of contrary thought and circumstances which protects the believer from the devouring gaze of the Enemy. The teaching model must show how to take life's ups and downs and use them to strengthen faith. The teaching model must explain how to study Scripture so one develops a growing awareness of God's goodness and love. The teaching model must demonstrate how to transform a general prayer life into a specific series of requests and answers so that faith is built. When Satan attacks, a simple and unshakable trust in Christ is essential.

6. The Word of God
The sixth piece of armor is the Word of God. It is the duty of the teacher to explain the true nature of this weapon. Many believe a Bible on the shelf is protection against satanic attack. The Greek word used for word is rhema which means spoken word. The Apostle Paul is making a distinction between the written word of God contained in the Scriptures and the Word of God spoken by those who believe and trust Him. When Satan seduces, tempts, and pressures the believer, he must have hidden God's Word in his mind or there will be no ability to withstand the pressure. The Word of God is a powerful tool when it is in the mouth and life of His servants. It is of no value when it is left unknown and unused on printed pages. The Psalmist echoes a similar sentiment when he says, *"Thy Word have I hid in my heart that I might not sin against Thee."* (Psalm 119:11)

There is incredible power in the spoken Word of God. Any accurate teaching of the armor of God must include how to make the Word of God a powerful agent in an individual's life. There are numerous memorization and meditation programs which demonstrate and encourage the average

Christian to have God's Word ready to be used. The teaching model must help believers realize the incredible power in God's Word when spoken by them.

In order to really wield the Sword of the Spirit effectively, you must have it memorized and ready for use. God wants you to internalize the Word of God. The spiritual discipline of Biblical Meditation is incredibly lacking in our day. It is this discipline of hiding God's Word in our heart so the Holy Spirit can direct it through us out to the situation or person who needs it. It is the word pressed in our soul that will become the weapon when we are spiritually attacked. This discipline is so crucial and it has had such a formative element in my own Christian growth that I have written a book discussing and giving exercises about Biblical Meditation: *They Laughed When I Wrote Another Book About Prayer...Then They Read It.*

Let me give you a few exercises that will begin the process of putting the Word of God in your soul.

Slow repetition: Read slowly out loud the classic passages of Christian truth: The Lord's Prayer; The Beatitudes; The Ten Commandments; The Fruit of the Spirit; The First and Second Great Commandments; The Ladder of Virtue.

Memorization: Memorize a verse or section of Scripture that deals with an issue, problem or dream you are interacting with.

James 1:19	**Anger, gossip, pride**
Ephesians 5:25	**Marriage improvement**
Proverbs 18:1	**Divorce, big decisions**
Romans 12:1,2	**Temptation, loving God**
Philippians 4:6-8	**Worry, movie guide, thought life**
Romans 6:1-12	**Temptation, Christ's power**
Colossians 3:12-15	**Positive qualities, what to do each day**
1 John 1:5-2:2	**Getting rid of sin, forgiveness**
Exodus 20:3-17	**Ten Commandments, right and wrong**
Proverbs 15:1-4	**Calming anger, speaking well**
Ephesians 1:18-21	**Christian power and prestige**
Ephesians 3:14-21	**Love, strengthened with power**
Matthew 5:3-12	**How to be like Christ, how to act**
Galatians 5:22,23	**What God will prompt you to do**

Bible Study: Study a passage of Scripture and unlock the truths, insights, wisdom, and life change in it. Use the inductive method of observation, interpretation, and application.

Personalize: Write out a verse of Scripture with your name inserted into the verse and using personal pronouns whenever possible.

Confessionalize: Take a Scripture passage and press it through your will by agreeing with its proclamations and agreeing where your life measures up and doesn't measure up to the standard in the verse.

Visualize: Take a verse of Scripture and picture that verse taking place with you right in the midst of it. Take a verse of Scripture and picture yourself actually doing the ideas and commands of the Scriptures.

Diagram or Draw: Make a diagram or drawing of the ideas in a verse. This may be like a schematic or more artistic. Some people are able to connect with a verse when they are using a pencil and paper as they engage on the verse.

Pray: Take a verse or section of Scripture and ask God to fulfill the ideas, promises, and blessings of that verse.

Journal: Write out your prayers to God and/or keep a journal of your interactions with Scripture. Writing down what God is saying and what you are observing about your life can be very insightful and helpful.

Sing: One of the most dynamic ways to connect the Scripture with the inner part of your person is to sing it back to God. The tune doesn't matter. Just sing the words and ideas of Scripture back to God.

Using these ways you will be ready to use the Word of God as a weapon in the midst of the spiritual battle.

7. Prayer

The weapon of prayer is often overlooked in discussions of the armor of God because it is not couched in the metaphor of a Roman soldier's armor in the Apostle Paul's discussion. However, prayer is one of the most important weapons which the believer can possess in warfare with Satan. Unfortunately, the average Christian is used to praying weak, ineffective prayers and tries to utilize these as weapons against the Enemy. Satan is unaffected by this type of prayer. Prayer as a weapon in the warfare with Satan must be specific, doctrinal, and based on the Holy Spirit's promptings. A nonspecific prayer for traveling mercies will not accomplish much in the battle. Mark Bubeck in his two books, The Adversary and Overcoming the Adversary, provides help in explaining and rediscovering effective praying in a demonic context. Although these books are most often used by pastors and reinforce the defacto expert model, these books and their prayers are quite helpful for all Christians. When average Christians learn to pray in this powerful way, they are released like tigers into the battle. I have seen mild-mannered and somewhat meek individuals transformed into great spiritual warriors through prayers of this nature. The teaching model must incorporate practice sessions to listen to believers praying in this new way. Without these practice sessions, the ideas do not become practiced techniques.

Those who utilize the teaching model are often guilty of not praying diligently before, during, and after their seminars. This leads to devastating effects in the conferences and churches where the seminar was held. Those involved in any form of demonic work must practice what they preach. They must understand and utilize the weapons which the Lord provided. Prayer is a primary weapon which must be used. When used properly prayer can create a climate of liberty and freedom for those who come to the teaching session. Prayer by the leaders can be used to draw to a conference those under demonic influence. Prayer by the leaders of a church can protect the church and dilute the Satanic outrage involved in exposing his strategies. Prayer by the leaders can sensitize them for the specific direction God may give during the conference. In the church I served, I went through four major upheavals in a very short period of time and many families left. While the surface causes were different in every case, each came at a time of intensive teaching on spiritual warfare without adequate prayer by the leadership of the church. A number of pastors have become excited about the arena of spiritual warfare, but they do not adequately petition the Lord in a powerful way. Therefore their churches are devastated in the process. A very large church in the Los Angeles area began a series on spiritual warfare. The teaching was accurate and effective, but there was not sufficient preparation in prayer for the series and the church experienced numerous problems. This is not to suggest churches should avoid the subject but rather prayer must be more than just a doctrine. It must be a practiced and honed skill by the leadership of the church.

There are also many other ways of praying that will strengthen our connection with God and bring us His wisdom, His help, and His comfort when we need it. Let me suggest a few different ways of expanding your prayer life.

Confession-based prayer -- in which you would let Christ search your life and see if there is any sin in your life. This is usually aided by a list of topics to go through like the Ten Commandments, the seven deadly sins, the fruit of the spirit, the deeds of the flesh in Galatians 5:19-21, the list of sins in Rom. 1.

Holy Spirit-based prayers: This is where you let the Holy Spirit prompt you to pray for people, organizations, goals. or events. Just listen to Him prompt you.

Scripture-based prayers: This is where you pray the prayers of Scripture or you read a passage of Scripture and pray the ideas, truths, and wisdom of that verse into people's lives.

Service-based prayers: This is where you would listen for how God would want you to serve and then while you are serving in that way, talk with God about the people, organizations, goals, and ideas that come to your mind.

Worship-based prayers: This is where you praise, adore, give thanks, and bless God for who He is and all the things He has done for your life.

Fellowship-(Intercession)based prayers: This is where you pray for others or with others.

Entreaty-based prayers: This is where you pray for specific personal blessing you need or righteously desire.

Request-based prayers: This is where you would ask God for specific items, wisdom, blessings, changes, etc., in your life and in the lives of others.

Church-based prayers: This is where you talk with God about your church or the churches in your region or nation in general.

Authority-based prayers: This is where you pray for and with those who are in authority over you. This would include family authorities, governmental authorities, spiritual authorities.

Evangelism-based prayers: This is where you would pray for specific people who do not know the Lord that they would be given grace to hear and receive the gospel. Also you would pray for people groups who are without the gospel.

Communion-based prayers: This is where you would interact with God regarding Christ's death for you and your continuing need of God's grace and forgiveness.

Abstinence-based prayers: This is where you would launch your prayers during a time of fasting or silence or solitude or sleep deprivation. These types of prayers can increase the effectiveness of prayer.

Need-based prayers: This is where you pray for the real needs of people. What they really need to feel the love of Christ. Sometimes people don't realize what they really need.

Generosity-based prayers: This is where you pray for generosity to come to an organization or people to be generous. This may involve a specific project or general giving for ministry.

Wisdom-based prayers: This is where you would pray for wisdom about a specific problem you might be encountering. You would pray as you look at Proverbs and Psalms for the answer to your prayers.

Doctrinal-based prayers: This is where you would speak to God about the truth of the ten basic Christian doctrines.

Healing-based prayers: This is where you would pray for people to be healed in some specific way. This might include physical, mental, emotional, spiritual, relational healing.

Gift-based prayers: This is where people are encouraged to pray out of the their spiritual gift and for people who need the benefit of that spiritual gift.

Relationship-based prayers: Ten Relationships: this is where prayer in each of the ten major relationships of a person's life would be prayed and listening to God's direction in those arenas. God, Self, Marriage, Family, Work, Church, Money, Society, Friends, Enemies.

Work-based prayer: This is where prayer would be specifically directed at the situation, people, plans, and organization of work.

Beatitudes-based prayers: This is where the Beatitudes are used as a filter or prompt to pray for people and organizations.

Morality-based prayers: Ten Commandments: This is where the Ten Commandments are used as a prompt to pray for certain needs and possibilities.

Financially-based prayers: This is interaction with God about the finances of a family, group, organization, or event. The thoughts, feelings, and facts are laid before the Lord and wisdom, generosity, and stewardship is asked for in these areas. There are only three areas of problem with money: income, management, and generosity and each of these should be explored with God in prayer.

Marriage-based prayers: This is interaction with God about your marriage. This is where you talk back and forth with God about what you need to do to inject more love into your marriage. It means you bring up to God what you need in your marriage. There are only five problems in marriage and the answers to those five problems are in the Scriptures.

Compassion-based prayers: God's heart moves out in compassion for those under the burden of sin. This is interaction with Him about those people. It may be you have been particularly sensitized to one group of people victimized by the problems of sin or it may be that you need God to show you where His heart is breaking in your world right now.

Family-based prayers: This is interaction with God about your family. This would include your immediate family and your extended family. Remember, prayer is talking and listening to God back and forth on these subjects. You are not leaving a message on God's voicemail but instead dialoguing with Him about family.

Personal-based prayers: This is interaction with God that is centered on your life. It could move through the ten relationships; it could move through the spiritual, mental, emotional, volitional, physical, and even nutritional aspects of your life.

Enemies-based prayers: This is prayer specifically directed at those who are in opposition to you, who do not seem to want your best, who are in competition with you. This also may involve prayers about those who oppose God's designs and righteousness.

Wound-based prayers: This is prayer based upon Jesus' statement in Matthew 5:5: Blessed are those who mourn for they shall be comforted. We all live in a sinful world that will wound, hurt, and disappoint us. It is only as we grieve these wounds and process the pain involved in them that we will be able to overcome them, learn from them, and keep them from holding us back.

Friendship-based prayers: This is prayer that approaches Jesus as our friend (Hebrews 4) who has experienced every temptation and troubling situation we are experiencing. This is allowing Jesus to hear our prayers as a friend and as a counselor. We are not asking him to be the solution to our prayers as much as we want to talk with Him about these difficulties.

Community-based prayers: This is prayer directed at the problems, issues, and situations that exist within the community at large and need to be addressed. This may involve asking for a leader to be raised up or monies or organizations to attack these problems.

Leadership-based prayers: This is prayer focused on the future and what can be accomplished in a righteous direction. Often we do not sit down and look at a year from now or three years from now and contemplate what could be different and what would need to happen to make that new possibility a reality.

Written prayers: This is reading out loud prayers that have been written and can usually carry more depth and detail than spontaneous prayers can.

Deliverance prayers: This is prayer that is designed to set a person free from an attachment to sin, a spiritual tormentor, an addiction, a wound, or a toxic person.

Personal development: This is an application of Psalm 37:4 where God says if we delight in Him He will give us the desires of our heart. This type of prayer walks through what is the desire of our heart in all ten major relationships: God, Self, Marriage, Family, Work, Church, Money, Society, Friends, Enemies.

CRITIQUE

Having examined and explored the teaching model, it is time to turn a more critical eye to this resourceful and flexible model. The teaching model has become a favorite model in working with many aspects in the church, not just spiritual warfare. The strengths and weakness discussed here are in regard to deliverance but could also be voiced about the teaching model in other areas of the church.

Strengths

1. The teaching model explains vital information to the believer involved in the battle with the Enemy.

The greatest strength of the teaching model is its vital information is obtained by those who need it most—the average Christian. Often in the other models the believer is uniformed as to why and how certain things are done. The teaching model can clear up the mysteries surrounding Satanic involvement in the believer's life. This model can show people the beginning and end of Satan and his minions. The believer can learn the strategies and devices of Satan in a non-threatening environment. One fellow, whose family was under Satanic attack, was ecstatic about a clear explanation of the armor of God. He saw how he could protect his family from further satanic attack. His wife saw a way to be free from Satanic oppression through meditating on the positional truths of the Christian.

2. The teaching model carries the potential of showing the believer how to practice the essential spiritual truths.

One of the great possibilities of the teaching model is the application of truth. Following a time of exposure to truth is the perfect time to lead people through a practical involvement in truth. If one is teaching on the weapon of peace with God and it is explained that confession and repentance is an essential part of using this weapon, the teacher can lead the group in a period of private self-examination and then confession. It is also possible that, following a session explaining this piece of armor, the teacher asked those assembled to write a list of those with whom they are not at peace. This list then becomes a list of contacts for the next week to make peace. There are numerous applications possible for each lesson, but the chance to change a life immediately following the session exists. In a seminar conducted by Dr. Ed Murphy, he dealt with sexual sin and its ramifications in the demonic realm. At the end of the session he instructed the audience to bow their heads and pray out loud the prayer of confession. He led the prayer for the whole group and following the prayer he commanded, "In the name of Jesus, if any demons have been harassing individuals, they must leave as their ground was canceled." This was a helpful and insightful way to apply the truths he just taught.

3. The teaching model does not pursue direct contact with satanic entities.

The teaching model is not interested in contacting demons but in educating the Christian about the truth. The teaching usually takes place in a group setting where there is rarely demonic manifestation. This model is safe for many who may think they are experiencing demonic bondage. It is also safe for those who are desiring a deeper understanding of all the truths of the Bible. In my years as a pastor, I have seen a number of people who were greatly helped by teaching in this manner. These people would never come to me personally and ask for help in this area. The teaching model is a safe and appropriate means of help for many within the congregation. The teaching model is a "user friendly model" in that no part of the model is designed to frighten or over involve any individual. It is a non-threatening way to understand the warfare in the spiritual arena.

4. The teaching model can be graded so one understands basic concepts before moving on to more complex and difficult ones.

The teaching model lends itself to progressive learning in the spiritual war. Few people are ready to handle all the types of Satanic and demonic workings which are going on in the world. A crash course usually overwhelms the listener. The teaching model can easily be organized in prerequisite jumps which slowly build a framework for understanding this complex area. This graded approach is unique to all the models and can educate the mass of the congregation as well as begin to identify those who God may have selected for a more extensive ministry in this area. It is unfortunate the teaching model is used almost exclusively as a remedial method for those already suffering severe oppression and not as an educational and training method for the entire church. Building a proper Christian understanding of the world is the responsibility of the teacher. There are a number who are using this graded approach to spiritual warfare and are having great success in educating the general Christian on spiritual warfare.4

5. The teaching model is rooted and grounded in Scripture.

All the concepts grow out of Scripture. The teaching is expositional in nature. The teaching model is strong and balanced because it begins with the Scripture and then reasons to experience. A number of the other models start with experience and reason back to the Scripture. The teaching model begins with clear, sound exegesis of the Scripture and then makes conclusions about the world and the demonic realm. All the concepts from Satan's origins to the armor of God are taken from Scripture. Average Christians are far stronger in their faith when they have a clear nail in Scripture on which to hang their actions. The Scriptures are living, active, and endowed with the breath of God and are a means of growing in Christ.

6. The teaching model has strong scriptural support.

The New Testament supports the teaching model. In II Timothy 2:24-26, the apostle states, *"And the Lord's bond servant must not be quarrelsome, but be kind to all, able to teach, patient when wronged, with gentleness correcting those who are in opposition, if perhaps God may grant them repentance leading to the knowledge of the truth, and they may come to their senses and escape from the snare of the Devil, having been held captive by him to do his will."* The concept is that God's servants are to present the truth and pray that God grants them repentance so they can escape the snare of the Devil. The ability to teach is a prerequisite to helping those caught in the Devil's trap.

In John 8:31-33, Jesus states the key to true freedom: *"If you abide in My word, then you are truly disciples of Mine; and you shall know the truth and the truth shall make you free."* The truth can free a person from bondage. In every area of life it is objective truth that frees a person from the bondage of superstition, intimidation, and confusion. The truth must be communicated in order to be effective and that communication is teaching. There is an inherent power in truth, Jesus says, which will transform a life. It is clear from Jesus' statement that freedom depends on the possession of truth. If the truth about the Christian life is unknown, then one can never be free.

One of the sad but clear facts of deliverance is that many who are miraculously and dramatically delivered from demonic bondage slip back under Satan's control because of their lack of willingness to embrace the truth. One woman, who God delivered, slipped back six years later into a pagan lifestyle, divorcing her husband, and denying God. She never fully embraced the truth about the Christian life or the fact that she had been bound by the Devil. She was taught a lie concerning her deliverance process (that there were no demons; it was an emotional/psychological release), and this gave Satan the room he needed to slip in and slowly erode her Christian life.

Weaknesses

1. The teaching model tends to be long in explanation and short in application.

The great weakness of the teaching model is the tendency to spend all the available time in explanation and save no time for application. Unless the truth is shown to be practical, it is not helpful. Unless the teaching period contains ways to practice the truth, the teaching model is guilty of inoculating against the truth. Often those who hear good teaching on spiritual warfare believe they have conquered another area of the Christian life. This can lead them to believe they do not need to pursue growth in the spiritual area.

The reason for this lack of application is a radically flawed understanding of teaching. Teaching in a Western context means disseminating information rather than causing someone to learn as it does in the Hebrew. One has not taught if the students have not learned. If the students do not practice the truth that was explained, then the teacher has not adequately taught them. The weakness of Western teaching methods will continue to plague the church until those involved in teaching take full responsibility for teaching.

2. The teaching model is not action oriented.

The teaching model does not lend itself to taking action in an individual case. When the demonized present themselves to those using the teaching model there is often little direct action or help. They may be referred to a tape series or a book so their understanding of truth may be increased.

3. The teaching model is a slow process and those seeking help need some immediate help and support.

The teaching model does not offer much direct, immediate help. One well-known deliverance expert who uses the teaching model was approached by a woman needing help. He began to counsel her and asked her to repeat biblical truths about herself. She did and felt a measure of relief. She was pronounced free from demonic bondage as she lived in the truth of those statements. She was, however, not free and could not maintain a clear grip on the biblical truths under the relentless pressure of the demonic voices. This type of episode is continuously repeated as those who are demonized often need more individualized help than the teaching model can offer.

4. The teaching model does not usually supply the support staff to help implement the needed changes.

One of the greatest dangers in having a ministry in the area of spiritual warfare includes the overwhelming requests for help. If the teaching model is adopted, it is easy for one person to treat hundreds if not thousands of people. But there may be no thought given to the follow-up process. Since the teaching model often rejects the other models, it cannot train people to handle demonic situations other than through teaching. The teacher must assume responsibility for training people in this vital area.

5. The teaching model can elevate the teacher so pride can become a major problem.

The teaching model tends to put one man or one woman on a pedestal, drawing attention to the teacher and his/her solutions for demonic deliverance. The natural inclination to elevate the gifted teacher is magnified because of the intensity of the need, and individuals can almost worship the teacher. Worse yet, the teacher can succumb to the mind-numbing accolades and be an easy prey to Satan.

There can also be a hardening of the viewpoint and an unwillingness to learn from others because "I am the teacher." When a teacher decides his/her method is the best, divisions, strife, and jealousy can result. The danger of pride and arrogance is present in each method, but one is regularly confronted with inadequacies in the other models. The teaching model elevates in an insulated way and arrogance can creep in.

Limitations

1. The teaching model is limited by the teacher.

The teaching model can become an exchange of information with little action or it can be a liberating interaction with the truth of Scripture. The teacher in the teaching model limits or releases this model. In some instances the teacher gives too much information and the truth can be lost. Some teachers take full responsibility for interaction with the truth and liberation takes place. The teacher can set aside time to apply the truths that were explained or the entire time can be filled with more information. It is best to apply the information immediately after it is shared.

2. The teacher in the teaching model can destroy the benefits of the information by focusing too much attention on themselves.

This form of pride often slips up on those who are involved in this area, causes many to begin to trust the teacher and his/her ideas and plans as the only means for deliverance. Years ago I was caught in this trap of believing I needed to be the main, if not the only, mouth-piece of hope and help to those bound by the Devil. A number of people attached themselves so strongly to me. they cut ties with all other teachers on all other subjects. This set up their ultimate downfall. Having become attached completely to me, these people had no answers if I did not possess the answers. As a young man with limited experience, there were a number of areas (from raising children to running a church) for which I did not have answers. Because of my lack of answers, the demons suggested I was unreliable. This left these people without their other support systems and Christian teachers. In a few cases it caused people to walk away from church and the Lord for a long period of time.

SUMMARY

The teaching model is an excellent part of an effective spiritual warfare ministry. Great care and diligence given to a full-orbed teaching program goes a long way to reducing the sensational deliverance sessions. It is essential to realize those who may be best at teaching biblical material about Christ's victory and Satan's origin and ultimate demise are not equally gifted at working through deliverance on an individual level. The teaching model is not sufficient in and of itself to deliver all those who have come under bondage of the Devil. There is a need for other forms and techniques of deliverance than just the teaching model.

8

PUTTING ALL THE TOOLS IN THE BAG

Many people are using a system for life that was handed them by their parents or others, but it is dysfunctional and consistently giving them bad results. They do not realize a different kind of life is possible. Many people have embraced at least one, if not many, lies the Devil is peddling and it holds them back from achieving their potential. Many people are held in bondage to fear and do not understand how to move forward to get beyond the fear to the wonderful life waiting outside of the prison of fear.

In order to break satanic bondage, it is crucial to recognize whenever there are demonic problems, there are many areas which must be dealt with in order to ensure complete and permanent freedom. The following chapter offers suggestions on how to strengthen the various methods to bring about total release from demonic control. All the various techniques that have been discussed in this book have their place in setting people free in Christ. No one technique or methodology is best in every situation and for every person who wants to help. God has equipped each person with spiritual gifts and placed them in unique settings to apply the healing of the work of Christ. The more we take a full biblical view of deliverance, the more complete will be the application of Christ's victory on the cross.

In the midst of a normal premarital counseling session with a couple (we will call them Bill and Robin), Bill broke out in sardonic laughter and began to ridicule Christ and the Bible. He began referring to himself in the third person. He declared power over Bill. I realized a demon was manifesting. Years before I would have called the demon to attention and initiated a power encounter. This manifestation would have been the beginning of a number of days of intensive spiritual struggle. This time, however, I spent some time in prayer, estimated Bill's understanding, and surveyed all the methods which have been discussed in this book. As I paused to pray, it seemed clear Bill was not ready for a power encounter. It also seemed the Lord was not directing a frontal assault on the wicked spirits in Bill's life at this time. Bill needed to become a much stronger Christian. This type of evaluation, prayer, and mental survey of the various methodologies is called the inclusive model.

The inclusive model gives the control of the spiritual battle to the Lord to use any possible applications of biblical truth. The inclusive model does not prefer one model over another, but realizes one biblical technique may be more appropriate in a particular situation. In this model. Christians act like spiritual doctors regarding deliverance and need to have all the equipment Christ provides in their medical bags. They must be patient and not rush to a diagnosis or to a cure. In Bill's case I stopped the manifestation and bound it in Christ. I let Bill know what was happening and he needed to become stronger in his faith before we would deal with this problem. I recommended several books I thought he should read. I wrote out several prayers for him to pray at various points throughout his day. I briefly spoke about his position in Christ and the need for him to strengthen himself in Christ. I then returned to the premarital session.

The next four months for Bill were a time of growing and strengthening his understanding of his position in Christ, in the premarital sessions we dealt with how to handle unresolved hurts of the past, as memories of childhood sexual abuse still haunted him and controlled his thinking. When the demonic problem came up during counseling, I assured him the Lord would let us know when it was time to renew the battle in earnest.

The battle was renewed on the last day of the premarital counseling. There was a strong demonic manifestation, and it was clear the Lord was directing me to confront it. I took authority over the demon in Christ, prayed for guidance, and commanded it to leave (exorcism model). In a minute or two it did leave. Another spirit manifested and I followed the same plan. I threw it out in the authority of Christ. When a third manifestation came up, I prayed and felt led to confront it in the same way. This demon, however, did not leave, and the battle became a power encounter with the power of Christ causing the demon to reveal its source of power, sin, and ground. The ground was of such a nature it could not be dealt with quickly, so after two or three hours the manifestation was shut down. I sent Bill home with a description of his position in Christ and gave him an assignment of writing down the sins in his life he had not confessed to the Lord. For the next two weeks we were involved in canceling ground through the resistance model's formula of confession. No demonic manifestation was allowed. Bill worked through the various issues that allowed Satan a foothold in his life. Bill and his fiancé worked through the issues that this demonic encounter produced. He and Robin went on to be married and have stayed married and positively impacted many for Christ.

The process of deliverance is not easy or quick. One must be dependent upon the Lord and willing to learn new truths from the Scriptures. It is imperative Christians be fully prepared when they face the coming satanic decades. It is shameful Christians have sought to exclude certain methods and certain techniques from the Lord's hands because it was not culturally acceptable.

The rest of this chapter presents ways to rehabilitate the various methods and guard them from their own weaknesses and limitations. I am not advocating a one, two, three step process which should be used in every case. The Lord directs those in His church to use new ways to apply these biblical methods. The following updates can encourage the church in this coming age.

All of the problems people have are not spiritual. There are emotional, mental, relational, volitional, physical and spiritual. If we are going to help people claim what God has for them (John 10:10; Ephesians 2:10; John 5:8) then we need to think more comprehensively than Christians sometimes do when they are involved in spiritual warfare. We must see spiritual warfare as a part of a holistic approach to allowing the person to claim the abundant life God has for planned for them. They have a destiny the devil is trying to rob from them.

The following chart shows the different tracks or approaches that are needed to help a person fully embrace the truth of their freedom in Christ and the life God has for them. Notice, I recommend having a spiritual mentor who will walk with the person through the prayers and development of their freedom in Christ.

Helping People Maximally

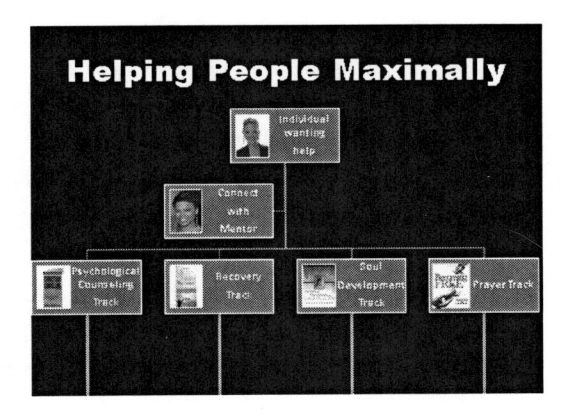

[Diagram: Individual wanting help → Connect with Mentor → Psychological Counseling Track | Recovery Track | Soul Development Track | Prayer Track]

Each of these different tracks is a part of freedom. They help the individual work forward towards a Holy, Righteous, Positive, Loving life.

Let me suggest some resources under each heading I have found helpful as a person walks into the wonder of Christ's love. There are all kinds of resources being produced that have workbooks and study guides to help a person grow in the outworking of their faith. The resources I have listed are in no way an exhaustive list, but I have found these to be helpful in developing a holy, righteous, positive, and loving life. These resources are not theory books but practical works that will help equip a person for the Christian life. Some of these resources are now considered older resources and some are ancient. There are new resources that are also helpful, but the church has been around for 2,000 years, and in this time God has raised up many wonderful men and women to provide insight and counsel.

The Prayer (Deliverance) Track

Many people need to be prayed for and prayed with to release them from the work of sin and the demons in their life. There are a number of wonderful works that have exercises and spiritual workouts that can help a person process through this critical need. Some of these resources are for those who have mild issues of demonization and some are for those who have severe issues of demonization. Bondage Breakers by Neil Anderson; Victory Over Darkness by Neil Anderson; Becoming Free by Gil Stieglitz; The Adversary by Mark Bubeck; Occultic Bondage and Deliverance by Kurt Koch.

Soul Development Track

The development of a soul that is really free to live a righteous, joyful life is one that understands how to love. Jesus says we need to love God, others, and ourselves to have the richest kind of life. It takes His power and grace but it is worth it. Everyone -- until the day they are taken to heaven -- needs to continue to grow in these various areas of love. The resources included here have been very helpful and come from many different theological backgrounds. Enjoy.

Developing love for God at new levels: *Experiencing God* by Henry Blackaby; *Celebration of Discipline* by Richard Foster; *Spiritual Disciplines of a C.H.R.I.S.T.I.A.N.* by Gil Stieglitz; *Knowledge of the Holy* by A.W. Tozer; *The Pursuit of God* by A.W. Tozer; *Knowing God* by J.I. Packer; *Desiring God* by John Piper

Developing righteous love of self: It is easy to think of ways to selfishly love ourselves, but it is often hard to think of the things our spirit, mind, emotions, will ,and body actually need in order to be ready to live out the Christian life. If we are going to be ready to love God and to love others, we must have our own righteous needs met.

Here is a list of resources that can help you understand how to meet the needs of your spirit: *The Dream Giver* by Bruce Wilkinson; *Death by Love* by Marc Driscoll

Here is a partial list of resources to help you understand how to meet the needs of your emotions: The Emotionally Healthy Church by Pete Scazzero; Emotionally Healthy Spirituality by Pete Scazzero

Here is a partial list of resources to help you understand how to meet your volitional needs: *Happiness is a Choice* by Minireth and Myers; *Decision Making* and the *Will of God* by Friessen; *Learned Optimism* by Martin Seligman.

There are numerous exercise and nutrition programs to help you meet the needs of your body. Make sure you also look at a healthy sleep and rest cycle so you are not weary. I would also recommend the book Margins to deal with the effects of our overstimulated culture.

Here is a partial list of resources to help you understand how to meet your spouse's needs and thereby build a great marriage: *Love and Respect* by Eggers; *Falling in Love*, Staying in Love by William Harley; *Becoming a Godly Husband* by Gil Stieglitz; *Becoming a Godly Wife* by Gil and Dana Stieglitz; *Marital Intelligence* by Gil Stieglitz

Here is a partial list of resources to help you understand how to meet the needs of your family and build a lasting and loving family: *Parenting with Love and Logic* by Foster Cline and

Jim Fay; *Roots to Grow* and *Wings to Fly*; *Becoming a Godly Parent* by Gil Stieglitz

Here is a partial list of resources to help you understand how to meet the needs of your friends so you can have more friends and develop a deeper bond with them: *Friendship Factor* by Alan McGiinnis; *Bringing Out The Best in People* by Alan McGinnis; *How to Win Friends and Influence People* by Dale Carnegie.

Here is a very partial list of ways to improve your meeting the needs of those at work. *How to Win Friends and Influence People; The Winning Attitude* by John Maxwell; *There Is No Such Thing As Business Ethics* by John Maxwell.

Here is a partial list of resources to improve your involvement and love for the church: *The Anatomy of a Church* by John MacArthur; *The Purpose Driven Church* by Rick Warren.

Here is a partial list of resources to help you have a biblical perspective on money, wealth, possessions: *Financial Peace University* by Dave Ramsey; *Crown Financial Ministry* books and tapes; *Money, Wealth and Possessions* by Randy Alcorn.

Here is a partial list of resources for loving those who become consumed with opposing, competing, or annoying us: *Forgiveness* by David Augsburger; *Total Forgiveness* by David Augsburger.

The Recovery Track

Here is a partial list of resources for helping people who are in need of recovery because of deep wounds and/or addictive behaviors that are destroying the life they could have: *The Emotionally Healthy Spirituality* by Peter Scazzero; *Celebrate Recovery* manuals, books and tapes; *The Genesis Process* by Michael Dye and Patricia Fancher

The Psychological Track

Here is a partial list of resources to help identify and heal dysfunctional mental patterns and harmful family programming: *The Emotionally Healthy Church* by Pete Scazzero; *Christian Counseling* by Gary Collins; *Uncovering the Mystery of MPD* by Jeff Friesen; *No Condemnation* by Bruce Narrimore; *Inside Out* by Larry Crabb: *Why Am I Afraid to Love* by John Powell

THE SPECIALIST MODEL

The specialist model is deliverance that is directed by a gifted, knowledgeable, or experienced person. The techniques of this type of deliverance could be strengthened through incorporation of the following suggestions.

1. Releasing people to become specialists.

The early church realized it had a demonic problem and willingly allowed some of its people to specialize in this area of ministry. They were called exorcists. This is an unacceptable title today, but the need for these people increases every day. The church must release its rationalistic grip on people and begin to identify, train, and sanction a new host of "exorcists." These people could be called counselors or prayer team leaders. Whatever they are called, they are needed. The Lord always meets our needs, so I can only conclude there are a number of lay people ready to address this problem. They only need to be identified and trained.

2. Providing training manuals which include prayers and remedies.

There is a need to revive the training manual format which was used so effectively in the early church. There is a plethora of books being written on this subject with much helpful information contained in them. The problem is they tend to push only one technique or one method. There is a need to condense and combine the helpful and valuable material in these books into manuals which can be given to those called to a ministry in this area. A group of books could be assigned presenting the different approaches and rounding out a person's understanding of the area. I would include the following books in this assignment: *The Adversary and Overcoming the Adversary* both by Mark Bubeck; *Demon Possession and the Christian* by Fred Dickason; *Power Evangelism and Power Healing* both by John Wimber; *Deliverance from Evil Spirits* by Scanlan and Cirner; *Victory over Darkness and Bondage Breakers* both by Neil Anderson; *The Transformation of the Inner Man* by John and Paula Sanford; *Occultic Bondage and Deliverance* by Kurt Koch; *War on the Saints* by Jessie Penn Lewis. These books discuss deliverance from different and, in some areas, antagonistic perspectives; but they strengthen the Christian worker's grip on the liberation that is available in Christ. While I cannot embrace all the contents of each book, this bundle of books forms a fairly complete perspective on "Christian" deliverance.

3. Incorporating an elder or spiritual warfare pastor.

In the coming days the church will either demonstrate the power of Christ over the supernatural world or become static on the secular world's radio. Therefore, I believe just as most churches have a youth pastor or youth department staffed by a lay person, each church will need a spiritual warfare department overseen by a pastor, lay elder, or trained lay person. This must become an ongoing ministry in the functioning of the church. Demonic manifestation is too often a surprise because there is no organization in place to deal with the problem. Some churches are already moving in this direction, and I applaud the effort. Some churches have pastors who are presently carrying the ball alone. Pastors, you must train others to carry the load or this area will swamp your other responsibilities.

4. Training and collecting teams.

The specialist quickly comes to the understanding he/she cannot perform alone. There is a need for a sensitive and supportive team to surround those involved in this ministry. My experience is there are spiritually sensitive people who would delight in being a part of this type of ministry. God may give one person the gift of discernment of spirits, another the gift of mercy to empathize with the sufferer, and another may be called to a ministry of inner healing through prayer. Still, another might be called to a teaching ministry in the area of the believer's position in Christ or the great doctrinal truths or others might be called to do battle in prayer during sessions. These types of gifted people must be collected into teams so the most effective ministry can take place.

5. Providing the means for Christians to receive help.

Unfortunately, there are few ways for those suffering under spiritual bondage to declare their problems and get help. New pathways must be developed for the oppressed to receive help. Some churches offer specialized seminars, regular times of confession, and support groups under the guidance of a sensitive, spiritually mature person. Altar calls and preassembled prayer teams are also other ways to make help available for those who are struggling. I know of one church that offers a video presentation on deliverance every Friday night, followed by a time to consult a prayer counselor.

6. Suppressing demonic manifestation and allowing people the room to choose.

It can be very important for the specialist to bind the demonic influence in the person who is afflicted. The more room and power the demon exerts in the person, the worse it is for the person. It is often very helpful to have a person gifted in prayer to pray that all the demonic activity would be bound in the person and that the only direction that a demon could move is out of the person. It is the suppression of the demonic work that will allow a person to choose to fully embrace Christ or to continue following the influences and voices they currently hear. I have included a sample prayer for binding the enemy that may be working in or on a person:

"Dear Heavenly Father,

I come in the name of the Lord Jesus Christ and bow in surrender to You, Almighty God. I thank you, Heavenly Father, for the victory you have provided through the Lord Jesus Christ. I realize the only reason why we can be forgiven and freed from our sins and their consequences is the life, death, and resurrection of the Lord Jesus Christ. I ask you to bind any demons working in, on, or around this person (or use their name) for a period of 60 days (you could go up to two years) so they can decide if they want to follow the Lord more fully.

I would ask you would allow this person the privilege of repentance and receive your abundant grace to move in a completely new direction free from the spirits that now trouble them. Please do not allow the demons to move or influence this person in any way as they learn, embrace, and practice using the grace of Christ. Thank you for the power of the cross and your love for this person specifically. They have a destiny planned by You and still possible, and it does not include wicked spirits. Thank you for the power and authority you have given to me as a Christian to bind the enemy and give this person the time and room to more fully embrace the Lord Jesus Christ.

In the Name of Jesus Christ the Lord,

Amen."

THE EXORCISM MODEL

The exorcism model is interested in tormenting the demons who have attached to a person so they will leave or be forced to leave. This model is not interested in the reasons why the spirits are present. The following suggestions strengthen the exorcism methodology and its implementation:

1. Develop faith to utilize a word of command.

It seems that large parts of the church are unable to believe God can remove demons just through a word of command. This lack of belief in the authority of Christ severely reduces the church's effectiveness in the world. There are a number of ways to develop the faith to actually use a word of command in this culture. The first and typical means is to spend time teaching on it. The scriptural basis for the word of command must be explained. Christ's life, death, ascension, and glorification are the ground basis for the word of command. Scriptural examples must be shown such as Paul and the demon-possessed slave girl in Acts 16. Historical and present-day examples should also be shared. It is important to develop a picture in the mind of the student that this is possible.

A second way to develop faith in the power of a word of command is to demonstrate its effectiveness. People need to be exposed to demons being expelled this way. When it is possible to witness an activity accomplished, people immediately have greater confidence in the practice.

Other ways to inculcate faith in the word of command include listening to tapes of this process and assigning books where this procedure is discussed and reported. Using the word of command in an actual demonic situation also develops faith. It is important to mention, at this point, that no one will use this procedure if there is no sense of permission in our churches.

2. Explain and distribute godly music.

If the power of the exorcism model is ever to be unleashed on the church, then the power of godly music must be taught and demonstrated. In order to make our homes and churches safe havens, people must understand the type of music demonic forces do not like. Praise to God -- especially of a soft and melodious nature – is hated by demonic spirits. A seminar to emphasize the power of melodious praise to irritate demons can be very effective in creating a "safe zone." The point of a seminar would be to stress the power of praise music. If a discussion of music spends too much time on wrong types of music, then there will be disagreements and arguments and the real point will be missed.

3. Encourage the use of Scripture tapes.

Another powerful tool in spiritual warfare is using Scripture tapes as background "noise" during the day. Christians should be encouraged to let the Bible tapes play in their homes. There are a number of good readings of various versions. The problem is many Christians do not understand the value of allowing the Scripture to play as the background noise of the day. Many assume if a tape is playing, then full attention must be given to it. The use of Scripture in this way is not so much for the conscious mind as the subconscious mind and to signal spiritual forces which may be invisibly present. Wicked spirits do not want Scripture to be constantly spoken, read, or heard in any form.

4. Educate the counselee and the counselor about the strengths and the weakness of the exorcistic techniques in working with demons.

When the exorcist techniques are used, it is designed to excite and torment the demons. This usually causes the person whom they are attached to feel agitation, pain, difficulty, and the like. Too often the demonically-afflicted person is led into a exorcistic deliverance model without realizing all that will take place. It is usually best to have the person make progress in their faith before an exorcistic methodology is pursued. It is the faith of the individual that will help the process move forward.

It is also important to caution those who do not typically work through these kinds of overt spiritual experiences to not shy away from commanding the demons to leave through your authority in Christ. This is an appropriate way of working with wicked spirits at Christ's direction. The Lord Jesus Christ may whisper to your soul this spirit just needs to go and should be commanded to leave right now. Do not leave this beyond the realm of possibility.

5. Teach and give written copies of strong doctrinal prayers.

The church has become weak because most individuals do not understand the truth or the power of the doctrines of the Bible. The truth of who Christ is and all He did in salvation sets people free. It is important to give people written prayers that are full of doctrinal truths. At the beginning the person may not even understand all the truth in the prayer they are praying, but it will slowly seep into their mind and protect their spirit.

While I love spontaneous prayers, there is also something wonderful about written prayers. Written prayers speak of deep things and request profound needs the baby Christian may never think to pray. It is these truths and requests that need to be inserted into the prayers people pray.

6. Make sure the people on the prayer team are righteous and understand the power of Christ's and their righteousness.

The righteousness of Christ is the only protective gear the Christian can really use when they are battling against the spiritual forces of wickedness. All Christ did in His life, death, and resurrection is available to Christians. It is His work that sets us free and allows us to walk in freedom. It is also true our righteousness allows us to fill out the protective suit of Christ's righteousness more effectively than if we remain indolent and apathetic in righteousness. It is important the people who would be a part of a prayer team would not be openly in rebellion against God. This seems obvious, but people do not always realize what is involved in being within the boundaries of basic morality. People need to be told they cannot have activities and behaviors that are currently outside the lines of the Ten Commandments if they want to be helpful on a prayer team. If there are areas of open sin in the individuals of a prayer team, that person will be attacked or the team will be ineffective. This can never be forgotten as we would attempt to do battle against wicked spirits.

7. Identify and make use of the more exorcistic spiritual gifts.

The Holy Spirit has given spiritual enablements to the church to help set people free from demonic influence and strongholds. The power of these gifts are demonstrable. These gifts while controversial include prophecy, wisdom, discernment of spirits, knowledge, faith, tongues, and interpretation of tongues. These gifts of the Holy Spirit work like a hot knife through butter in the spirit realm. They are guided by the Holy Spirit when tested and used properly. These gifts make a huge difference when used intelligently against wicked spirits.

THE POWER MODEL

The power model is the type of deliverance which seeks to demonstrate openly the power of Christ over the power of wicked spirits, usually through power encounters. The following suggestions allow the brashness of the power model to be utilized effectively in the church:

1. Do not hide the reality of the spiritual battle from the average congregation. Talk about it.

Without over-sensationalizing the encounters, the average Christian needs to be informed of the reality of the spiritual battle. This is not being done in the majority of the churches across America. There are appropriate opportunities in sermons and lessons to give illustrations from the front lines of the spiritual war. Amazingly enough, the average Christian does not hear about the reality of the battle. There is, as Wimber labels it, the problem of the "excluded middle"! This will only be overcome when the church hears from its leaders in non-sensational ways about the ongoing battle.

The danger on the back side of this problem is to overdramatize or constantly be relating these "hair-raising" experiences. Encounters with evil spirits must be blended into the whole of the Christian experience and not become the whole. Similar to the war in Iraq dominating the television and radio news in 1991, spiritual warfare can dominate the church if the whole Christian perspective is not shared.

2. Allow power battles to take place within the ministry of the church. Do not stop them as embarrassing or theologically unneeded.

There is a great need to give permission for Christ to demonstrate His power over Satan in this day as a part of the ministry of the church. I was part of a team that was ministering to a woman in the mid-west. We began by using an office in her church, but then it became apparent the demonic counseling was not welcome in that church. There needs to be an understanding that wholeness (including deliverance) is the church's business.

3. Utilize the demons on occasion to speak out their own doom.

A major problem in using the power model is directly speaking to demons and gathering information from these known liars. (John 8:44) This process, however, can be sanitized and used on occasion to provide helpful information. Just as a general would not want to rely completely or largely on information from captured POW's, so those working in this area should not rely solely or too much on demonic information. However, it is possible at times to obtain helpful information from demons which directly contribute to their destruction. This type of information gathering should be done as a last resort or if the Lord seems to direct it. The questions must relate to those areas which will accomplish the destruction of the demons (i.e., name, ground, work, date attached). Evil spirits must not be allowed to ramble on about other things or about the people on the prayer team. The Devil is a master at pride and can use this to puff up the team members.

4. Do not shy away from those who have obvious demonic problems.

The church of Jesus Christ was designed by the Lord to be a refuge for the hurting. Yet, at times, the hurting are made to feel they have no place in church. The American church especially has become a haven for suburbanites looking for another program. This causes the demonically oppressed to feel unwanted or to leave un-helped. Those within the church must be compassionate to those who are struggling in the most severe ways. Some people are in desperate need of the liberating power of Jesus. They find no help from the church because it shies away from them. The church must be willing to ask some spiritual warfare questions before desperate people are handed over to secular counselors who will not explore the spiritual dimension.

5. Identify those with strength of personality or temperament who could be used in this ministry.

The early church found those most successful in deliverance over the long haul were those with strong personalities. God made some people dominant, powerful, and strong. What better place to unleash this fury than on the Enemy. Strong people can create havoc in a church if they do not have an outlet for all their God-given energy. When these people are trained and unleashed against the demonic hordes, they are extremely useful and come to understand their dependence upon the Lord. Most churches have at least one strong or dominate personality. God does not waste temperament or giftedness, which suggests He may want a deliverance ministry in many churches. I am not suggesting just because someone has a strong personality he/she should be rushed into this most sensitive and delicate area. A strong temperament is only useful when it has been broken by the Lord and when it responds to His promptings.

6. Allow people to make mistakes by trying... Let them exercise their spiritual muscles (I John 2:12-14).

One of the primary principles of training people to do anything is that people learn the most by doing. This means trying and failing and trying again. Churches often ignore this idea and only allow the paid professionals to do ministry. Humans are, on the whole, afraid of mistakes and failure. If people are not allowed to experiment with the weapons of warfare Christ provided, then they cannot expect proficiency when the war commences. The suggestion in I John 2:12-14 is maturity in Christ comes through engagements with the Enemy and learning to overcome him by using the Lord's strength and His Word. If this is true, then it is no wonder there are so many immature Christians in churches. I can remember turning one deliverance session over to a fellow who had watched me on numerous occasions. He was rather nervous but did an admirable job and learned valuable lessons in the process of being the specialist.

THE RESISTANCE MODEL

The resistance model is the type of deliverance which seeks to resist Satan and his hordes through confession of sin and daily living in positive righteousness. The following suggestions are offered as a help to strengthen aspects of the resistance model:

1. Have regular times of confession.

One of the needs in the Protestant church is to provide a time, place, and trained counselor to help people work through their sins. If those in the congregation knew the pastor or a trained counselor was scheduling times at the church where they could be led through confession, more confession would take place. There could also be retreats which stress the need for confession. These retreats could be a day or a week, examining each area of life to uncover sin and acknowledge it before God. I believe the church shies away from these practices because of the connection to Catholicism. However, it is a helpful practice in eliminating an overabundance of un-confessed sin and giving the Devil handles in the life of the believer. These sessions should stress confession is made to God and not to a man. It is God who forgives; the counselor is only present to assist confession and provide information as needed.

2. Distribute sheets on "How to Clean Out Your House."

Average Christians need to know the importance and process of making their homes a sanctuary instead of a battle ground. Sermons, classes, announcements, and bulletin updates should keep Christians alerted to the dangerous material that could be brought into their homes. After I talked about this area in a sermon, one couple went through their house and removed a number of objects (tapes, statues, pictures) which had provided the Enemy a launching pad for spiritual attack. After clearing out the house, the couple found their teenage daughter became more submissive and cooperative toward the family. A number of months later when the girl's attitude abruptly changed again, the mother found her daughter had purchased and was listening to a tape of a secular heavy metal band. When the daughter was confronted and the tape destroyed, the girl's attitude again became submissive and cooperative. Clear, practical direction on cleaning out one's home is needed

3. Place a greater emphasis on positive righteousness.

There is a great need in the church to teach and preach what Christ desires. Too often only the negative is spelled out. Positive righteousness includes: how to become a mature Christian; how to be a godly husband/wife; how to apply God's principles to finances and money; and how to be a wise parent. The church should emphasize the positive actions Christ desires. It is now possible to conduct video Bible studies taught by some of the national Christian experts in the church. This is one way of returning the church to a proper emphasis on positive righteousness.

4. Develop posters, flyers, or banners on the demonic sins.

Churches often miss subtle ways to emphasize the truth. Posters, flyers, and banners which indicate the connection between sin and demonic oppression can help in educating people on the need to resist sin. The church needs to improve the visual medium like the Byzantine and medieval church did with pictures, carvings, and stained glass. Posters, flyers, and banners offer an inexpensive substitute for the Sistine Chapel ceiling. These types of information could be used effectively around the Halloween time when people are alert to the spiritual world.

5. Talk openly and repeatedly about the Ten Commandments and Christian morality.

It is important people realize why God tells us about the Ten Commandments and the moral boundaries inherent in those prohibitions and directions. Each of the commandments marks a minimum boundary that will produce freedom from oppression in some direction. God is telling us that crossing these moral lines produces spiritual, emotional, mental, relational, and even physical decay and oppression.

Our culture has become ignorant of the effects of sin. Even the Christian church has begun to play fast and loose with the reasons to stay away from sin. We see sin as God's problem with something we are doing instead of our selfish pursuit of actions, words, and attitudes that will stain us, destroy us, and bring wicked spirits to feed off of our selfishness. Sin is a blight, an oppression of others. It is destructive in its selfishness. It robs us from being in the right place at the right time to receive God's blessing.

THE COUNSELING MODEL

1. Educate and employ trained counselors for recovery from deliverance.

More and more Christian counseling services are open to the spiritual dimension in their counseling. These counselors can be used for work in deliverance. If a working relationship is established between the church and these counselors, the problems of the afflicted can be broken down into manageable sections and cured. I find Christian counselors are open to helping Christians in this area if those involved in deliverance are sensitive to the expertise and limitations of the counselors. I explain to these professionals what I believe is going on and how I think their expertise fits. They are usually willing to accept these referrals and work with me.

2. Recognize and develop those gifted in inner healing.

I have only ministered in churches which do not emphasize the charismatic gifts; yet I do not find a lack of people specially equipped by God to sense deep inner hurts and pray for God to heal those wounds. These people often need to be encouraged and directed, but they usually become excellent prayer warriors. It is often the warm and accepting atmosphere created by these people which allows the oppressed to receive the ministry of the Lord.

3. Realize people are full of patterns, programming, and dysfunctional memories.

One of the significant discoveries of the last one-hundred years is the extent of family programming. The Scriptures expose this pattern development and programming inheritance (Exodus 34:7), but it has been far more extensively explored and its power has been exposed. Those who seek to help others must understand the way the person you are trying to help is programmed by their past decisions and their family background. There is a reason why this person is where they are in life.

When we help people unwind those patterns and realize they have a choice about how they make decisions and how they interact with others, we are helping them make a huge step toward the life God wants for them. In many cases, people have never seen a healthy normal way of acting in a given circumstance. People will revert to old patterns if they do not have a new pattern to follow. Demons just exploit old patterns and seek to help a person continue to be dysfunctional so their hold can grow stronger.

4. Dismiss simplistic methods in deliverance.

All deliverance involves three problems: demons, sin, and deception. Deliverance almost always involves a number of complex issues. Unless God does an instantaneous miracle to heal a person, the process will involve injecting truth into the person's life until complete freedom results. Psychologists have often criticized Christians for seeking simplistic and unrealistic solutions to complex problems. This has been true. In order to help people maximally, the gains of psychology must be incorporated. Even the apostle sees spiritual warfare as a battle for the mind. (2 Corinthians 10:3-5)

5. Develop lay counseling training, active listening courses, and a network of small groups with counselors and support systems.

The epistle to the Hebrews suggests the church needs to assume the responsibility for strengthening the knees that are weak and the bones that are out of joint. No specific prescription is given as to how this is to take place, but it is clear from the context that the Lord wants Christians to help other Christians. There is a need for support systems in the church so Satan can be effectively resisted. Those with spiritual problems (including alcoholics, sex addicts, drug abusers, child abusers, etc.) are sick and need help. They first need salvation in the Lord Jesus Christ.

They also need a support system which will stand with them "in the evil day" (Ephesians 6:11) when they are tempted to return to the chains which held them.

Lay counselors can help unburden the staff of a church and provide powerful and practical help for those in crisis. Improving the skills of dedicated Christians in the congregation is time extremely well spent.

THE TEACHING MODEL

The teaching model seeks to deliver people from demonic bondage through understanding and applying biblical truth. The following suggestions are offered to strengthen deliverance through this method:

1. Develop an ongoing teaching and discipling program which stresses the great doctrinal truths of the Christian faith.

In the past thirty years the church has made great strides in the application of biblical truth to practical living. There is now a plethora of marriage, finances, and family classes. The problem is that good, strong theology is often left behind. Many Christians today have no understanding of justification, redemption, or regeneration. These and many other crucial concepts are left behind in the search for practical truth. The difficulty is these truths are the basis for victory over Satan. The church needs to continue its current practical emphasis but also teach solid theology. I am amazed at the strong response to theology in our church. A course in theology is at present the most well-attended Bible study in the church. Theology refers to an understanding of the essence, attributes and names of God, the many aspects of salvation, and one's position in Christ. If the church is going to build spiritual warriors, theology is essential spiritual food that must be added back into the believer's diet.

2. Teach regularly on the Armor of God.

There is a regular need to teach the concepts of truth, righteousness, peace, faith, salvation, the Word of God, and prayer. The armor of God does not have to take the form of a class on how to combat Satan and his hordes. It can be one application from a sermon or a topical study on each concept. When these concepts are regularly taught and imbibed by the church, the Devil has less opportunity to prey upon Christians.

3. Have a regularly scheduled "Our Position in Christ" and "Understanding Salvation" classes.

The Christian's position in Christ is another neglected area of teaching. Unless Christians are told what is available to them in Christ, they will not be able to utilize their position. I find these courses to be startling to many people. One fellow nursed a deep-seated fear all his life. He saw fear of this kind could not come from Christ. Since he was in Christ, he no longer needed to be afraid. Eliminating that one fear began a new confidence in the man's life.

4. Develop a layered approach to spiritual warfare.

I trained my congregation to resist Satan in a number of ways, and some of my attempts have ended in disaster. One time I taught an extended Bible study on Satan and deliverance which was open to the entire church. People who were fascinated by Satan and demonism enrolled in the class. I saw the Devil work by causing confusion and fear toward this type of approach, which divided the church. A better approach is to have a prerequisite process in which people are trained in the fundamentals of the faith before they are ever exposed to the details of spiritual warfare. Training deliverance teams requires intensive training classes as a final disciplining process. The information in this book can form the basis for this intensive course.

5. Separate the class for those who need to be set free from the class for those who want to learn.

I have settled convictions that it is not profitable to invite those who are struggling with demonic oppression to the same class in which people are being trained. If the two classes are kept separate, the training class can help those who are struggling. There is then no confusion in the learning process. This creates the need for a regularly scheduled time for those who need help with spiritual oppression. Many times spiritual oppression is addressed only in individual counseling. If, however, there is a regular time to learn about deliverance, then the counseling load is reduced. Much of what could be said to an individual can be relayed to a group. Individual counselors are needed to follow up the process of deliverance with each person.

SUMMARY

The inclusive model is not meant to suggest a rigid format for setting people free. It is an attempt to take the strengths from each model and utilize them to liberate those suffering from demonic oppression. I believe when the methods are grouped and used as strands of the same cord, the weakness of each individual model is limited and the overall strength of Christ in deliverance is demonstrated. In other words, I believe when we allow the Lord to use all the tools He wants, then He will set people free and bring glory to His name.

Notes

Forward

1. Oesterreich, Traugott Konstantin. **Demon Possession.** Chicago: The De Lawrence Company, 1935, Inside Cover.

Introduction to Spiritual Warfare

1. Ferguson, Everett. *Demonology in the Early Church*. New York: Edward Mellen, 1984, 106.

2. Tunnel. Joseph, *The Life of the Devil.* New York: A. A. Knoph, 1930, 221

3. White, John. *Problems and Procedures in Exorcism*, ed. John Warwick Montgomery. *Demon Possession: A Medical, Historical, Anthropological, and Theological Symposium*. Minneapolis: Bethany Fellowship, 1976, 281

4. Anderson, Neil. Unpublished notes given at Talbot School of Theology. *"Since I Am in Christ, Who I Am."* These now appear in a modified form in Dr. Anderson's books, *Victory over Darkness* and *Bondage Breakers.*

Chapter 1: Seeing the Whole Picture

1. Turmel, Joseph. *The Life of the Devil.* New York: A.A. Knoph, 1930, 221

2. Alexander, William Menzies. *Demonic Possession in the New Testament*, its relations historical, medical, and theological. Edinburgh: T&T Clark, 1902; 223.

Chapter 2: SPECIALISTS: Ghostbusters to the Rescue

1. The names and at times the gender have been changed to protect those involved in the illustration.

2. Scanlan, Michael and Cimer, Randall J. *Deliverance from Evil Spirits: A Weapon for Spiritual Warfare.* Ann Arbor: Servant Books, 1980, 68-69.

3. Alexander. *Demonic Possession.* 223.

4. ibid.

5. ibid.

6. ibid.

7. Kelly, Ansgar. *The Devil at Baptism: Ritual Theology and Drama.* Ithaca: Cornell Univ. Press, 1985, 236-238.

8. Alexander. *Demonic Possession.* 223.

9. Bubeck, Mark. *The Adversary.* Chicago: Moody Press 1975. 122.

10. Turmel. *The Life of the Devil.* 220.

11. Koch, Kurt. *Occultic Bondage and Deliverance.* 87.

12. Koch, Ibid. 87,88.

13. Kelly. *The Devil at Baptism.* 239.

14. Bubeck. *The Adversary.* 144-148.

15. Bubeck, Ibid. 144.

16. Turmel, *The Life of the Devil.* 218-219.

17. Rockstad, Ernest. *Counseling in Demonic Crisis. Deliverance Papers* Andover: Faith and Life. 1983. 1-2.

18. Koch. *Occult Bondage and Deliverance.* 99-102.

19. Koch. 99-102.

20. Turmel, *The Life of the Devil.* 219-220/

21. Turmel. *The Life of the Devil.* 219.

22. Rockstad, Ernest. *Enlightening Studies. Deliverance Papers.* Andover: Faith and Life. 1983. Introduction.

23. Rockstad, *Counseling in Demonic Crisis.* 8.

24. Bubeck, *The Adversary.* 123-124.

Chapter 3: EXORCISM: Making the Demons Tremble

1. Oesterreich, Traugott Konstantin. *Demon Possession.* Chicago: The De Lawrence Company. 1935.

2. Turmel. The Life of the Devil, 218, 219.

3. Rockstad, Ernest. *Resources for Conflict and Conquest.* Deliverance Papers. Andover: Faith and Life. 1983. 2.

4. Kelly. *The Devil at Baptism.* 245.

5. Bubeck. *Overcoming the Adversary.* 116.

6. Turmel. *The Life of the Devil.* 233.

Chapter 4: POWER: Flexing Your Spiritual Muscles

1. Koch. *Occultic Bondage and Deliverance.* 109.

2. Oesterreich, Traugott Konstantin. *Demon Possession*

2. Womber, John. *Power Healing* San Francisco: *Harper* and Row. 1988. 194.

3. Murphy, Edward. *Lectures at Biola University.* 1981.

4. Wimber. *Power Healing.* 233.

5. Wimber. *Power Healing.* 233.

6. Rockstad. *Counseling in Demonic Crisis.* 4.

7. Rockstad. *Dealing with Demons by the Transfer Method.* Andover: Faith and Life. 1983. 1-4.

8. Wimber. *Power Healing.* 237.

9. Ibid., 238.

10. Leahy, Fredrick Stratford. *Satan Cast Out.* Carlisle: Banner of Truth Trust. 1975.

11. Wimber. *Power Healing.* 231.

Chapter 5: RESISTANCE: Building the Impenetrable Fort

1. Scanlan and Cirner. *Deliverance from Evil Spirits.* 56.

2. Ibid., 56-57

3. Kelly. *The Devil at Baptism.* 136.

4. Stieglitz, Gil. *The Spiritual Disciplines of a C.H.R.I.S.T.I.A.N.* Thrive Publication, Carson City, Nevada 2010. 20, 21.

5. Stieglitz, Gil. *The Spiritual Disciplines of a C.H.R.I.S.T.I.A.N.* Thrive Publication, Carson City, Nevada 2010. 22, 23.

6. Rockstad, Ernest. *Some Practical Suggestions Regarding Spiritual Warfare. Enlightening Studies in Spiritual Warfare* Andover: Faith and Life. 1983. 1.

Chapter 6: COUNSELING: The Battle for the Mind

1. Collins, Gary. *Psychological Observations on Demonism.* ed. Montgomery, John Warwick. *Demon Possession: A Medical, Historical, Anthropological, and Theological Symposium.* Minneapolis: Bethany Fellowship. 1976. 237.

2. Bernier, Annie and Dozier, Mary. *The Client–Counselor Match and The Corrective Emotional Experience: Evidence from Interpersonal and Attachment Research.* Psychotherapy: University of Delaware. Theory/Research/Practice/Training. Educational Publishing Foundation. 2002. Vol 39, 1, 32–43 .

3. Bernier, Annie and Dozier, Mary. Cited in *The Client–Counselor Match and The Corrective Emotional Experience: Evidence from Interpersonal and Attachment Research.* Berzins, 1977; Beutler, Clarkin, Crago, & Bergan, 1991; Flaskerud, 1990; Nelson & Neufeldt, 1996. Psychotherapy: University of Delaware. Theory/Research/Practice/Training. Educational Publishing Foundation. 2002. Vol 3, 1, 32-43.

Chapter 7: TRUTH: Exposing the Truth and the Lies

1. Barnhouse, Donald Grey. *The Invisible War.* Grand Rapids: Zondervan. 1965. 21-43.

2. Bubeck. *Overcoming The Adversary.* 75-76.

3. Spurgeon, Charles. *Lectures to My Students*. Grand Rapids: Zondervan. 1972.

4. These experts in spiritual warfare would include Dr. Ed Murphy, Dr. Neil Anderson, Dr. Mark Bubeck, and Dr. Timothy Warner.

Chapter 8: Putting All the Tools in the Bag

1. Wimber, John. *Power Evangelism*. San Francisco: Harper and Row. 1986. 75-86.

BIBLIOGRAPHY

Alexander, William Menzies. *Demonic Possession in the New Testament: Its relations historical, medical, and theological.* Edinburgh: T & T Clark. 1902.

Andersen, Neil. *The Bondage Breakers.* Eugene: Harvest House. 1991.

Andersen, Neil. *Victory over Darkness.* Eugene: Harvest House. 1991.

Barnhouse, Donald Grey. *The Invisible War.* Grand Rapids: Zondervan. 1965.

Bubeck, Mark. *Overcoming the Adversary.* Chicago: Moody Press. 1984.

Bubeck, Mark. *The Adversary.* Chicago: Moody Press. 1975.

Calvin, John, John T. McNeill, ed. Translated by Battles, Ford Lewis. *Institutes of the Christian Religion.* Philadelphia: Westminister Press. 1960.

Dickason, Fred. *Demon Possession and the Christian.* Chicago: Moody Press. 1987.

Ferguson, Everett. *Demonology in the Early Church.* New York: Edward Mellen Press. 1984.

Jones, Alan Hugh. *A Psychological and Theological response to a case of demon possession with Particular Reference to the Theology of Reinhold Neibuhr.* D.min Dissertation. Claremont School of Theology. 1977.

Kelly, Henry Ansgar. *The Devil at Baptism: Ritual Theology and Drama.* Ithaca: Cornell Univ. Press. 1985.

Kelly, Henry Ansgar. *The Devil, Demonology and Witchcraft.* Garden City: Doubleday. 1968.

Koch, Kurt. *Occultic Bondage and Deliverance.* Grand Rapids: Kregel. 1971. Leahy, Fredrick Stratford. *Satan Cast Out.* Carlisle: Banner of Truth Trust. 1975.

Montgomery, John Warwick. *Demon Possession; A Medical, Historical, Anthropological, and Theological Symposium.* Minneapolis: Bethany Fellowship. 1976.

Murphy, Edward. *Spiritual Warfare.* Audio Tapes, San Jose: Overseas Crusades. 1988.

Oesterreich, Traugott Konstantin. *Demon Possession.* Chicago: The De Lawrence Company. 1935.

Orr, James. *International Standard Bible Encyclopedia.* Vol. 4. Grand Rapids: Wm B. Eerdmans. 1939.

Peck, M. Scott. *The People of the Lie.* San Francisco: Harper and Row. 1985.

Penn-Lewis, Jessie. *War on the Saints.* New York: Thomas E. Lowe, Ltd., 9th ed.. 1973.

Phillips, McCanlish. *The Spirit World.* Wheaton: Victor Books. 1972.

Phillpott, Kent. *A Manual of Demonology and the Occult.* Grand Rapids: Zondervan. 1974.

Rockstad. Ernest. *Deliverance Papers.* Andover: Faith and Life. 1983.

Scanlan, Michael, and Cimmer, Randall J. *Deliverance from Evil Spirits; A - weapon for spiritual warfare.* Ann Arbor: Servant Books. 1980.

Sheed, Francis Joseph. *Soundings in Satanism.* New York: Sheed and Ward. 1972.

Spurgeon, Charles. *Lectures to My Students.* Grand Rapids: Zondervan. 1972.

The Life of J.O. Fraser. Chicago: Moody Press. 1964.

The New American Standard Bible. LaHabra: Lockman Foundation. 1961

Thiessen, *Lectures in Systematic Theology.* Ann Arbor: Wm. B. Eerdmans. 1949.

Tunnel, Joseph. *The Life of the Devil.* New York: A. A. Knoph. 1930.

Unger, Merril. *Demons in the World Today.* Wheaton: Tyndale House. 1971.

Unger, Merril. *What Demons Can Do to the Saints.* Chicago: Moody Press. 1977.

White, John. *When the Spirit Comes with Power.* Downers Grove: InterVarsity. 1988.

Wimber, John. *Power Evangelism.* San Francisco: Harper & Row. 1986.

Wimber, John. *Power Healing.* San Francisco: Harper & Row. 1988.

About the Author

Gil Stieglitz is an internationally recognized author, speaker, catalyst, counselor, professor, Pastor and leadership consultant. He is Executive Pastor of Adventure Christian Church, a mega-church of 4,000 in Roseville, California. He teaches at Christian Universities and graduate schools in practical theology (Biola, William Jessup, Western Seminary). He is the President of Principles to Live By, an organization committed to teaching God's principles in a life-giving way. He sits on several boards, including Thriving Churches International, a ministry extension of Bayside Church, and Courage Worldwide, an organization that builds homes throughout the world to rescue children forced into sexual slavery. He has been a denominational executive for fifteen years with the Evangelical Free Church of America and was the senior pastor of a vibrant church in southern California for seventeen years.

He has a Master's Degree in Biblical Exposition and a Doctorate in Christian Leadership with a special emphasis in Spiritual Warfare.

Other Resources by Gil Stieglitz

BOOKS

Becoming Courageous

Deep Happiness: The 8 Secrets

Developing a Christian Worldview

God's Radical Plan for Husbands

God's Radical Plan for Wives

Going Deep In Prayer: 40 Days of In-Depth Prayer

Leading a Thriving Ministry: 10 Indispensable Leadership Skills

Marital Intelligence: A Foolproof Guide for Saving and Strengthening Marriage

Mission Possible: Winning the Battle Over Temptation

Spiritual Disciplines of a C.H.R.I.S.T.I.A.N.: Intensive Training in Christian Spirituality

They Laughed When I Wrote Another Book About Prayer ...Then They Read It: How to Make Prayer Work

Touching the Face of God: 40 Days of Adoring God

Why There Has to Be a Hell

If you would be interested in having Dr. Stieglitz
speak to your group, you can contact him
through the website
www.ptlb.com

CPSIA information can be obtained
at www.ICGtesting.com
Printed in the USA
FSOW01n1406170316
18026FS